BANKSTERS

As RTÉ's business correspondent, David Murphy has been in the front line of the banking crisis on a daily basis – breaking stories on television and radio about a financial sector slipping from confusion into chaos. The 2008 winner of the UCD Smurfit Business School Business Broadcast Journalist of the year, he is a former deputy business editor of the *Irish Independent*. He also devised and presented a weekly business show on NewsTalk radio.

Martina Devlin is a best-selling author and award-winning journalist. She has written six books, was shortlisted twice for the Irish Book Awards and won a Hennessy Literary Award. A weekly columnist with the *Irish Independent*, commenting on news and current affairs, she also writes a column for the *Sunday World* magazine. Previously, she spent seven years in London working for the Press Association. She is 2009 writer-in-residence at the Princess Grace Library in Monaco.

BANKSTERS

HOW A POWERFUL ELITE SQUANDERED
IRELAND'S WEALTH

David Murphy &
Martina Devlin

HACHETTE
BOOKS
IRELAND

First published in 2009 by Hachette Books Ireland

1

A CIP catalogue record for this title is available from the British Library.

The publishers would like to thank the *Irish Times* for permission to
reproduce the photograph of Seán Quinn, and the *Irish Independent* for kind
permission to reproduce all of the remaining photographs in this book.

ISBN 9 78 0340 99482 5

Typeset in Sabon by Hachette Books Ireland
Printed and bound in Great Britain by CPI Mackays, Chatham ME5 8TD

Hachette Books Ireland policy is to use papers that are natural, renewable and
recyclable products and made from wood grown in sustainable forests. The
logging and manufacturing processes are expected to conform to the
environmental regulations of the country of origin.

Hachette Books Ireland
8 Castlecourt Centre
Castleknock
Dublin 15, Ireland
A division of Hachette UK Ltd
338 Euston Road, London NW1 3BH

www.hbgi.ie

Contents

*To Betty and Jerry Murphy,
with love and gratitude*

Authors' Note

We interviewed key sources connected with banking while writing this book. Many are not identified. People spoke freely, and shared more valuable insights, if allowed to remain anonymous. In addition, a number of those interviewed still work in the financial sector. For those reasons, many of the quoted observations in this book are not attributed. We weighed it up and decided it was a necessary evil to present the most accurate possible flavour of events and motivations during the banking crisis.

We would also like to recognise that many people of integrity work in the Irish financial institutions and have done nothing wrong, but have been tarnished with the misdeeds of their superiors.

Timeline

March 2007	House prices start to decline nationally.
August 2007	Shares begin falling as credit crunch bites.
14 September 2007	Run on Northern Rock.
15 July 2008	Seán Quinn sells 10 per cent of Anglo stake.
7 September 2008	Fannie Mae and Freddie Mac nationalised.
15 September 2008	Lehman Brothers collapses.
29 September 2008	Irish bank shares drop sharply.
30 September 2008	Government guarantee for banks.
24 October 2008	Iceland gets International Monetary Fund (IMF) bailout as its banks collapse.
3 December 2008	Anglo presents fictitious results.
18 December 2008	Seán FitzPatrick resigns from Anglo.
19 December 2008	David Drumm resigns from Anglo.
21 December 2008	Government to recapitalise banks with €7.5 billion.
16 January 2009	Anglo nationalised.
13 February 2009	Three executives resign from Irish Life & Permanent.
24 February 2009	Fraud Squad raids Anglo.
25 February 2009	Brian Goggin gone, Bank of Ireland names new chief executive.
7 April 2009	Emergency budget announces new National Asset Management Agency (NAMA)to buy bank debts.

PART I

The Stakes

Prologue
The One-Night Stand

'Politics is the art of looking for trouble, finding it everywhere, diagnosing it incorrectly and applying the wrong remedies.'
Groucho Marx

29 September 2008

The Irish Stock Exchange, 8.00 a.m.–5.00 p.m.

Fear gripped the markets. This was a day like no other.

On trading floors across Dublin's stockbroking houses, it was a bloodbath as hoards of wealth accumulated over decades suddenly melted away. Stockbrokers' screens turned red and stayed that way: share prices were in free fall. Traders screamed prices at each other, frantically trying to deal with an avalanche of sellers and a scarcity of buyers. This was not simply a case of investors offloading shares on a bad day – something fundamental had gone wrong. The volume of transactions was exceptional, everything was spiralling out of control. The speed of the slump, as well as its ferocity, was unprecedented. Terms such as 'carnage' were bandied about – for once, they were no exaggeration. Fright spawned panic.

The blue-chip banks, regarded as the nexus of Ireland's boisterous economy, were collapsing like matchsticks. Irish Life & Permanent lost a third of its value, AIB was down 15 per cent, and Bank of Ireland had 17 per cent lopped off its price. Hardest hit was Anglo Irish Bank. Its share price suffered a loss of almost half its value in one day, plummeting by 46 per cent. Depositors were removing their money in droves, alarmed that the bank was teetering towards collapse. It became a self-fulfilling policy – as news of jumbo withdrawals from Anglo circulated among traders, the rate of sell-off accelerated.

Billions of euro had been withdrawn from the Irish banks since 15 September – the day US investment bank Lehman Brothers folded. Minister for Finance Brian Lenihan knew he had to halt the decline. If one of the major banks went bust, no international financial institution would risk advancing money to an Irish lender again. And the Irish economy would career off a cliff face. The minister acted quickly and decisively. The volatility of the situation meant no one could predict where it would all end. But a start would be made.

Government Buildings, 9.30 p.m.–midnight

A subdued group of supplicants gathered at Government Buildings. It was a delegation of four of the country's most senior bankers, and humble pie was a dish these executives were unaccustomed to sampling. Tonight they were in apprehensive mood, however. They knew exactly how vulnerable their institutions were – and the repercussions of collapse. The party consisted of Brian Goggin and Richard Burrows, chief executive and chairman respectively of Bank of Ireland, and Eugene Sheehy and Dermot Gleeson, chief executive and chairman of AIB. They had requested an urgent meeting to outline the severity of the crisis which was immobilising the entire banking system. In the preceding weeks, Irish banks had been struggling to convince investors they were solvent. But the wipeout on that day's stock market had sent them sprinting for shelter under the government's umbrella.

Rumours were circulating that Anglo Irish Bank would not be able to open for business the following day. Even as the four bankers had the chastening experience of being left to kick their heels for two hours – in the Sycamore Room, once a favourite spot of Charlie Haughey's – Anglo employees were on the town. They were giving the bank a send-off in the style of a wake, presuming it would have gone under by the time they sat down to breakfast the next morning.

Traditionally, when banks lend money, they take it from deposits. But the avarice that characterised the Celtic Tiger epoch meant that insufficient money was left on deposit to meet their ambitious plans to boost profits. It had all been doled out already, in an unhinged lending bender. Just about every senior banker in the State was infected by a virus that turned them greedy and irresponsible overnight. Regulation, which should have curbed their excesses, was so light as to be virtually invisible. So they borrowed from other banks. Generally those borrowings were short term, perhaps three months, although their purposes were long term – a thirty-year mortgage, for example.

The property crash was an instant sanity check. As the credit crunch gained momentum around the world, banks became reluctant to lend to one another. On the receiving end of this freeze were the Irish banks, regarded as exceptionally vulnerable because of their hefty exposure to property. All at once, international banks stopped lending to Irish banks. These institutions now found themselves obliged to repay loans – but without the means to do so. This prompted the share-price collapse.

Watching bank shares keel over, investors were seized by

foreboding that banks themselves could topple. Corporate customers with considerable sums on deposit, hundreds of millions of euro, began to take their cash out of Irish banks and move it to more secure institutions. The entire financial system was teetering at the mouth of an abyss.

At 6 p.m., after the markets closed that Monday, Brian Lenihan hurried across to the Taoiseach's office from the nearby Department of Finance. Soon he was huddled in a kitchen cabinet meeting with Taoiseach Brian Cowen, Attorney General Paul Gallagher, Financial Regulator Patrick Neary and Governor of the Central Bank John Hurley.

A number of ministers, including Minister for Foreign Affairs Micheál Martin, Tánaiste Mary Coughlan and Minister for Transport Noel Dempsey, were put on notice that a Cabinet decision would have to be reached by telephone later that night. Such arrangements are known as incorporeal meetings when the Cabinet cannot be convened in time.

By then, the European Commission had learned 'something serious was up in Dublin' but not the particulars. Cowen fretted the press would hear about the plan early and, by leaking details, derail it.

The four bankers were finally brought into the Taoiseach's oak-lined office, dominated by a portrait of Éamon de Valera. Cowen and Lenihan listened intently to what the bankers had to report. They asked a few questions, but in the main they simply absorbed the stark communiqué. Bank of Ireland and AIB, once regarded as impregnable, only had enough money to continue operating for a matter of weeks.

'[They] made it clear to us that liquidity was drying up in the Irish banking system and the maturity dates for the various loans they need to fund their business were shortening all the time, and reaching dangerous levels of exposure,' Lenihan would later explain to the Seanad – in other words they were running out of cash.

AIB's Eugene Sheehy said of that meeting, 'Our interest in stability and the government's would have been very much aligned. That meant staying open for business.' He described his bank's liquidity on the night of the guarantee as €10 billion surplus to regulatory requirements. This is typical banker-speak. On the surface, it sounds fine. But scratch beneath it and a different story emerges. Investors were less worried about the night of the guarantee – and more concerned about the bank's future losses. (And they were right to be anxious: the 2008 results were dreadful.)

The steps to be taken were not discussed in front of the bankers. The four left the meeting, and in their absence the nuclear button was pushed. A daring plan was hatched to fully underwrite Ireland's entire banking network. Other non-Irish banks operating in the State would be considered on a case-by-case basis. Covered by this insurance policy were four banks: Bank of Ireland, AIB, Anglo Irish Bank, Irish Life & Permanent – owner of Permanent TSB – and two building societies: EBS and Irish Nationwide.

Guaranteeing the banks was an extraordinary step. It meant if any bank discovered it had unmanageable bad loans, the taxpayer would be liable. This was a highly probable scenario, since excessive lending was the order of the day – greased by the bankers' bonus culture which hinged on ever-increasing profits.

By now, the occupants of Government Buildings were without food or bottled water. Snacks and sandwiches brought in earlier had long since disappeared. Officials watched RTÉ's *Questions and Answers* and settled in for the long haul.

The bankers were escorted back into the meeting, the proposal was put to them and they were given time to consult with colleagues. Sheehy and Gleeson returned to the Sycamore

Room while Goggin and Burrows made telephone calls in the corridor before being offered the dining room for privacy.

Meanwhile, the kitchen cabinet made contact with other bank chief executives to tell them Christmas had arrived early. The mobile phone of EBS chairman Mark Moran rang but he was asleep and missed the call. In the morning, he picked up regulator Patrick Neary's message informing him the government was introducing a guarantee and that his building society would be included.

30 September 2008

Government Buildings, midnight–5.00 a.m.

The two Brians – Lenihan and Cowen – and their team turned the Taoiseach's office into a war room. They rolled up their sleeves and set to work ironing out details of the rescue package, attempting to plug loopholes and to second-guess drawbacks. For some time, they had been aware that radical action was needed but they had kept their fingers crossed it could be delayed until the weekend when markets were closed. Governments worldwide were reviewing how to safeguard their indigenous banking systems and how to protect deposits from public panic. It was hoped that US politicians would pass a $700 billion bailout bill under discussion in Congress in a move to restore fiscal stability. But a note sent in during one of the meetings on 29 September dashed expectations: the Washington vote had gone against the proposal (although compromises were made and it was passed the following week).

The team laboured until 3.30 a.m., drafting revisions. At one stage, the phrase 'serious disturbance in the economy' was removed, but it was returned because it offered some armour against a European Union (EU) challenge on state aid rules. Under EU law, member states have the freedom to intervene to prevent a systemic collapse in the national banks. However, mergers valued at €5 billion or more must be approved by Brussels.

The option chosen to avert Armageddon – a guarantee on 'the deposits, loans and obligations' of the six Irish banks – had been circulating within the Department of Finance, the Central Bank and Government Buildings for more than a fortnight. Economists had also mentioned it.

In the weeks leading up to the guarantee, the government had considered nationalisation of one of the banks – either running it as a going concern with new capital, or simply running it down. Department of Finance officials preferred the option of new investors for a disaster-stricken bank rather than a State takeover.

Cowen and Lenihan were operating in the dark to some extent: they realised there was a credibility gap in what bankers were admitting to regarding the extent of their bad debts. But how wide was that fissure? Nevertheless, they were between a rock and a hard place because the banks could not be allowed to fail. It was agreed the State had to guarantee the Irish banks and building societies without a clear idea of the cost to the taxpayer. Like the indulgent father of a winsome teenage daughter, the government was prepared to pay a bill regardless of the total.

Collective Cabinet responsibility meant that ministers had to be rounded up for an emergency meeting. While a number of senior ministers had already been put on notice, the Cabinet secretariat now contacted the remainder, advising them to be ready for the incorporeal meeting between 1 a.m. and 2 a.m. Even then, most ministers were not told exactly of the decision's scope. Minister for Defence Willie O'Dea was woken shortly after 1 a.m. by his ringing mobile, but it had gone to voicemail by the time he fumbled for it. The landline by his bed rang seconds later.

Green Party leader and Minister for the Environment John Gormley's mobile had run out of power, and the secretariat could not access him. In desperation, his garda driver was called, and despatched to the minister's home in Dublin's Ringsend. He was woken up and asked to ring the Taoiseach's office.

Ministers were now given details of the ground-breaking financial pledge which shouldered hundreds of billions of banking liabilities on to taxpayers. In return, the financial institutions would pay a fee for the cover enabling them to stay in business.

The cost was gauged at €440 billion on the basis that the banks had liabilities of €440 billion and assets of €500 billion. An asset's value is debatable, however: goods are only worth their resale price. The banks' problematic assets tended to be collateral pledged against loans by property developers, which meant their assets were often in property. And property was crashing. That figure of €500 billion was destined to tumble before the ink was dry on the guarantee.

Nevertheless, ministers assented unanimously, including the telephone participants. Micheál Martin gave his agreement from a private room in Newark Airport – he was en route back to Ireland from the United Nations General Assembly when he took the call.

Finally, at 3.30 a.m., Cowen encouraged Lenihan to go home and put his head down for a couple of hours. It had been an action-packed night – and a busy day stretched ahead of him.

And as Rome burned, Anglo Irish Bank's chairman Seán FitzPatrick slept soundly through it all.

The Airwaves, 5.00 a.m.– 8.30 a.m.

At 5 a.m., by prior arrangement, the Department of Finance briefed RTÉ's business correspondent David Murphy, this book's co-author. He had been alerted the previous night to expect 'something major coming down the track'. The department issued a press release at 6.50 a.m., immediately ahead of news bulletins at 7 a.m.

An advance copy of the blueprint for survival had been sent at 4.30 a.m. to the European Central Bank, followed by a call from Ireland's central banker John Hurley to its head Jean-Claude Trichet.

Lenihan now made telephone contact with the French finance minister and chair of EU finance ministers, Christine Lagarde. He also spoke with Luxembourg's Prime Minister Jean-Claude Juncker, Europe's veteran fixer and head of an informal grouping of eurozone finance ministers. Speaking mainly in French, in which he is fluent, Lenihan relayed Ireland's decision. Europe's response was tetchy. It wanted all the countries within the Commission to keep in step, and Ireland had struck out on its own. Lenihan argued he had to intervene to save the banks – crisis point had been reached.

Next, the Minister for Finance was interviewed on RTÉ's radio news programme *Morning Ireland*. As Irish citizens boiled their kettles and brushed their teeth, preparing for work, they learned that their reputations had been harnessed to lend credibility to the banks – now regarded as cancers in the global marketplace.

The minister's work was far from done. After going off air, Lenihan called Enda Kenny while the Fine Gael leader was walking around TV3 waiting to appear on its *Ireland AM* breakfast show for a prearranged interview. Cross-benches support was important. He also phoned Labour Party leader Eamon Gilmore. Conversations later took place with Fine Gael finance spokesman Richard Bruton and his Labour counterpart Joan Burton.

Bedlam erupted in Britain at the news: there were reverberations for its own banking system. All the Irish banks had a British presence, and Bank of Ireland also had a savings scheme with the British Post Office. To avail of the guarantee, depositors would simply have to take their money out of a British bank and place it in an Irish one.

Government Buildings, 8.00 a.m.–6.00 p.m.

The stock markets opened at 8 a.m., and it was immediately clear that the plan was working. As the markets gave the deal a cordial welcome, a halt was brought to the share-price decline of all the major financial institutions. Shares in Anglo Irish Bank rose by 40 per cent, AIB by 20 per cent, Bank of Ireland by 18 per cent and Irish Life & Permanent by 13 per cent. In a matter of minutes, they had regained the catastrophic losses of the previous day.

In the Sycamore Room, Fianna Fáil ministers gathered for their usual pre-Cabinet breakfast meeting. Many were flabbergasted by the night's dramatic events. An exhausted Cowen made no effort to hide the gravity of the situation. One of those present reported the Taoiseach as saying, 'We came very close to the brink.'

Britain's Chancellor of the Exchequer, Alistair Darling, called Lenihan in the first of a series of phone conversations that day. It was not an amicable exchange. Demanding a reversal of the decision, Darling warned that money would flood out of British banks. Lenihan's response was that he had to guard Ireland's interests.

British Prime Minister Gordon Brown rang Brian Cowen later. While expressing concern, he did not ask for the guarantee to be overridden – although he did urge Cowen to throw a lifeline to UK bank subsidiaries operating in Ireland. Perhaps conscious of the lack of warning from Downing Street when it nationalised Northern Rock a year previously, Cowen replied that Ireland had to look to its own. Brown did not let the issue rest. He proceeded to complain twice about

Ireland's banking guarantee, in telephone calls to President of the European Commission José Manuel Barroso.

At 9.30 a.m., Lenihan held a press conference at the Department of Finance. His eyes were red-rimmed from lack of sleep yet he was in feisty form. The atmosphere in the room was tense, and he faced a barrage of questions about how the government had reached its decision and what it would mean for the taxpayer. He insisted that the failure of an Irish bank would be an 'economic catastrophe' and would 'paralyse trade in this country'. The measures were aimed at providing stability in the banking sector, he stressed.

Uproar broke out when, after half an hour, he stood up and said he had to attend a Cabinet meeting. The interrogation was only getting into its stride. But the minister was needed at Cabinet to notify his colleagues about details of the guarantee.

There, Lenihan went through the draft legislation line by line. Tánaiste Mary Coughlan and Minister for Agriculture Brendan Smith, both representing border constituencies, peppered him with queries. They had already been contacted by mobile phone by infuriated Ulster Bank executives, as they were driven to the meeting in their ministerial Mercedes.

Lenihan indicated that Irish-regulated banks were first in line for protection, and he would wait and see about other banks operating in the jurisdiction. Quizzed about the emergency plan's cost, he told colleagues the banks would be levied if one of them did collapse. These payments would be used to pay the defunct bank's debts before the State had to settle a bill.

Bank share prices were now surging. Lenihan had two further conversations with the British Chancellor of the Exchequer that day. By their final encounter, Darling had withdrawn his demand to abandon the guarantee. He had accepted either that the Irish government had no choice or that he had no power to have the decision rescinded.

Later that day, the European Commission held a press conference in which Dutchwoman Neelie Kroes, European Commissioner for Competition, slated Ireland for not alerting the Commission until after the event. Ireland was seen as a solo operator and not a team player, in a union which prized collaboration.

Despite reservations about the strain it would put on the public purse, the electorate welcomed Lenihan's reincarnation as the Rambo of the Oireachtas. It was a relief, finally, to have someone make a decision and push it through with a certain panache. Months of government inaction had bred uncertainty and trepidation. Lenihan was only four months into the job, and hopes were raised – perhaps unrealistically – that he might fill the leadership vacuum.

Meanwhile, around the world, investors, banking experts and policy-makers scratched their heads and tried to fathom what exactly Lenihan had announced. If banks were in trouble, why not give them a once-off injection of capital? Why had the Irish State backed itself into a situation where it was now liable for an unpredictable avalanche of bad debts from a property bust? Why were investors so worried about the banks when the Financial Regulator, as well as the bankers, had worn themselves hoarse insisting there was no cause for alarm?

And, significantly, why were there so many rumours about Anglo Irish Bank?

Leinster House, 6.00 p.m.–midnight

Deputies were summoned to the Dáil to discuss the legislation on the State guarantee. But the Bill proved to be unready, and the Dáil was suspended for three hours. At 9 p.m., it was suspended again to allow the government yet more time to prepare the legislation, which had encountered an eleventh-hour hitch.

At 9.45 p.m., TDs were given copies of the legislation still warm from the printers. 'It's like being asked to read the Lisbon Treaty in fifteen minutes,' remarked Fine Gael's enterprise spokesman Leo Varadkar. At 10 p.m., Brian Lenihan unveiled the formal details of the guarantee to deputies. For some, it smacked of another period of easy money for profligate bankers. It was argued that greed and recklessness were being rewarded – profit-hungry bankers had landed their financial institutions in a black hole and were adopting a Pontius Pilate approach to the consequences.

Taoiseach Brian Cowen denied he was just doling out money. He said the move allowed banks to access credit on the international markets and would facilitate economic life in the country. He maintained that the taxpayer was not exposed.

The Opposition was furious it had been left out of the loop, complaining that the legislation was the most momentous in the Dáil's history yet there had been no consultation before the bailout decision was reached. However, Fine Gael's finance spokesman Richard Bruton supported the legislation, saying it would help copper-fasten the financial system. But Labour spoke against it, to Lenihan's annoyance. The party's leader Eamon Gilmore pointed out that it would increase the cost Ireland paid for its borrowings.

'This legislation is not about protecting the interests of the banks. It is about the safeguarding of the economy and everybody who lives and works here,' Lenihan said, defending the guarantee passionately. The message was that everyone in the economy would benefit from the legislation, not just the banks.

The debate ended just before midnight – the government pushed it through. After passing through the Dáil, the legislation proceeded to the Seanad for a debate that lasted into the early hours of the morning, and it got the nod there, too.

The guarantee was a done deal. A blank cheque had just been handed to the banks.

1

The *Riverdance* Generation

*'If you can count your money, you don't have a
billion dollars.'*
Oil tycoon, John Paul Getty

One of the sacred truisms of the boom was that Ireland had
thrown off the weight of its impoverished history. The 1980s
were stitched into the tapestry of the bad old days and would
never see the light of day again. Dynamic Celtic Tiger cubs
had triumphed over a recurrent pattern that had bedevilled
generations: too many people, too few jobs. The past was a
foreign country and had nothing to teach. Or so it was
thought.

But when the economy crashed in 2008 and 2009,
unemployment surged again. At the beginning of 2009,
around 1,000 people a day were losing their jobs. And the
lessons of the 1980s became chillingly relevant.

The boom had lasted so long that many had either
forgotten or had never experienced gloomier times.
Astronomical economic growth had supplied luxury cars,
house extensions, multiple foreign holidays – an unimaginable
level of affluence. At first it was pinch-me-I'm-dreaming

territory. But prosperity soon became the norm – and a dangerous assumption was made that life would always glow with promise. Sensible habits were jettisoned. No more economising, shopping around, saving up to buy: credit took care of everything. Greed, it seemed, had an Irish passport.

But history repeated itself – with a vengeance. And as Ireland's economy slammed into reverse, it became brutally clear that some of the conditions allowing the economy to flourish had disappeared. Recreating the magic potion would take years.

Learning the lessons of the 1980s is crucial. Ireland hauled itself out of a swamp before, and we need to see which building blocks worked and why. What were the measures taken to pilot the country towards the boom?

The 1980s was Ireland's lost decade. By the late 1980s, it was a land of dole queues, derelict sites and vacant business premises with hoardings over the windows. It was a land of instant coffee for breakfast, Tayto crisp sandwiches for lunch and Pot Noodles for dinner. It was a land of low expectations and high emigration – a bleak economic backwater.

For a thirteen-year period, economic growth had averaged a miserable 2 per cent. In 1987, the average income hovered at around two-thirds of the British equivalent. But the cost of living was not one-third cheaper: on the contrary, less money had to stretch further.

Here was a nation which seemed doomed to raise its young for the export market. The fit, the educated and the ambitious opted out. The brain drain was a particular loss, with graduates making a beeline for airports and ferries, leaving home to work in London, in Sydney and in the Holy Trinity of New York, Boston and Chicago. Once they shipped out, few returned. There was nothing for them to come back to.

External perceptions about the country were negative,

with the Troubles dominating the headlines. Investors were underwhelmed – they gave Ireland a miss.

The nadir for Ireland was 1986. Everything that could go wrong had gone wrong and the State was in pandemonium. Unemployment soared to 17 per cent. One per cent of the population was emigrating every year. The Industrial Development Authority (IDA) tried to spread the message of its energetic pool of skilled workers with a poster of young graduates at key locations, including Dublin Airport. 'We're the young Europeans,' cried the slogan. Within a year, all the graduates featured in the photograph had emigrated. There were no jobs for them in Ireland.

Previous administrations, wrestling with the conflicting demands of tackling unemployment while retaining enough popularity to stay in office, hired more public servants to reduce dole queues. This policy resulted in a spectacular level of borrowing: almost 130 per cent of Ireland's entire national income.

Attempting to tame the turmoil, the Fianna Fáil government hiked tax rates on alcohol and tobacco as well as on television sets and other consumer items. Unsurprisingly, smuggling across the border from the North of Ireland was rampant.

Taxes were so crippling that workers demanded pay increases, despite enormous levels of unemployment – a condition that usually acts as a check on wages. The top rate of income tax was 65 per cent, and the tax on company profits was 50 per cent. This compares with a 41 per cent income-tax top rate and just 12.5 per cent for company profits less than two decades later, in the Tiger era.

So how did Ireland make the transition? The government embarked on a programme of national recovery. In an attempt to create order from the rats' nest that defined the public finances, a freeze on public-sector recruitment was introduced. Its architect was the pragmatic Minister for Finance

Ray MacSharry, who came to be known as Mack the Knife. Cost-cutting policies pushed through by him led inexorably to slashing both public spending and jobs.

His decisions were unpopular and caused pain, but, significantly, they had the backing of his party's main rivals. Fine Gael committed itself to the Tallaght Strategy, a policy under which it pledged not to oppose economic reforms in the national interest that were proposed by the Fianna Fáil minority government. Social partnership was another plank in the national recovery; it delivered industrial peace so that potential employers did not need to worry about strike action disrupting productivity. Workers were promised income-tax cuts in return for wage restraint, which kept Irish salaries lower than in other economies chasing similar job projects.

Other initiatives included the International Financial Services Centre (IFSC) in Dublin's Docklands. It was set up in 1987 and became outstandingly successful in the field of banking, insurance, stockbroking and fund management. People were dubious at the outset, however. It was primarily due to financier Dermot Desmond's persistence – and the cooperation of then leader of the Opposition, Charlie Haughey – that this ambitious project to set up a world centre for financial services became airborne. A 1986 feasibility study concluded that a financial district was not viable. But Desmond refused to take no for an answer. He approached Haughey, and the politician later included the IFSC in his manifesto ahead of the 1987 general election.

Haughey was voted into office, and that same year the IFSC was given the green light. In time, half of the world's top fifty banks would open operations there. In the decade to June 2007, it would contribute €6 billion to the economy, excluding the taxes of those it employed. In a rare interview, with *Business and Finance* magazine in 2004, Desmond said, 'no other politician in Ireland would have built the IFSC but Charlie Haughey.'

Four years later, banker Seán FitzPatrick also paid tribute to the visionaries who established the IFSC. In a March 2008 UCD business alumni presentation, the banker said that the IFSC was a radical vision and 'would never have happened unless certain individuals had dared to dream'. He did not name Haughey – he is not readily invoked in Ireland of the Hundred Thousand Tribunals – but FitzPatrick cited state agencies, bankers, stockbrokers, politicians and civil servants.

FitzPatrick said, 'Back in 1987, Ireland was seen as a hopelessly delinquent economy. Our public finances were a joke, the IMF was hanging around waiting to move in and take over, unemployment was up at 20 per cent, inflation was still in double digits, the business failure rate was simply horrendous.

'The very idea of seeking to plant an international financial services industry in such unpromising soil was seen by many as the stuff of madness at that time. Not only were we caught in the throes of recession from which the rest of Europe had long since recovered, we had one of the most penal and irrational tax systems. Oh, and our banking and financial services sector at that time wasn't much to write home about either.'

Some things take to change better than others.

An educated labour force was among the stepping stones, aided by the far-sightedness of earlier policies such as free secondary schooling introduced in 1966. Irish education standards were high relative to those in other English-speaking countries.

Improvements in the technical-education area as a result of EU investment also played a key role in up-skilling the workforce. By the millennium, five times as many Irish people were in third-level education as forty years before.

The promotion of competition stimulated development. Ryanair, a low-cost airline modelled on Southwest Airlines in the US, gained access to the Dublin–London air route in 1985. This had been controlled by the duopoly of State airlines Aer Lingus and British Airways. The brash young competitor drove a coach and four through fares and expanded the market by 65 per cent in two years. Tourist numbers and revenue grew, and the benefits of competition were extended to other regulated sectors.

Other dynamics included EU membership, access to the Single Market and Ireland's status as an English-speaking country in the eurozone. English was the lingua franca of the international business community.

Finally, Ireland was not some crackpot state, and it had institutions underpinning the rule of law and public administration. The financial system was also efficient – at least back then, before bankers threw out the rulebook on lending.

These measures helped lay the foundations for the Celtic Tiger and the golden age that roared in with it.

During the 1980s, the 64,000-dollar question was: where would all the jobs needed to achieve full employment come from? The government's concerted wooing of foreign multinationals was the special ingredient in the mix. Ireland paid court to US multinationals with all the persistence of an impassioned suitor – achieving spectacular results from the late 1980s onwards.

The role of the IDA became pivotal when the conditions to attract these multinationals fell into alignment. It had been plugging away for decades, luring foreign companies to set up in Ireland. But in the springtime of the boom, it was suddenly in a position to present Ireland as an über-appealing place for multinationals to do business. And the Celtic Tiger burst on the scene with all the pizzazz of *Riverdance*. Lights, camera, action.

The IDA's philosophy was simple. Hook a whale, and minnows will follow. Its instincts were spot on. A flood of international corporations, especially from the US, opened plants and offices in Ireland, and smaller companies operating in similar fields tagged behind. They saw giants such as Microsoft able to make money in that small island on the edge of Europe and fancied some of the same. Within a few years, a clutch of household names were conducting business from Ireland.

Imagine an average office worker. Sitting on his or her desk are three items: a can of Coca-Cola, a computer and a printer. The computer is built by Dell which, despite a round of devastating job losses, continues to employs hundreds in Limerick and Cherrywood, County Dublin. The computer runs on an Intel chip developed and manufactured in Leixlip, County Kildare. The software is from Microsoft, which has an operation in Sandyford, County Dublin, where software is developed, tested and adapted for different markets. The home page on the internet browser is Google's, which has an operation in Dublin's south inner city. The printer is made by Hewlett Packard, a major employer in Leixlip. Coca-Cola, the world's largest drinks company, has a manufacturing and innovation facility under way in Wexford, with the first workers hired on site in 2009.

Barely a week went by without US executives, still bleary from their overnight flights, holding press conferences to announce more jobs. They were always upbeat, articulate and ultra-smooth. Business parks, office blocks and internet connectivity popped up wherever they stepped.

Commentators and politicians sometimes indulged in bunkum about the lure of the Celtic mists and a diaspora keen to invest in Ireland for nostalgic reasons – to give something back to the old country. The US executives did not contradict them. But, despite giving the impression they came bearing gifts, they were in business to make money. The bottom line was always their motivation: they were in Ireland because they had cut a sweet deal with the IDA.

Jobs were created. More jobs than anyone had ever conceived. The State moved towards 3.6 per cent unemployment, widely regarded as the lowest it could possibly go. As with the Aegean stables, it was as if a vast river had been diverted to run through Ireland – this one carrying jobs. As late as 2008, some 135,000 people were employed directly in 1,000 IDA-backed companies, with a legion more employed indirectly.

During the boom, the agency was led by Kieran McGowan, who received plaudits for working with successive governments to implement far-sighted policies. His successor was Sean Dorgan, a bright man with the aura of a parish priest. A speech he gave in 2006, entitled 'How Ireland Became the Celtic Tiger,' returns to haunt him, and others who made a similar analysis: 'In just over a generation, Ireland has evolved from one of the poorest countries in Western Europe to one of the most successful. As a result of sustained efforts over many years, the past of declining population, poor living standards and economic stagnation has been left behind.'

Regardless of who held the steering wheel at the IDA, it was adept at spotting new trends which would yield jobs. As wages in Ireland rose, it was inevitable that old-style assembly jobs would divert to countries where the work could be carried out for less. So the IDA looked for high-skilled, high-paying jobs for the workforce. An agricultural economy had undergone a dramatic reinvention and was selling itself as a hub for industries with names such as nanotechnology, life sciences and biopharmaceuticals.

The outbreak of job announcements was unprecedented. It became so repetitive that the media and the general public lost interest. One RTÉ reporter, covering the announcement of

1,000 new technology jobs at the height of the boom, was dismayed to find it did not even warrant a headline on the evening television news bulletin.

At virtually every media conference, an identikit phrase was trotted out by the US executives in their button-down shirts. Asked why they chose Ireland, their response was invariably 'the young educated workforce'. One-fifth of the population was under the age of fifteen. Ireland had its baby boom later than other developed countries, between 1965 and 1980. This bulge in the population fed into the labour market from the late 1980s onwards. Young workers were available just as the economy was taking off, and many had been through third-level education. From 1990 to 2005, employment soared from 1.1 million to 1.9 million – solving the persistent problem of emigration.

But there was more to the boom than a ready labour supply. Ireland had a 10 per cent tax on profits for manufacturing companies, as well as companies operating from the IFSC. Eurocrats in Brussels applied pressure to change this regime, insisting it was unfair. In 1993, Ireland responded with a rate of 12.5 per cent tax on company profits across the board. (Ireland has a history of using its tax system innovatively to develop international businesses. The first duty-free zone in the world was set up in Shannon in 1947.)

Behind the scenes, the art of accountancy was kept busy-busy-busy. The bait of low tax rates was not the only enticement for multinationals. Also on offer were grant assistance from the energetic IDA plus the freedom to repatriate profits. A disproportionate share of firms relocating to Ireland were drawn by legitimate mechanisms to reduce taxes.

Meanwhile, a rising tide lifted a flotilla of boats, and US multinationals were not the only job creators. Law firms, accountancy practices, estate agencies, architects, insurance companies and stockbrokers hired staff. Hotels, catering companies, restaurants and pubs boosted their payrolls. Newspapers were splitting at the seams with situations vacant.

For the first time in Ireland's history, emigrants could return home to a job, and immigration figures would soon outstrip those for emigration. In 2000, Mary Harney, then Minister for Enterprise, Trade and Employment, memorably described Ireland as closer to Boston than Berlin. 'As Irish people, our relationships with the United States and the EU are complex. Geographically we are closer to Berlin than Boston. Spiritually we are probably a lot closer to Boston than Berlin.' Few disagreed with her.

The return of the Wild Geese, a phenomenon for which politicians were not slow to claim credit, contributed to the feel-good factor sweeping the State. In 1999 – coincidentally the year in which return migration peaked – Harney gave an interview to the Australian network ABC Radio National. In it she spoke of the importance, both symbolic and economic, of the homeward flight of the émigrés.

'Emigration was a big political issue,' she said. 'During the seventies and eighties, we constantly had scenes on our television of Christmas and Easter and after the summer period, of children leaving home – going away to America, to Britain, to many parts of Europe and other parts of the world, to Australia.

'The families were broken up. Parents had invested heavily in the education of the children. They could no longer sustain schools, post offices, football teams, because the young people had just gone. So now, people are coming back, a thousand people a week are coming to live in Ireland.'

Her comments about the leakage of Ireland's youth, and the empty gaps they left in society, referred to pre-boom days. Ironically, however, they held up a mirror to the post-boom period, because the spectre of emigration returned with stupefying speed.

In the ABC Radio interview, Harney explained how Ireland was attracting emigrants home. 'We have what's called the Millennium Fund, where we're trying to encourage Irish people who are fairly advanced in technology, in particular, to come back and consider establishing a company in Ireland,' she said. 'But I think the reputation of the country now is the big attraction – as the Celtic Tiger. We are the second biggest exporter of software in the world after the United States. They know about the opportunities – they are coming back in search of them – and we want to encourage more of them back. It's a good time to come back here.'

What a difference a decade makes. Some of those returned emigrants have had to pack their bags again, in light of the crash. As economist David McWilliams put it, 'My generation don't want to be the first generation who have had to emigrate twice in their working lifetime.'

But it happened to some of them.

What was the banks' position during the bonanza? In the early days of regeneration, conservative banking held sway. Nothing was left to chance. Banking was similar to the civil service, a safe job for life. Never mind the tedium, think of the pension. There was no hint of the buccaneering bankers who would emerge.

The number-one priority was ensuring that loans were repaid, and chances were never taken with a bank's funds. Bankers backing a business customer's application for a loan were grilled by the credit committee, made up of senior executives. 'At Bank of Ireland, going to a credit committee was like swotting for your Leaving Cert,' said Adam McNulty, former equity fund manager in Bank of Ireland's Asset Management Team, who also worked in a variety of roles at the bank. 'I dealt with investments on the agricultural side, people like Greencore and Diageo, big meat plants. It would take a lot of work to get a loan of €10 million to €50 million from the credit committee. It meant a full presentation.'

While the banks were lending judiciously, they were not necessarily paragons of virtue. They actively helped people evade tax by issuing bogus non-resident accounts so that clients would not pay tax on the interest on their savings. Customer service frequently covered a variety of mechanisms to keep money away from the eyes of the taxman – for example, in the Isle of Man.

Officially, though, prudence and caution were the watchwords. Some branch managers even took a parish-priest approach to customers. In 1999, a young woman known to one of the authors was scolded for cashing in a mortgage with her ex-boyfriend and applying for another with her new partner. The money was lent by EBS – but with a moralising lecture attached.

Prudence and caution served bankers well throughout their history, but they were no match for the property epidemic. In 1994, economic growth had jumped from 2 to 6 per cent and by 1995 it had reached almost 10 per cent. From that point on, the economic marvel gathered a head of steam.

Along with job creation came increased demand for living accommodation, and the property market spread its wings. Prices ratcheted upwards, partly because available stock was in short supply. In March 1996, when prices began their dramatic rise, the average three-bed home cost €75,000. Within four years, the average price had doubled to €150,000. Just two years later, in 2002, it had climbed to €182,000. At this point, the Central Bank began to chafe. Later that year, it wrote to banks and building societies expressing concern about the increase in mortgage lending. It said credit conditions could be one of the factors influencing what it described as the 'rapid acceleration in residential property prices'. The Central Bank pointed out that prices were already high by international standards – even before the latest acceleration.

It was also becoming alarmed about fatter pay packets across the board. During the boom of the nineties and noughties, there were more jobs than people to fill them, which resulted in a skills shortage and spiralling wages. Big corporations favoured Ireland because pay was comparatively low. But this state of affairs was changing. Multinationals were notoriously fickle. If wages and costs grew too steep, they would have no hesitation in folding their tents and moving elsewhere.

But the party was in full swing now; nobody wanted to listen to pessimists with their brimming basins of cold water. The government ignored the Central Bank. And its citizens took their prompt from Dáil Éireann.

The Central Bank was unable to take any action to influence consumer behaviour. The normal handbrake by which countries dampen growth – control over interest rates had been passed to Frankfurt and the European Central Bank. Europe was not about to reduce interest rates for the benefit of Ireland and its 4 million inhabitants. It had bigger fish to fry: the need to stimulate the German economy of 80 million people. Ireland pumped up the volume unchecked, while the Central Bank wrung its hands helplessly from its ivory tower in Dame Street.

'There has been a lot of revisionism going on at the Central Bank since the crash,' observed a retired senior banker. 'The main analysis from the Central Bank was always for a soft landing. Only its worst-case scenario was for a dramatic fall in house prices.

'But at the time of the boom, we had an extra million people wanting housing. The planning system did not deliver serviced land in the right place at a reasonable price for new homes. That is why you suddenly had so many people living in County Carlow and County Kildare.

'I am astounded that between 2004 and 2007, commercial lending in the banks grew so much. You have to ask yourself some serious questions about why this was. But part of the problem comes from the recommendations on banking laws from the Basel Committee on Banking Supervision, Basel II. It basically said "do more lending with less capital".'

While the Central Bank bit its lip and wrote letters, its sister organisation, the Financial Regulator, asked the banks to stress-test mortgage applicants to see if they could cope with a 2 per cent increase in interest rates. Unfortunately, that test was deplorably weak because interest rates rose by 2.25 per cent from January 2006 to July 2008. Higher rates piled on pressure for thousands of young couples who bought at the top of the property boom. The regulator did attempt to introduce measures to cool the runaway lending to developers, but they were watered down after lobbying by bankers.

Bankers, builders and property developers were on an out-of-control binge, aided and abetted by incompetent regulation and a complicit political establishment. But it looked as if they were having a ball – and virtually everyone in the country wanted to gatecrash that party. It was made deceptively easy. 'Come On In, The Water's Lovely' was the new national anthem.

Prices for a family home in Dublin reached parity with Beverly Hills. It was instant-millionaire status – on paper. Initially people blinked as house prices turned crazy, but the euphoria generated by all those zeros on a price tag meant that soon everyone wanted a piece of crazy for themselves.

During Leaders' Questions in June 2006, then Taoiseach Bertie Ahern was actually boasting about Ireland's turbo-charged house-building programme. 'Investment in infrastructure, streamlined planning and more effective use of land have produced record housing output. Almost 81,000 houses were built in 2005 whereas ten years ago the figure was fewer than 30,000. As a result, we are producing new houses at a much faster rate than other countries.

'Home ownership is rising, and some twenty new homes are produced annually per 1,000 of population compared to five per 1,000 in the EU. Thankfully, unlike in large parts of the EU, people are buying houses.'

Yes, people were buying, but anyone who took out a mortgage in 2006, when the country's prime minister was hustler-in-chief for the property push, has reason to be less than pleased. In June 2006, when the Taoiseach was talking up the market, the average national house price was €299,000. By December 2008, eighteen months later, average house prices were €261,000 nationally, according to the Permanent TSB/Economic and Social Research Institute (ESRI) House Price Index. And 2009 saw an even steeper decline.

Throughout the noughties, despite countless warnings, property prices continued in overdrive. Greed and recklessness smothered prudence and caution, and the banks were lending merrily. During the boom, house prices trebled over an eleven-year period. Instead of dampening the market, the government continued its policy of stimulating yet more investment in property. At one point, twenty different tax incentives were offered for people to purchase houses or apartments. These breaks encouraged developers to build, lubricating the boom. By early 2007, the average house price had ratcheted up to €311,000.

Perpendicular property prices were a problem for many would-be buyers, especially couples on the average industrial wage. Renting was rarely an option, however. Housing stock in the rental market was tiny and demand was huge, frequently making it as expensive to rent as to buy. As for public housing, the waiting lists were prohibitive. People had to buy – come hell or high water.

Despite deterrent prices, the queues of potential buyers did not thin out. The history of the Irish people gives them an unusual attachment to home ownership. Pre-Independence, the bulk of land was owned by outsiders who were often absentee landlords. Tenants had sparse legal protection and were rarely sure of the roofs over their heads. Race memory – indeed, family memory – meant that, given the opportunity, an Irishman or woman would always seek the security of owning the land on which they lived. Home ownership for its citizens was one of the fledgling Free State's stated goals. In the early years of independence, it was never more than an aspiration for many. But home ownership became an attainable target during the boom, when jobs and mortgages were plentiful.

One person's home is another person's investment opportunity. And so, during this period of soar-away prices, investors entered the market and began snapping up houses – manipulating prices inexorably upwards. Investors had a ready supply of tenants from Poland and the Baltic states – new admissions to the EU – who were arriving in Ireland in droves. This spawned a cycle of workers coming to Ireland to join the building industry and building homes which they themselves rented.

Developers also stepped in, building houses at a ferocious rate. Land prices rocketed: if agricultural land was rezoned for housing, it could expect up to a tenfold increase in value. Some developers made gargantuan profits overnight, even allowing for land price rises. Shopping centres, housing estates and apartment blocks sprang up, sometimes in areas without schools, roads or other infrastructure. Ireland was building as never before – at rates that outstripped the US, the UK and Europe.

Observers sometimes refer to the crane index to assess economic development. By that pointer, Ireland was flying. Cranes jostled for space on the skyline. Pneumatic drills and the whine of circular saws operated late into the night.

An oligarchy of developers emerged, men permanently on the lookout for greenfield sites to develop. Typically, they socialised with politicians – the corps with the power to rezone land. It was a recipe for corruption on an epic scale. In the Dáil in 2006, socialist TD Joe Higgins described the recent funeral of Charlie Haughey in scathing terms, 'The VIP pen in the Donnycarney church was like a major house builders' convention.' Later in the same speech he thundered, 'The clatter of developers' helicopters as they descend on the Fianna Fáil tent at the Galway races is drowning out the calls from tens of thousands of young people and their parents to stop this scandal of unbridled profiteering in the housing market.' Higgins was treated as a maverick playing to the gallery. Taoiseach Bertie Ahern accused him of trying to bring the country back to the poverty-stricken days of the 1930s.

In September 2005, some 12.5 per cent of the entire workforce was employed in the construction industry – one in four males. Two-thirds of them were assembling houses, according to Davy stockbrokers. 'In employment terms, the construction sector is now almost as large as the entire manufacturing sector,' noted Davy's chief economist Robbie Kelleher.

But these new developments were not necessarily in the capital, where the jobs were centred. Dublin was already built up, and few first-time buyers could aspire to a three-bed house with a garden there. Ireland was introduced to the concept of the commuter belt. Workers eager for a toehold on the property ladder were coaxed to buy in Meath, Wicklow and Kildare – sometimes further afield – and to travel daily to work in Dublin.

Resentment festered that couples born and raised in the capital were priced out of that market. The example was routinely taken of a guard and a nurse, both with safe public-service jobs and pensions, whose combined salaries could not stretch to a family home in the city. In the main, however, people were too preoccupied with commuting to work so they could service their enormous mortgages to raise these complaints beyond a mutter.

In 2007 alone, 90,000 new homes were built. Houses were mushrooming so fast that the Electricity Supply Board could barely get them connected in time for occupation. By this stage the Central Bank was sounding like a broken record, continually repeating its concerns about the economy's overdependence on the construction sector. It moaned, 'While it is understandable that resources have been moved into this sector in recent years, it is equally clear that the rate of expansion cannot be maintained.' Central bankers were right: the property market was dangerously overheated. But people paid as much attention to central bankers as the Trojans did to the desolate forecasts of their priestess Cassandra.

The wooden horse was already inside the city gates.

2

Nobody Shouted Stop

'Against stupidity, the gods themselves contend in vain.'
German poet-philosopher, Friedrich von Schiller

Ireland had morphed from Éireann to Irelandistan in the space of just twenty years. It was under the spell of turbo capitalism. The country was a textbook example of how to take an economy which was once the financial leper of Europe and transform it into the boy wonder of modern economics.

By 2006, the decade-long boom was reaching its crescendo. There was near consensus inside Ireland that the State was unassailable; observers in the wider world were less convinced. Only the previous year, the *New York Times* had described Ireland as the 'Wild West of European finance' – an assessment which partly prompted the creation of the office of the Financial Regulator. Many outsiders wondered how long house prices could continue to rise and how an economy could survive by using a property bubble as an engine for growth.

Sceptics called it a bubble, observing that it was only a matter of time before it popped. But Nostradamus figures had been insisting for years that the boom cycle could not continue indefinitely, and still their doomsday predictions had not come true. Ireland's leaders shook off negative appraisals. Begrudgery, they shrugged. Any criticism from within or without – 'Liechtenstein on the Liffey', for example – was routinely ignored. As far as the bankers, builders and property developers were concerned, the Irish economy was still theirs for the trashing.

On 7 April 2006 came the most important gathering in the corporate calendar. Anyone who was a player wanted to be seen here. The occasion was the Irish Management Institute Conference, a gathering of the key people in Irish industry and a peerless networking opportunity. Politicians had an appetite for hobnobbing with the captains of industry in attendance. High-flying businessmen (who literally did fly in to these events) were lionised as society's wealth creators. These were the men to whom others bent the knee.

Among those putting in an appearance was the boyish former Aer Lingus chief executive Willie Walsh, who had been snapped up to lead British Airways. Here was a man who symbolised everything to which delegates aspired. His appointment as head of the largest airline in Europe was yet another reason for Ireland's business elite to preen. It was one more pointer that the Irish had finally arrived on the international stage. The little country with the big self-image was finally punching above its weight.

The conference took place in the glorious setting of Druid's Glen in County Wicklow, amid the five-star luxury of the Marriott Hotel and Country Club. Delegates had a view of the lush, rolling hills of the golf course from the hotel's windows. Indeed, for those who wanted to skip the speeches, a session on the links was a useful way to conduct business.

Bertie Ahern, still in his Lord-of-all-Creation incarnation, arrived by helicopter to address the conference. The weather was unseasonably warm, adding to the impression of Ireland as a state which had not only discovered an enchanted formula for prosperity but could also control the climate.

At Druid's Glen, Ahern gave an interview about the property market which can only be considered bizarre in view of its timing and subsequent developments. He launched a ferocious onslaught on those who suggested that property prices were about to fall. Pointing to predictions of a downturn in 2005 which had failed to materialise, the Taoiseach claimed that such abysmal advice had deterred people from buying homes. This led to them losing their chance to scrabble for a toehold on the property ladder.

He shook his head in a parody of grief over missed opportunities: 'If you had taken the advice of a year ago you would have lost a lot of money. Everyone said we would see a huge downturn in 2005 linking into 2006. They were entirely wrong. Really, we should have an examination into why people got it so wrong. In my view, there is no great problem, and the bad advice of last year given by so many has made some people make some mistakes – that maybe they should have bought last year.'

In fact, he was reacting to warnings from the State's own Central Bank. A charitable interpretation might suggest Ahern was offering reassurance in the manner of early English mystic Julian of Norwich: 'All shall be well, and all shall be well, and all manner of thing[s] shall be well.' Then again, there is a time for confidence – and a time for caution. Nine unbroken years in power had convinced the Taoiseach and his ministers that they knew better than the experts.

One of the most significant contributions at the conference came from Finn Lyden, managing director of SIAC Construction. During an interview (with David Murphy), he revealed his reservations about a specific aspect of the property boom which had become widespread, despite its potential for disaster. He said he was worried about homeowners taking equity from their houses to buy investment properties abroad. In Ireland at that time, many people hankered after an apartment in a European sunspot. It was yet more wide blue sea between an aspirant class and the caravan holidays of their childhood. Ryanair's expansionist chief executive Michael O'Leary had taken to quipping that as soon as he added a new route it triggered a property binge by Irish people. The real joke was that it occurred in locations people could scarcely find on the map – even while convinced they simply must have a place there.

Ireland could have been prepared for a downturn, if not a recession, but the government did not listen. Ministers bunged their ears and flatly refused to hear unpalatable truths. Yet, even as Ahern publicly questioned the forecasts of the Central Bank and heaped scorn on critics, some well-placed figures in the construction industry were also raising valid doubts. Finn Lyden, as head of one of the biggest construction groups in the country, deserved to have his apprehensions scrutinised.

Others, including the independent and well-regarded ESRI, *The Economist* magazine and a number of economists, were all hoisting the red flag. 'People talk about a Celtic Tiger; I prefer a clockwork mouse: we're fully wound up, and we're going to run down over the next decade,' ESRI economist John Fitzgerald cautioned, as far back as 1999.

In 2005, RTÉ's *Rip-Off Republic* series ruffled the feathers of the property industry, among others, by highlighting the cost of living and working in Ireland. Seán FitzPatrick led the counter-charge. In a speech delivered at the *Irish Times* Property Advertising Awards that September, he attacked the national broadcaster for giving Eddie Hobbs a platform.

'This is not good,' complained FitzPatrick. 'I'd genuinely worry that much of the nonsense he peddled would gain common currency, and that the wholly unbalanced Hobbsian perspective on Ireland of 2005 would fuel the anger of many of those who have failed to benefit from our economic success thus far.

'This could also support a political agenda that is far removed from any of our long-established political parties. Were that to happen, RTÉ should be held accountable, as the media generally must be, for the significant influence it has on the economic environment. This whole area needs attention.'

It is just one more example of the way opposing arguments were steamrollered. Everyone may as well have been whistling in the wind. Above all, the Taoiseach was intent on an aggressive defence of a property bubble which had released unprecedented tax returns for his government, delivering colossal popularity and power. He was on track to be returned as head of government for three consecutive terms, thanks to an electorate tipsy on the illusion of having a share in the pot of gold.

From a narrow, party-political perspective – as opposed to a standpoint concerned with a nation's well-being and future prospects – it was expedient to disregard warnings of a price slump.

Ahern went back on the offensive the following July in a speech to the Irish Congress of Trade Unions in the seaside town of Bundoran in County Donegal. Here he suggested he could not fathom how people who moaned about the economy did not commit suicide and be done with it. Referring to those who talked down the economy, Ahern said, 'Sitting on the sidelines, cribbing and moaning is a lost opportunity. I don't know how people who engage in that don't commit suicide.'

While he later apologised for his insensitivity regarding the issue of suicide, his strike was part of a concerted effort to drown out dissent. Non-believers in the myth of Ireland's economic miracle were not just discounted, they were ridiculed.

Ahern was at it again at the Cairde Fáil dinner in December 2007 in City West, fantasising about a 'slowing yet strong economic growth' and 'driving the Irish success story forward'. He referred to the 'need to protect Ireland's prosperity in the midst of economic downturn elsewhere in the world', as though Ireland was somehow immune to the international lurch into recession.

'Neither a borrower nor a lender be' – sound advice from Polonius in *Hamlet* but not really practical in the home-ownership field. Few people can buy a house without borrowing. By the middle of the boom, a disproportionate number of Irish people were in hock to the banks: they found themselves in a situation bankers call negative net cash, otherwise known as debt. In 1996, the average mortgage debt per head of population was €3,827. By 2006, this had soared to €29,078 and was growing every year by 24 per cent. Over a decade of uninterrupted growth, borrowings for home loans leapfrogged by 760 per cent. Wealth, or supposed wealth, was driven by property values. People imagined they were Aristotle Onassis because they bought and sold houses to each other at inflated prices. Only those who bailed out of the property market before the downturn benefited from the boom. And, even then, a number of those evacuees turned to the stock market . . . out of the frying pan into the fire.

Borrowers were not just signing up to mortgage debt. Spending quickly became habit-forming in a country with limited previous experience of disposable income. Traditionally, salaries had been too tight to allow for it. But credit, now readily available, caught fire. Such eye-popping figures were routinely spent on property that a distortion was caused: other expenditure seemed tame by comparison. EU Commissioner Charlie McCreevy later referred to the property boom as not just a bubble but a 'super-bubble', without mentioning that he, as Minister for Finance for seven years, was one of the people who had pumped it full of air.

In 1996, credit-card debt was €102 per person. Ten years later, that figure stood at €646. Ireland had the highest personal credit-card debt of any European country. Interest rates on credit cards are much higher than on other types of borrowing, but they proved no deterrent. The plastic fantastic bender indicated that we Irish were splurging on consumer goods, living it up like there was no Gomorrah.

Sales of hi-tech gadgets, fancy furniture and exotic holidays skyrocketed. Prestigious designer names from Tiffany to Dolce & Gabbana, from Versace to Jimmy Choo, set up camp to cash in. Smart gyms, spas and golf clubs had a membership glut. Hair and beauty salons were extending their hours and opening new branches as fast as they could raise signs over the doors. Whether opting for teeth-whitening or cosmetic surgery, buying state-of-the-art Gaggia coffee machines or installing electronic security gates, people were routinely living beyond their means. Money, and what it could buy, was worshipped. By the crest of the boom, personal credit reached one and a half times that of disposable income.

Car ownership went supersonic. As soon as homebuyers signed up for 100 per cent mortgages they were offered €25,000 car loans. Between 1996 and 2006, the number of cars for every 1,000 people rose from 292 to 420. Nor were motorists prepared to drive beat-up bangers. From 2000 to 2008, Jaguar increased its market share by one-third and Mercedes by a half, while the market share of Porsche tripled. 'There are more Mercedes per capita in Ireland than in Germany where they are made,' said Garvan Callan, head of wealth management at National Irish Bank, in a February 2008 report. The report also contained an acknowledgement that Ireland's wealth was primarily tied up in property.

And the fly in the ointment was that property values were falling.

No one paid any real attention. A fallacy had taken root that a foolproof formula had been invented for running a small, open economy. Ireland was riding the tiger. But there were no reins.

Warning voices were lost in the wilderness. Instead, the fantasy held sway that Ireland had evolved, in the space of a single generation, from among the poorest countries in Western Europe to one of the most affluent.

In 1996, weekly industrial earnings averaged €360 before tax. A decade later they were €601. They had not even doubled. So how were the waves of relentless expenditure powered?

By borrowing. Pawnshop economics had arrived.

An observer might imagine a steep rise in borrowing would be matched by a similar jump in wages. After all, money taken out on loan has to be repaid. But normal rules did not apply during the boom. Wages did rise quickly – in fact, more rapidly than should have been allowed for reasons of competitiveness. Salaries did not keep pace with borrowings, however. From 1996 to the peak recorded in house prices in January 2007, the cost of buying a home had risen by an astronomical 314 per cent.

These statistics were troubling for lenders. If salaries had not even doubled, how could they shift houses for many multiples again? Bankers did not want to turn off the mortgage loans' tap: it was too profitable, and their shareholders were too fond of the dividends they could pay out. Instead, banks made the unaffordable seem more manageable, offering loans of up to thirty-five and sometimes even forty years and 100 per cent mortgages.

In an effort to tot two and two up to five, banks, mortgage brokers and estate agents devised an 'affordability index'. This conveniently overlooked the massive sums people were borrowing, instead focusing on how much they would have to pay back every month. On this basis, manageable figures could now be presented to potential homeowners. Wide-eyed buyers were encouraged to concentrate on this massaged monthly repayment figure rather than on the chilling sum they were being charged for a property. As prices continued to surge, non-owners were continually reproved for failing to mount the property ladder. Those who hesitated were scolded as foolhardy and warned they would never own the roofs over their heads. This message was promulgated busily from the top down.

In 2006, during Leaders' Questions in the Dáil, Bertie Ahern praised the questionable lending policies implemented on his watch. The Taoiseach said that while house prices had risen, 'the cost of mortgage repayments, growth in incomes, employment, lower taxes, interest rates and availability of finance have had a positive impact on affordability. People are taking longer term mortgages, which reduces annual outgoings.'

So, that was all right then.

There was no recognition that people were being saddled with debts they would spend the best part of their lives repaying. Everything was upbeat. Longer mortgages were the perfect solution to unaffordable house prices – the government said so.

And so Irish citizens bought properties to live in, properties to rent out to others, properties to use as holiday homes . . . because they believed their investments were as safe as houses.

'Punters were banging on the doors for money. They were lying on their application forms,' said a former senior executive with Bank of Ireland. (Although in some institutions and mortgage brokers, customers were actively encouraged to boost their earning figures in numerous ways, including fictional bonuses).

He added, 'They were queuing up outside estate agents to buy. They were buying off plans – sometimes in countries they had never visited. For the Irish banks, there was a sense that if they did not lend in these circumstances, a foreign competitor might come in and do it instead. Their refusal would leave the door open.'

Those who predicted prices could not continue to rise were continually being proved wrong. The wise owls preaching restraint were right – but their timing was off. This allowed them to be derided as fuddy-duddy killjoys. Economists who took a realistically downbeat approach to growth were figures of fun, said the Bank of Ireland executive. 'We called them Chicken Lickens,' he recalled. 'We laughed about them thinking the sky was about to come crashing down around our heads.'

It seemed to be in everyone's interests to insist that the boom had plenty of oomph left in its engine.

The government became intoxicated on ever-increasing revenues from stamp duty. The Exchequer had never been so full. It was as if a giant ATM machine had been installed at Leinster House – no authorisation code needed.

The electorate was bribed with some of the bounty in a variety of ways, including a special savings scheme introduced in 2001. This was the SSIA (Special Savings Incentive Account), which gave savers a euro for every four they squirreled away over a five-year period. Minister for Finance Charlie McCreevy predicted it would encourage a savings mentality. Fat chance. It did act as an anti-inflationary measure to a certain extent, but there was less evidence it encouraged people to continue saving afterwards. A lusty spending spree poured forth from 2006 onwards when savings could be accessed. Money was also diverted into paying off credit-card debt, according to Central Bank figures, which showed a sharp drop coinciding with SSIA accounts maturing.

Why else were warning voices overridden? There was

always contradictory analysis. Economists working for banks and estate agents were forever churning out upbeat house-price forecasts. Journalists, who should have been asking sterner questions, allowed themselves to be distracted by an avalanche of pie charts and graphs from 'experts' insisting the only way was up.

Besides, newspapers were heavily dependent on revenue from property advertisements; they were panting to produce those glossy supplements which helped estate agents sell overpriced homes and investment properties. Anything connected with property was regarded as a guaranteed money-spinner, making daft prices palatable. For example, the *Irish Times* paid €50 million for the property website myhome.ie near the top of the boom in July 2006 instead of leveraging off its own brand name to set up a rival site at minimal cost.

While newspapers tended to corner the lion's share of property advertisements, the general advertising boom fed into television and radio. Television schedules were lopsided with programmes featuring couples renovating tumbledown hovels, trading up and buying places in the sun. Some shows even followed those dipping their toes into property development.

Just as the crane index showed how the geographical landscape had changed, there was also a gracious-living index. Interiors magazines were pored over. Backyards became courtyards. Bathrooms became wet rooms. People read about gas fires that doubled as art installations, about walls made from sheets of glass and about open-plan living. And they hankered after such luxuries.

Refurbishing their dream houses to opulent specifications meant even more borrowing. Welcome to Nirvana. Who knew it had to have underfloor heating?

Equity release became another way of accessing credit.

Same old serpent, different skin – debt by another name. Car salesrooms were thriving while some of the tiger cubs even parlayed their bank loans into yachts. As with cars, yachts depreciate the instant they leave the showroom. Factor in mooring fees, club charges, insurance, maintenance and the pressure to have top-of-the-range equipment on board. A rip in a sail could set back an owner €1,500. No wonder experienced yachtsmen admit that owning one is like standing in a shower tearing up money. During the recession, some sensational bargains in the second-hand yacht market quickly became available – and the used-car market was also a buyer's paradise.

In January 2007, 1,604 new Mercedes cars were registered, according to the Society of the Irish Motor Industry. By January 2009, that figure had plunged to 309. Over the same period, Porsche sales nosedived from twenty-one to two.

Lending practices grew lax at the height of the boom. 'It comes down to short-termism. Everyone was incentivised to look at the short term,' said a Bank of Ireland senior executive. 'The truth is we all knew the property market was overvalued. But we thought we could muddle through.'

Within months of that management conference in Druid's Glen, the first cracks were materialising. Towards the end of 2006, prices for new apartments began to fall in the capital. The drop was gradual at first – just 1 per cent. This was shrugged off as the Irish preferring their own front door. The received wisdom, from people contradicting the winds of change, was that the Irish had never taken to apartment life like other Europeans. There was talk of a correction in the marketplace, and some people were even prepared to concede that it might be for the best. Then the price decrease spread to homes outside Dublin.

Property developers were not yet alarmed – nor were estate agents, mortgage lenders or builders. These minor stirrings fitted into that comforting theory known as the soft landing.

The Ice Bar in Dublin's Four Seasons Hotel is plush, impeccably run and reassuringly expensive. Developers used to gather over drinks at the pale marble bar, under dramatic lighting, to bolster each other with the shared belief that prices would soon stabilise. Their self-confidence was mutually reinforcing. And so they continued to borrow and build – even as the economy started to undergo a pummelling that would lead to the grimmest housing collapse in history.

Their confidence was reinforced by the continued availability of money from the banks. Certain bankers were as obstinate as politicians in persisting with an upbeat assessment of the economy. 'It's not beyond the bounds of possibility that we actually talk ourselves into a recession, and I think that would be absolute sacrilege,' blasted Brian Goggin, then Bank of Ireland's chief executive, at the bank's annual results' announcement in May 2007.

If bankers saw early distress signals, they looked away. They were not about to surrender their gigantic lending spree. Gurus such as Charles Prince, US banking giant Citigroup's chief executive, helped stifle doubts. In July 2007, he dismissed fears that the party was over for the cheap credit-fuelled boom. In a memorable quote to the *Financial Times* in Japan (which he has probably regretted daily since then), Prince said, 'When the music stops, in terms of liquidity, things will be complicated. But as long as the music is playing, you've got to get up and dance.' Citigroup was 'still dancing', he said.

Anglo Irish Bank had always been shaking its tail feathers. Bank of Ireland and AIB, supposedly sedate grown-ups orbiting the Irish financial sphere, were jitterbugging just as energetically. Except the tempo was about to slow right down . . .

3

On the Northern Rocks

*'The bankers own the earth. Take it away from them,
but leave them the power to create deposits, and with
the flick of the pen they will create enough deposits to
buy it back again.'*
*Sir Josiah Stamp, President of the Bank of England in the
1920s*

Dublin, 14 September 2007

Writer Joe Armstrong was worried. He was one of thousands of Irish depositors in Northern Rock, a British bank which set up an operation in Ireland in 1999 offering attractive rates for savers. On the morning of 14 September, Joe heard the news that Northern Rock had received an emergency loan from the Bank of England the previous night.

Concerned, he tried to access his deposit account. 'I could understand the online account probably being bombarded with people trying to log on. But I tried several times, and then I tried ringing the helpline number, and I had no joy any time,' he said.

He was not the only fretful customer.

The lustre of an operation set up to deal with consumers over the telephone or via the Internet was diminishing as the hours went by, and nobody could access their accounts or reach anyone in the bank. Customers began to think that if the bank had no presence on Irish streets it might not be safe. Where was their money kept? Why did Northern Rock need an emergency loan? Anxiety levels multiplied. People were terrified they would never see their nest eggs again.

Northern Rock had total Irish savings of €2.4 billion, with €100,000 as the average deposit from an Irish client. Senior manager of the Irish operation Brian Kavanagh tried to offer reassurance, 'Northern Rock is a bank with assets of £113 billion sterling. We are a very big bank. As I am sure customers are aware, the Internet is very busy and, unfortunately, sometimes with the broadband you get through very quickly, other times it takes a bit longer. The lines have been very busy today, and we ask customers to bear with us.'

There had been jitters on the stock markets around the world over the previous six weeks, but few people had felt the effects. Experts wearing square glasses and stripy shirts had lined up before television cameras in hectic dealing rooms, explaining the source of the problem was 'the credit crunch' and 'sub-prime mortgages' in the US. For most viewers, none of this made sense. It was the first time many had heard these disturbing phrases.

Northern Rock's presence in Dublin amounted to one anonymous office, which did not even have the bank's name over the doorway. It was shared with a number of other businesses. The building was on Harcourt Street, around the corner from the National Concert Hall. This small operation was completely unprepared for what followed: the first run on a bank in Ireland in living memory.

As frustration grew that afternoon, people began to trickle into Northern Rock's office and to queue for up to two hours to retrieve their money. Mary O'Dea, at that time consumer director of the Financial Regulator's office, reassured customers that the bank remained solvent. But people wanted to hold their cash in their hands.

15 September 2007

Despite a meagre Irish presence, the bank had an extensive branch network across Britain and was one of the biggest mortgage providers. Its UK branches opened on Saturdays, and thousands of people took time out from washing their cars or doing the supermarket run to line up for their money.

In Ireland, consumers watched the television footage with horror. Meanwhile, the website remained frozen and call centres continued to be jammed.

That same day, EU finance ministers gathered in Porto in Portugal. The Northern Rock issue was raised by Ireland's Minister for Finance Brian Cowen with his opposite number Alistair Darling. The British Chancellor of the Exchequer reassured Cowen that the Bank of England was not going to let Northern Rock go bust. By this time, £2 billion sterling had already been withdrawn. Northern Rock was the first ripple in the financial sector's glass-smooth surface.

17 September 2007

From early morning, a huge queue formed outside Northern Rock's Dublin office. People brought sandwiches, portable seats, newspapers and flasks of hot drinks and settled in to wait. The weather was unusually cold and windy for mid-September, but depositors were undeterred. The queue was as wide as the pavement and stretched all the way up the street, around the Bleeding Horse pub and on to Camden Street, where a presidential cavalcade had brought President Bill Clinton to visit Cassidy's pub in more hopeful days.

The run on the bank was now in full swing.

One customer in his early sixties, familiar with the saying 'as safe as the Bank of England', remarked, 'I know the Bank of England has reassured customers everything will be OK, but all you have to do is look at the queues in every part of England.'

A middle-aged woman nearby said, 'They haven't handled it very well. Where are the staff with leaflets and emergency telephone numbers? You can't get online so everybody is anxious because there is no information.'

Another looked towards the top of the queue at the far end of the street and wondered, 'If everybody up there takes all their money out, how much will be left? Tomorrow it will be too late.'

Alarm was causing tempers to fray. A customer was openly hostile to the media, telling one reporter, 'Stop showing this on the television. It's only making things worse.' The journalist replied, 'If you weren't queuing there wouldn't be anything to show.'

Delays were aggravated by the fact that the public was filing up to withdraw savings from an administrative office rather than a high-street branch accustomed to dealing with customers. The office could not cope with wave after wave of customers emptying their accounts all at once. They were only allowed to enter the office in limited numbers, and many were left standing in the cold.

It was not just the clients who were fulminating. The Financial Regulator did not regulate Northern Rock, but its officials felt an operation which had taken on thousands of customers should be able to facilitate them if they wanted to withdraw their money.

The government and the Central Bank were concerned at the unfolding scenes. Such spectacles generated a sense of general panic. Brian Cowen appeared on the evening news bulletin, telling viewers to take reassurance from Alistair Darling's promise that the Bank of England would stand behind Northern Rock. But Cowen added, 'It is important they deal with people's queries as expeditiously as possible.' It was a nudge to the British financial establishment that Ireland was impatient for the mess to be sorted out. Northern Rock took the hint and dispatched staff from Britain to Dublin that evening.

18 September 2007

Again, that snaking queue formed outside the Northern Rock office from early morning. This time, the bank was ready. A slick public-relations campaign swung into action, offering tea and sympathy to customers. The company had also taken out newspaper advertisements apologising for the debacle. Customers were given withdrawal forms to fill out and told at what time their cheques would be available for collection. Staff from Northern Rock in Britain worked their way through the queue and by mid-morning it was almost gone.

However, the volume of cheques from Northern Rock now being lodged with other financial institutions was slowing down the entire banking system. There was a hiatus before the Northern Rock cheque appeared in accounts – and people leaped to the conclusion something was amiss. That delay was causing even more uncertainty, prompting Mary O'Dea to appeal to people for patience. She said, 'This is not a cause for concern. People's funds are still going through to their accounts but it is taking a little bit longer than it would for normal transactions.'

The situation was being managed – but it was a warning bolt. Northern Rock's troubles showed the banking system was heading into choppy waters. Its example would be repeated in future months across the globe.

Traditionally, banks took in deposits and lent out that money. They paid one rate of interest to savers and charged a higher rate to borrowers. The difference between the two rates created a bank's profit. But during a property boom there were not enough deposits to finance the demand for mortgages. Instead, lenders borrowed money from other banks and used those funds to make mortgage loans. This was not unusual: one bank borrowing from another had been common practice for decades. But suddenly bigger financial institutions which had been lending to banks with retail networks, such as Northern Rock, found they were experiencing high levels of bad debt. They reacted by increasing the interest rate at which they lent to other banks. Now, banks which offered mortgages found they were borrowing money at a higher rate than they were lending it. Instead of making money they were losing it. Rapidly.

Northern Rock found itself in just such a situation. This state of affairs could only continue for a short period before Northern Rock and similar institutions went to the wall.

The cause of these unexpected bad debts was the sub-prime lending crisis. It happened in the US, but its shockwaves travelled around the world. Normal mortgages, taken out by people who can pay back the money and who do not have a patchy credit history, are known as prime lending. Somebody with a poor credit track record is usually turned down by mainstream banks as a risky prospect. But these people became regarded as a lucrative new market and were targeted by other banks, although they would be asked to pay a significantly higher rate of interest. Frequently these mortgages were mis-sold to people who were duped into signing up to deals they would never be able to repay. Consumers were encouraged to focus only on the discount interest rates for the first year of their mortgages. After the honeymoon period expired, they discovered they were unable to make their payments.

In the US, the salespeople pushing such mortgages were often paid commission and were selling the home loan on behalf of another financial institution. They were the car salesmen of mortgages: once the deal was done, they were not responsible for the goods.

Lending money to people with no prospect of being able to repay it produces strictly short-term gains. Salespeople might not care about the medium to long term, but senior bankers are supposed to take an overview. Their vision was clouded, however.

The trail leads back to greed.

Northern Rock was no isolated situation. The following year, the US markets started wobbling.

The US, 11 July 2008

The first indications of trouble surfaced over the summer months, with US mortgage giants Fannie Mae and Freddie Mac brought under tighter government control. Confidence was waning in the two businesses, which were at the heart of the multi-trillion US housing market and underpinned its entire debt infrastructure. As property prices collapsed and foreclosure levels soared, consumers could not meet their mortgages.

The corporations lost more than $3 billion between April and June 2008 alone, resulting in a steep fall in their share values. On 11 July, President Bush was forced to wade in to the turmoil to calm fears, saying that the two banks were 'very important institutions'.

The problems came to a head as Fannie Mae and Freddie Mac tried to raise funds to cover their losses, but investors backed off, convinced they would be unable to honour their liabilities.

Fannie Mae is short for Federal National Mortgage Association, Freddie Mac for Federal Home Loan Mortgage Corporation. They are pivotal in supplying money for people to buy homes, but they do not lend directly to homebuyers. Instead, they buy mortgages, package most of them into bonds and sell them on to investors, which they guarantee.

They collectively own or guarantee more than half of America's $12,000 billion outstanding mortgages, and their failure would have a domino effect on the US and global economies. If they collapsed, mortgages would be more difficult to access, as well as more expensive, and an already enfeebled property market would face annihilation.

In the biggest state rescue in history, the US Treasury intervened and pledged trillions in financial guarantees for the duo.

7 September 2008

As Fannie Mae and Freddie Mac continued to teeter on the verge of collapse, the US government put both into a loose form of nationalisation. It promised cash, dismissed their chief executives and directors and eliminated future dividend payments to shareholders.

Henry Paulson, the US Treasury Secretary and a key creator of the rescue package, said it was highly unusual for a government to intervene where publicly traded companies were concerned. But he emphasised that the two struggling groups represented a special case because their survival was crucial to the health of the hardest-hit housing market since the 1930s.

'Our economy and our markets will not recover until the bulk of this housing correction is behind us. Fannie Mae and Freddie Mac are critical to turning the corner on housing,' he said.

Other governments around the world would soon be forced to undertake remedial action, pumping transfusions into a financial system that was growing increasingly sickly. They operated on the same basis as US politician John Lewis, who said during the Bush bailout bill, 'I have decided that the cost of doing nothing is greater than the cost of doing something.'

In Ireland, decisive action would also be taken. But nothing could prevent the Celtic Tiger from being exposed as a paper tiger.

PART II
The Players

4

Circle of Friends

*'Good people do not need laws to tell them to
act responsibly, while bad people will find a way around
the laws.'*
Plato

Ireland's success was as eye-catching as a comet. But like a
comet rupturing into fragments, the country's economic machine was also destined to shatter – and her bankers were among
those who contributed to that fate. Who were these men and
how did they come to dominate the banking firmament?

Best known among them was the perennially suave Seán
FitzPatrick, who was the developers' banker. Known to
everyone from taoisigh to bank clerks as Seánie, he was
routinely referred to as the country's richest banker. Born in
1948 in Dublin's Shankill, he studied commerce at University
College Dublin (UCD) and joined Anglo Irish Bank in 1974,
becoming chief executive twelve years later when the bank was
still a sleepy operation. Not for long. FitzPatrick brought
Anglo to the stock market, where its growth outshone the 'big
two' banks, AIB and Bank of Ireland. This was achieved by
ambitious lending policies which left the other banks under

pressure either to compete or to fall behind. In 2005, FitzPatrick stepped aside and took on the role of chairman. He also became a frequent – and charismatic – public speaker, sharing his vision as a financial guru, fêted wherever he went. It seemed as if he could do no wrong . . .

David Drumm of Anglo was the youngest of the crisis-hit chief executives, born in 1966 in Skerries in north County Dublin. He was viewed as FitzPatrick's puppet/protégé, which put him on his mettle to grow profits at an even faster rate than his predecessor. After leaving school, he qualified as a chartered accountant and gained valuable experience working with start-up companies before joining Anglo as an assistant manager in 1993. He caught FitzPatrick's eye, and four years later was sent to the US to build Anglo's Stateside operation from scratch. It was a test of his abilities, which he passed with flying colours, and in 2002 he was recalled to become head of lending. Three years later, he was the surprise winner of the race to replace FitzPatrick. But the compulsion to prove himself was to be Drumm's undoing.

Dapper banker Brian Goggin joined Bank of Ireland from school at the age of seventeen, in 1969. Later, he graduated from Trinity College Dublin with a Master's degree in management. Early in his career, he was pinpointed as a contender and powered his way through the ranks. In 2004, he earned the carrot of chief executive because of his solid, dependable reputation as a safe pair of hands. Yet, under his stewardship, the bank moved away from its conservative roots and lending exploded – rising from €67 billion in March 2004 to €135 billion in March 2008. It was a disastrous change of direction that left Goggin fighting to hold on to one of the most prestigious jobs in banking.

Eugene Sheehy's career was outside the norm for a senior banker. He had been a branch manager in AIB for years before finally being noticed in mid-stream. His chance to shine came when he was sent to the US in 2002 to act as head janitor, cleaning up after the Rusnak affair, when a rogue trader racked up losses of $691 million. Three years later, he was named chief executive. Born in Dublin in 1954 and schooled in Limerick, Sheehy joined AIB at the age of seventeen but took time out to do an M.Sc in organisation behaviour at Trinity College Dublin. Like Goggin, Sheehy was the archetypal insider. He was known for his people skills – and developers, in particular, benefited. He wound up as the banker holding more loans to developers than any other institution, a situation that would take more than his eloquence to adequately explain.

Michael Fingleton, boss of Irish Nationwide, was never going to blend in with Goggin or Sheehy. Known as 'Fingers', he was a generation older, and a more flamboyant character. Born in 1938 in Tubbercurry, County Sligo, he furthered his career in a seminary but left before taking vows. A degree in commerce followed, then he trained as a chartered accountant and later qualified as a barrister. He ran a one-man band at the building society, with virtually no middle management. In the course of a thirty-seven-year career there, Fingers made it his business to become well connected politically, and he was a regular on the social circuit. If his tentacles ran deep, his ambitions ran deeper still – but in the end he overreached himself.

Denis Casey of Irish Life & Permanent was an office boy made good. Born in 1959, he left school at sixteen. His first job was as a post-room boy before he trained as an accountant. He joined Irish Life, a life-assurance business, in 1980 and was made chief executive of the life company when Irish Life merged with Irish Permanent in 1999, forming Irish Life & Permanent. The workaholic Casey operated the life company, Ireland's largest, for six years until being shifted to run the banking division. In 2007, he became chief executive of Irish Life & Permanent. Under him, Permanent TSB cashed in on the boom in residential mortgages, maintaining its position as the country's largest home-loan provider. But the rock on which this high-flier perished was an unexpected one.

So much for the leading bankers – but who was charged with patrolling them?

Lecturer-turned-politician Brian Lenihan was no sooner named Minister for Finance – an unusual choice for the job – in May 2008 than he found himself battling one crisis after another. Born in 1959, he studied law at Trinity and lectured in banking law for eight years before winning his father Brian Senior's Dublin West seat in 1996. He is the son, grandson, nephew and brother of Fianna Fáil politicians. But his political pedigree was of little use to him when the banks helped to drag the economy over a precipice, and Lenihan found a plum ministry transformed into a poisoned chalice.

Regulator Patrick Neary was no match for the financial storms, or for the bankers who regarded unwise profit generation as nothing more sinister than 'game on'. He was chief executive of the Financial Regulator, a position that gave him a central role in the tangled web of scandals that vandalised the reputation of Irish banking. The Kilkenny-born public servant joined the Central Bank in 1971, after a year at UCD, and became regulator in 2005. After almost forty years working in financial regulation and the Central Bank, he left in a cloud of ignominy as politicians blamed him for a litany of failures. Commentators sneered that he must have sat in his office combing his trademark moustache while the country went up in flames. A decent, trustworthy man had become persona non grata.

Cork-born John Hurley was a civil servant to the core, who took an academic approach to his role – but someone more sceptical was needed for the challenging times he encountered.

After qualifying as a barrister, he joined the civil service in 1963 and went on to become Secretary General of the Department of Finance. He was appointed Governor of the Central Bank in 2002 and played a pivotal role in devising the State guarantee to the banks. Conscientious, meticulous and above all conservative, he was bright enough to be concerned about the property bubble . . . but not assertive enough to stop it.

The Salaries

The pay for the luminaries of Irish banking peaked in 2007, as banks gorged on over-lending and boosted profits to their zenith.

Kingpin was **David Drumm**. That year, then chief executive of Anglo Irish Bank, he earned a prodigious €4.6 million package. This is the highest deal commanded by any Irish banker, and it included a €2 million bonus. The 2007 annual report said he was paid €3.3 million – the substantially higher figure was only revealed twelve months later. Drumm received an additional €1.3 million cash payment in lieu of a contribution to his pension after the end of the financial year, propelling his combined pay and conditions to the figure of €4.6 million.

Drumm decided to opt for the payment because the government had set a surcharge on accrued retirement packages that exceeded €5 million. He did nothing wrong by taking the money, which was taxed. However, in its 2008 annual report, Anglo said it would no longer allow executives to choose cash instead of pension contributions.

In 2008, Drumm's total remuneration was €2.2 million. He was obliged to resign in December following the controversy over secret loans to directors at the bank, among other scandals.

Anglo's 2008 annual report also showed a payment of

€3.75 million to executive director **Tom Browne**, who retired in November 2007, 'in recognition of his contribution'.

Considerable public tumult was stirred up by gargantuan pay awards to bank chiefs in 2007 being swiftly followed by a guarantee and bailouts from the taxpayer for their institutions in 2008 and 2009.

When Minister for Finance Brian Lenihan introduced the guarantee in September 2008, he promised to rein in bankers' pay. He set up a committee to examine the issue, composed of Vivienne Jupp, a former executive with consultants Accenture, ex-Comptroller and Auditor General John Purcell and Eddie Sullivan, a former senior official at the Department of Finance. The trio set a series of caps on bankers' packages in March 2009. Pay was stipulated at:

–€690,000 for chief executives at AIB and Bank of
  Ireland;
–€545,000 for Anglo Irish Bank and Irish Life &
  Permanent;
–€360,000 for the two building societies, EBS and
  Irish Nationwide.

But Lenihan thought this was still excessive, in light of decisions taken in Germany and the US to limit bankers' pay at lower levels. He wrote to the financial institutions asking them to set a €500,000 boundary in the four cases where caps exceeded that amount.

The committee recommended that no bonuses be paid for 2008 and 2009 and for the duration of the State guarantee, which expires in September 2010. It said that bonuses may be appropriate in the future but advised a string of caveats:

–Bonuses should not be contractual; they should be
  discretionary.
–Bonuses should not exceed 80 per cent of basic pay

(unlike Drumm's, which was double his basic pay).

–Bonuses should not be pensionable.

–Bonuses should not be structured to encourage banks to run unacceptable risks.

At AIB, chief executive **Eugene Sheehy**'s total package was €2.1 million in 2007. His pay for 2008 was €1.1 million. This followed a 10 per cent pay cut in September 2008 and a 15 per cent reduction in January 2009, which decreased his basic salary to €696,000 by the end of the year. He waived the right to share options and said that he would not accept any bonus for the remainder of his tenure. The government capped his salary at €500,000.

Bank of Ireland's then chief executive **Brian Goggin** was paid €2.9 million in total for 2007. His base salary from April 2008 was set at €1.1 million. **Richie Boucher** replaced Goggin in February 2009, and his salary was capped at €500,000.

Irish Life & Permanent's then chief executive **Denis Casey** was paid €1.36 million in 2007. He took a pay cut from January 2008, which slimmed down his salary to €890,000, and his wages were to be frozen for 2009. He resigned in February 2009 amid uproar over the series of deposits to Anglo Irish Bank, totalling €8 billion, that helped Anglo fake its accounts. Irish Life & Permanent's incoming chief executive will be subject to the government cap of €500,000.

The only lender who tried to buck the trend of truncated pay packets between 2007 and 2008 was Irish Nationwide chief executive **Michael Fingleton**. Despite the economic and banking crash, his package remained at €2.3 million. His deal for 2008 included an incentive bonus of €1 million paid to him in November 2008, just weeks after his building society was covered by the State guarantee. This was highly contentious because no other chief executive of an Irish institution covered by the guarantee took a bonus for 2008. The banks had all suffered enormous setbacks and could not justify it.

The government made repeated demands for Fingleton to return the €1 million bonus and, in March 2009, he finally caved in. Pay at Irish Nationwide was subsequently capped at €360,000.

In September 2007, EBS chief executive **Ted McGovern** stood down after a series of boardroom rows – some of which converged on executive pay. McGovern was paid €677,000 for nine months' work that year and received €1.86 million as an early retirement package. In January 2008, he was replaced by **Fergus Murphy** who was paid €490,000. That figure was reduced to €440,000 after a 10 per cent pay cut in 2009. The government capped his salary at €360,000.

The days of telephone-figure take-home pay for senior bankers were finally over.

5

Leader of the Pack

*'Yes, as through this world I've wandered I've seen lots of
funny men/ Some will rob you with a six-gun, and some
with a fountain pen.'*
From 'Pretty Boy Floyd' by Woody Guthrie

Seán FitzPatrick is a modern Jekyll and Hyde. The man who
built up a sleepy bank into Ireland's third largest lender was
undoubtedly a talented financier – some say he was the
outstanding banker of his generation. The business sphere
does not often throw up celebrities, but he was one of the few.

In the heyday of the property boom, FitzPatrick became a
byword for success. He was hailed as a shining example of
what people could achieve if they believed in themselves.
Conviction was always FitzPatrick's special talent, but he was
also a hard worker and put his back into creating a successful
bank which lent to small to medium businesses, in turn
facilitating the property boom.

Here stood a virtuoso salesman. He could have sold anything with conviction: it just happened to be a bank which he
pitched so persuasively. He had missionary zeal about all
aspects of banking and spoke fervently, and often, about

corporate values. But for all his insistence on integrity, both personal and corporate, a vein of ambivalence ran through FitzPatrick's honour code. Lauded by admirers as a financial visionary, he was ultimately exposed as a pretender. Anglo Irish Bank ended up being taken into State ownership, with nationalisation of FitzPatrick's bank estimated to cost the average family €20,000. So much for the wealth-creator.

No man can be held single-handedly responsible for the banking crisis which has attacked the fabric of Irish society, raised taxes and unemployment, ended careers ignominiously, levelled egos and eroded certainties. Global forces did play a part. But Ireland was caught in a pincer movement between extreme economic conditions worldwide and a property bubble at home, fuelled by political desire for tax receipts and the reckless behaviour of the banks.

Irresponsible bankers were one matter; corrupt ones were something else entirely. The culture FitzPatrick spearheaded at Anglo Irish Bank had serious implications, not just for his own bank but for all of Ireland's financial institutions. Some followed his ethos, lambs to the slaughter, on a tide of unrealistic optimism and a thirst for short-term gain – whatever the cost.

Author Tom Clancy said the difference between fiction and reality was that fiction had to make sense. Seán FitzPatrick's story is too incredible for fiction. The one-time shooting star of the financial world self-immolated. Icarus-like, he aimed too high – and fell to earth as Public Enemy Number One.

Christmas 2008

In the approach to Christmas 2008, Seán FitzPatrick was running around in ever-decreasing circles. During the middle of the month, it was becoming blindingly obvious that his options for keeping his bank afloat and scandal-free were limited. The festive season was quieter than usual as people knuckled down to the austerity of the new world order. Still, some social events were unavoidable, and must have strained FitzPatrick's already taut nerves as he tried to keep up appearances.

On 17 December, he attended an annual Christmas dinner for Anglo pensioners at the bank's headquarters on St Stephen's Green. It was held in Heritage House, a Georgian building incorporated into the bank's headquarters.

'That night Seánie looked well shaken,' said a guest. 'He spent a lot of time outside on his mobile phone. People thought it was to [chief executive] David Drumm, who was not there, although he attended in previous years. At one stage Seánie was heard to lose it on the phone and start swearing, in a way that was unlike him. But he made a speech, as he usually did, and spoke about tough times, and he also managed to crack a joke.

'Everybody knew there was trouble. But he kept up a good front. He was still hoping to raise funds at that stage. He said Anglo needed to get new capital and that the next few days were crucial. The sense was that the team was working around the globe trying to sort something out and that there might be some news by the weekend. This was a Wednesday. On Thursday he was gone. Clearly that was someone in denial.'

On 18 December, FitzPatrick was forced to resign as chairman of Anglo Irish Bank. He fought tenaciously to the end, but the game was played out.

The credit crunch had focused an unusual level of attention on the bank that he operated as if it was a private concern. Once the State was obliged to intervene in September and to guarantee Anglo, along with five other financial institutions, it was inevitable that the bank's books and lending arrangements would be scrutinised. And Anglo was a Frankenstein bank.

FitzPatrick had not been his usual ebullient self during the autumn of 2008, but this was hardly surprising. Bankers had the wind knocked out of their sails by the speed and force of the global downturn. The Minister for Finance himself had noticed that FitzPatrick was uncharacteristically subdued. As early as November, Brian Lenihan commented privately, 'I used to think I was supposed to genuflect when Seánie FitzPatrick entered a room, but he has been a lot more contrite lately.' It was an astute observation.

FitzPatrick had every reason to beat his breast. Though among his many, undisputed talents was the ability to maintain a façade, cracks occasionally showed. One such occasion was the morning of Friday, 21 November 2008, a bright, clear autumnal day. FitzPatrick's ready smile and the charm that was second nature to him were both present, and he was as approachable as ever. But an uncharacteristic nervous tension rippled just beneath the surface.

Troubles were on his mind. He had just stepped off a conference stage – shared with former Taoiseach Bertie Ahern – at Leopardstown Racecourse. The event, 'Wicklow Showcase', was organised by Wicklow County Council to persuade businesses to locate in the county. And who better to sell the message than the county's favourite son, Seán FitzPatrick?

FitzPatrick was a born orator and at ease in front of an audience. His speech was as engaging as ever. Afterwards, he declined to be interviewed for television. But he always wanted people to like him, and it was not in his nature to refuse requests. So he agreed to speak privately with one of the authors about the recapitalisation negotiations between the Minister for Finance and bankers. As he talked, expressing reservations about letting private-equity groups invest in banks, FitzPatrick was edgy and preoccupied.

Within four weeks, he and his chief executive were gone from the bank. Anglo was exposed as a renegade operator – one of the banks guilty of 'economic treason' according to impassioned language in the Dáil. Within eight weeks, the government was forced to nationalise it. Its misdemeanours caused multiple resignations from the galaxy of corporate Ireland – fatally wounding Ireland's reputation as a sound financial system. On that day back in November, FitzPatrick was still hoping to pull the wool over people's eyes. He remained optimistic that his cloak-and-dagger arrangements with the bank would remain clandestine. But by Christmas 2008, the naked capitalist was stripped bare to the world.

If one banker can be said to personify the hubris of the Celtic Tiger, that man is Seán FitzPatrick. Most countries have produced a single figure identified inextricably with the credit crunch. The US has Lehman Brothers' Richard Fuld – dubbed 'the Gorilla' for the way he stalked the trading floors. Britain has Sir Fred 'the Shred' Goodwin of the Royal Bank of Scotland, owner of Ulster Bank. He won his nickname for his enthusiastic cost paring policies. And Ireland has Seán FitzPatrick, known not as an awe-inspiring ape or a remorseless shredder but as the considerably less macho Seánie Fitz. It could conceivably be the name of a pantomime character. Indeed, in the best traditions of pantomime, people tended to be looking in the wrong direction where Seánie Fitz was concerned.

FitzPatrick did not have a glitzy lifestyle. What he did possess was a hankering to become legendary in financial circles: to be a Tony O'Reilly, a Denis O'Brien, a Dermot Desmond. (He particularly admired Desmond.) Why such hunger? He had already turned Anglo Irish Bank into a star performer. At a UCD business alumni talk in March 2008, he offered some insight for his motivation: 'None of us can afford to rest on our laurels, no matter how gilded they may be. Because once we stop moving and progressing, we quickly get overtaken and eventually left behind.'

FitzPatrick was still an active man in his fifties when he stepped down as chief executive and became chairman of Anglo in 2005. When he then disposed of half his holdings in the bank, it was the largest transaction at the time by any individual on the Irish Stock Exchange. It was worth €100 million – even bigger than anything Michael O'Leary had done. The Ryanair chief executive used to sell Ryanair stock every year, offloading between €30 million and €50 million. He would always issue a health warning, saying he was diversifying his portfolio and that nothing should be read into it. But FitzPatrick outdid O'Leary on that occasion – a tall order, in anyone's book.

'A number of people said to him he was mad to become chairman,' recalled a former senior figure at the bank. 'I was there when someone said to him, "Why not stand back? What's the difference between €100 million and €150 million?" He just shrugged and smiled.

'But he did not seem capable of sitting back and enjoying the fruits of his success. He did not enjoy his money. That's a sad note to consider on the human side of things.'

FitzPatrick was horrified at the prospect of becoming yesterday's man. Retirement was anathema to him, for all his smokescreen talk about being able to travel and to enjoy lie-ins. He was nowhere near ready to swap his bow ties and cufflinks for Bermuda shorts and flip-flops. He wanted to make his mark – not just in banking but beyond it, to prove he had business acumen in a range of fields. And, indeed, Seán FitzPatrick of Anglo Irish Bank did make his name. For all the wrong reasons.

Anglo Irish Bank was an entirely different creature to any other bank. Analysts tended to describe it, with some justification, as 'unique'. It was a small, ambitious lender which, like Topsy in *Uncle Tom's Cabin,* seemed to have 'just growed' – and kept on growing. Its model was deceptively simple. It had no branches: instead of building up a network of expensive retail outlets, it concentrated on the niche market of lending to small businesses. This was traditionally a high-risk sector avoided by the established banks. Initially, they were sniffy about Anglo, considering it brash and an upstart. Its success left them still regarding it in the same way, but they could no longer afford to be sniffy.

Anglo Irish Bank was the creation of one man. The bank was started in 1964, while FitzPatrick was still a schoolboy, but he was the highly motivated architect of its success. Over thirty-three years working there, he transformed it from a tiny operation with three people and one low-key office into a significant player with loans of almost €72 billion.

FitzPatrick had the aura of a cult leader – as well as the rampant self-belief. His staff adored him and were proud of their charismatic figurehead. 'I put him on a pedestal, and I wasn't alone,' said a former senior executive at Anglo.

FitzPatrick always presented himself as a sprat taking on the whales of other financial institutions, and there is some truth in this depiction. He saw himself as an innovator while his rivals played it safe. They lacked the grit to take chances, while he was willing to sail close to the wind to attract business. But he denied his loans were risky and claimed that he took a 'belt and braces' approach to the loan book. Former staff say they liked to do deals but they always made sure they were secured – and that a fee was paid. All the same, a saying grew up in the industry: 'If you can't get it, you can get it from Anglo.'

FitzPatrick's Anglo Irish Bank reached maturity just as the Celtic Tiger was let out of its cage. Many of Anglo's customers, to whom the larger banks had been reluctant to lend, suddenly blossomed as the owners of businesses worth hundreds of millions of euro. As Anglo's customers grew exponentially in a booming economy, the bank expanded with them. Firing on all cylinders, it started snapping at the heels of AIB and Bank of Ireland.

The Anglo effect was to leave shareholders in other banks dissatisfied with the returns on their investments. Investors complained, and applied pressure. Chief executives started becoming nervous. These institutions were achieving healthy double-digit growth, but Anglo was hitting 50 per cent growth, and shareholders in other organisations were impressed. Bankers could not figure out how Anglo was doing it, but demands to match Anglo's performance were endemic, and chief executives caved in to them.

Bank of Ireland's former chief executive Mike Soden has admitted that he was impressed by FitzPatrick at the height of his bank's success. 'At the time I thought they were fantastic. They were able to make decisions a lot quicker than we did. They had a culture of putting their customer first.

'I was one of the few people that ever complimented Seán FitzPatrick on his results. I couldn't understand how he did it. We analysed their activities up and down, round and about,' he revealed in March 2009, on Eamon Dunphy's RTÉ radio show.

Hiring excellent people was the lynchpin of FitzPatrick's success. His team prided itself on a rapid turnaround: potential borrowers could have an answer in twenty-four hours. His policy was to surround himself with able lieutenants whose judgement he trusted, to pay them well – and to let them get on with it. He was no micro-manager.

A former Anglo executive said, 'If you were prepared to work, he was a superb guy to work for. He nurtured you, and paid well above the going rate. He didn't go for yellow-pack staff, he chose good people. There was no union, but he looked after you.

'Anglo was much faster at reaching decisions than other banks. Seánie delegated those powers. When you went in for a loan, you were dealing with a decision-maker as opposed to walking into a branch of one of the big two banks looking for a deal of half a million, with nobody authorised to sign off on it. Anglo could sort you out in a day or so. They worked faster and more efficiently, and they got good bonuses for it.

'There is nothing wrong with that model. When Seánie got away from that core ethos and that model – that's when he ran into difficulties.'

He went on, 'It was mainly a property bank. Bricks and mortar gave the bank a lot of consolation. It's an asset, you can touch it and see it, and hopefully it won't go down in value – and it didn't for ten or fifteen years.'

In the early 1990s, when AIB and Bank of Ireland still had their horns pulled in, Anglo was building business with loans to developers. Other banks raised their eyebrows, but FitzPatrick's comfort blanket was fee commission. There was a 1 per cent arrangement fee per loan, so a €3 million application would generate €30,000 in commission, which was loaded on to the loan. Fee income went straight into the accounts.

'The developer was delighted, and Anglo was delighted. If you offered Seán FitzPatrick fees every year instead of interest he'd have gone for it – he much preferred it,' said the former Anglo executive.

Many of the builders Anglo dealt with were already successful, but AIB and Bank of Ireland remained cautious. They regarded their enterprises as dubious prospects.

'Builders like the Durkans who were not getting looked after by AIB on some projects went to Anglo,' said the Anglo executive. 'FitzPatrick helped to create a lot of wealth for a lot of high-profile people like Bernard McNamara, Ulick McEvaddy, Gerry Gannon and Dermot Desmond. Desmond had made a name for himself already, of course, but the IFSC was not successful early on. Seánie organised finance for it in its early days.'

As the underdog developed into an extremely profitable bank, its success bred jealousy: Some faceless competitors tried to smear its reputation by circulating rumours of financial improprieties. There was never any substance to this, and it can be attributed to sour grapes on the part of banks left looking like stuffed shirts by Anglo.

'In the early days, AIB and Bank of Ireland were suggesting that Anglo were pirates and telling people their money wasn't safe there. Seán FitzPatrick drove to the offices of both CEOs and had it out with them – threatened to sue them,' recalled the former Anglo executive.

The malice of the rumour-mongering demonstrates the uphill battle that FitzPatrick faced. But he was ultra-competitive. In a January 2005 interview with the *Sunday Times*, he said that the loan book was built on word of mouth. Anglo bankers were salesmen, in the image and likeness of their leader. They were hungry. Persistent networking – his ability to forge bonds and tap into connections – propelled the bank forward. 'It was twenty-four-seven selling, taking every opportunity, with friends, casual acquaintances, old university pals, at dinners, the rugby club, the golf course. It was non-stop,' recalled FitzPatrick. Senior staff were also encouraged to socialise with developers and with other clients. This was part of Anglo's 'relationship management' culture with customers.

'Seánie would know the clients but he was at arm's length. His skills were that he was good at making a profit and at looking after staff and customers well,' said the former Anglo executive. 'Anglo used to bring customers to property shows in Monaco, to golf trips in Spain, to the Ryder Cup in the US. It was all very positive. People liked working there. There was a can-do attitude.

'Seánie carried that attitude with him when he moved over to become chairman. It was at that point he had a vision to be a very big player in his own right, and he all but achieved it. Except for the unravelling. Until then he was very successful at running the bank.'

So where did it all go wrong, and how did he end up breaking the bank he loved? Did he come to regard it as his personal creation, to do with as he wished? That is how another senior banker sees it: 'Seánie told me he treated investors' money as if it was his own. That's frightening, when you think about it.'

FitzPatrick exuded a positive aura which beguiled investors and customers alike. Small, slightly stocky and suntanned, in his uniform of blue business shirts, pink ties and double cuffs that could slice butter, he had an avuncular appearance – the favourite relative who would slip you a few notes with a nod and a wink. He could well afford to: when he stood down as chief executive in 2005, he was Ireland's best-paid company boss with a salary of €2.6 million. In 2008, his personal wealth was estimated at €55 million according to the *Sunday Times* 'Rich List'. One banking chief executive described him as 'always hail fellow well met, always king of the castle'. But FitzPatrick did not have an extravagant lifestyle. His office was spartan. He encouraged people to switch off the lights when they left work, to make sure the heating was turned off on bank holidays – wastefulness was frowned on when he was growing up. His civil-servant mother's influence was extensive, and he often cited her strictures on honesty and economy in speeches and interviews.

One of his few indulgences was his black Mercedes CL 500, with its five-litre engine capable of going from 0 to 60 mph in six seconds. (Bankers and politicians share a love of Mercedes.) Another mark of his success is his home in the Wicklow seaside town of Greystones. FitzPatrick lives in a tasteful, creeper-covered house with tall chimneys which would not be out of place in an Agatha Christie novel or in the genteel Home Counties universe of the film *Brief Encounter*. Situated on a broad, tree-lined avenue, the building conjures up a sepia-tinted world of white gloves and afternoon tea. The substantial gardens are filled with mature plants and trees, including a yew in the front, as well as a decorative lamppost.

No mean streets these, the road (named after a pioneering female Victorian mountaineer from the area) exudes prosperity. All the properties along it are detached, and are identified by name rather than by number. It is close to the sea and to the main street in Greystones, yet it has a secluded feel. More importantly for FitzPatrick, an avid golfer, it is a stone's throw from Greystones Golf Club, which is at the top of his road.

A friend said, 'He loved golf, and every so often he'd go off on a golfing weekend, but it wasn't to anywhere glitzy, it was to Wales, and he'd get the car ferry and stay outside Cardiff with a bunch of nice, regular guys.' But FitzPatrick had a less orthodox streak, too, and was known to bet hundreds of euro on nearest-the-pin shots on his local course.

The friend noted that FitzPatrick, who captained his school's junior and senior rugby teams, was a passionate rugby fan and sponsored the sport. The evidence is there at the approach to Greystones, where its rugby club carries a prominent sign advertising Anglo Irish Bank's sponsorship. FitzPatrick played until the 1970s, in centre position for Greystones and Bective, one of Ireland's oldest rugby clubs. Later, he became an enthusiastic spectator as well as corporate sponsor. Wicklow GAA was also sponsored as part of his drive to project the bank's brand.

The house is the most visible symbol of his success, born out of long working hours. He used to rise at 6 a.m. and was available on the phone from shortly afterwards. Employees spoke of receiving early morning calls as he drove to the office. 'His work ethic was immense,' said the former senior figure at Anglo Irish Bank. 'He worked every hour of the day. He would be available most mornings before 7 a.m. on the phone travelling in, and worked till 9 p.m. at night – perhaps longer. He worked on the weekend as well.'

But while he worked diligently and networked even more diligently, FitzPatrick was also a family man. He has been married since the age of twenty-six to Caitriona (née O'Toole), known as Triona, a former secretary. They have three adult children: a daughter, and two sons, Jonathan and David. Jonathan, born in 1977, works for Digicel as head of marketing in Vanuatu in the South Pacific. Denis O'Brien, with whom FitzPatrick had professional dealings, owns the mobile-phone company. David, three years younger, is based in Anglo Irish Bank's New York office.

FitzPatrick is a Type I diabetic, which means he must take daily injections of insulin. On one occasion in 2007, at a business meeting, he began to show signs of his condition. One of the people at the meeting said, 'He just started blanking out. At first he could not take in information and continued to ask the same question over and over. Then he started to fall asleep. I knew what must be going on and I rang his wife Triona. She told me to run out and get a can of Coca-Cola, rouse Seán and get him to drink it, which I did. Then he came around. It could have been serious if I had not acted.'

While he stepped down as chief executive in 2005, he stayed on as chairman. This was an unusual step – it is not illegal, but neither is it considered good practice because it prevents new blood coming on board. 'Seán FitzPatrick is the consummate professional. So how on earth did he become chairman after he was chief executive? That was stupid,' said the chief executive of one of the bailed-out financial institutions.

After becoming chairman, a less time-consuming position, FitzPatrick started joining other boards. By 2008, he was on the boards of Aer Lingus, packaging empire Smurfit Kappa and food group Greencore. There seemed to be no stopping him. The outsider had become the ultimate insider.

The son of dairy farmer Michael and his wife Johanna, he was an unexceptional student at Presentation College in Bray, managing one honour in his Leaving Certificate (in French). He was more interested in playing rugby than in swotting. He managed to scrape a place at UCD studying commerce, and after sitting his degree qualified as a chartered accountant in 1972. But chartered accountancy was soon abandoned for banking.

At the age of twenty-six, he discovered his niche. In 1974, he joined Irish Bank of Commerce Anglo, immediately phoning his mother to describe his office with thick-pile carpet and free newspapers. Through a series of mergers and disposals, it was sold to a French bank, and FitzPatrick found himself at Anglo Irish Bank.

He was vaulted into the chief executive's role in 1986, at a time when Ireland was in the doldrums. That year, he brought the bank to the stock market. In 1987, it had profits of €1.6 million. By 2007, they had skyrocketed to €1.2 billion, an increase of 60,000 per cent. This stellar growth outstripped Ireland's own economic phenomenon. But, as it says in the small print of every financial product, past performance is not a guide to future performance.

By 29 September 2008, his dreams of a place in the Irish entrepreneurs' hall of fame were in jeopardy. Deposits, the bedrock of any bank, were rapidly leaving Anglo as rumours circulated it could be close to collapse. That month alone, €4 billion was withdrawn. A sense of panic pervaded Anglo's St Stephen's Green offices as executives scrambled to secure funds to avert catastrophe. 'I was very fearful during [that] week,' FitzPatrick would say soon after.

There is a normal arrangement between banks that they lend money to each other, to facilitate liquidity and the smooth functioning of the market. The Central Bank actively encouraged banks to do this during the crisis. It is called inter-bank lending, and the money is only parked in the borrowing bank for a few days. It is not used to inflate a bank's position and does not appear on its balance sheet as a customer deposit – except in Anglo's parallel universe.

The books were cooked to create the illusion that everything was healthy at the bank, when the opposite was true. An underhand scheme was devised whereby Anglo transferred €8 billion to Irish Life & Permanent. In return, Irish Life & Permanent sent the money back to Anglo in two tranches to make it appear as though new business was coming in. The second transfer took place on 30 September 2008 – just hours after the State guarantee was introduced.

Instead of showing the funds as a short-term deposit – inter-bank lending – Anglo took the fraudulent step of classifying it as a corporate customer deposit. This implied it would remain in the bank for a much longer period. Its impact at this critical time immediately before the bailout, when Anglo's accounts were under the microscope, was to give the deliberately misleading impression that it was generating new business.

This amounted to market abuse. The timing of the money from Irish Life & Permanent was material for another reason. 30 September was the final day of the financial year for Anglo Irish Bank. This meant that the sum of money in the bank at the end of the day's business would be published in its annual report and pored over by investors. Anglo duped shareholders into believing that money in accounts had grown, when the opposite was true.

The accounts were not just window-dressed to make them look presentable; they were faked. Such deceit had to originate in the institution's upper echelons. The risks were titanic – but the stake for which they were playing was the bank's survival.

Anglo was not the only bank in the wrong. Irish Life & Permanent, run by the ambitious Denis Casey, had been concerned that if Anglo went under, it would precipitate a domino collapse of the entire Irish financial system. Even so, Casey's over-enthusiasm to ride a white charger to the rescue was naive in the extreme and broke all the rules.

By evening on 30 September 2008, after one of the most heart-stopping days of his banking career, FitzPatrick was able to breathe a sigh of relief. The accounts would pass muster, and the bank would survive. No wonder, when he gave an interview on Marian Finucane's radio show a few days later, he thanked the Irish people – although he should have been expressing his gratitude to Casey as well.

Casey would live to regret his helping hand, however.

'I am saying thank you unashamedly, because we owe our lives to the government and what they did. We are incredibly grateful for it [the guarantee],' FitzPatrick told listeners to the RTÉ show. He had actually been invited by a listener to apologise but declined on the basis that he had done nothing that warranted an apology. He offered his thanks instead. It was a bravura performance, especially considering the sheer quantity of buried bodies that remained to be dug up. His voice husky, he called the guarantee the most important decision made since the foundation of the State from an economic perspective.

A vein of buoyancy ran through his words that belied the sombre reality of Anglo's situation. Listening again to that

October 2008 radio interview in the light of subsequent events, his capacity for deception was astounding. 'Anglo is a very well-capitalised bank,' he insisted. In fact, it was bleeding deposits – only a few weeks earlier, depositors had withdrawn €4 billion.

FitzPatrick refused to take any responsibility for the runaway lending that had bloated the property bubble: 'This was not a shameful position to be in.' 'Have we been reckless? No, we haven't.' 'This is a systemic problem worldwide.' And, 'This was not caused by any one bank.' It was a global crisis, an international liquidity crisis . . . nothing to do with him.

That night, FitzPatrick made a speech at the annual La Touche Legacy Seminar in County Wicklow. It caused considerable surprise among the audience, with its range of socially controversial demands. He exhorted the government to tackle the 'sacred cow' of universal child benefit, State pensions and automatic medical cards for the over-seventies in the forthcoming budget. The conceit of his attack – he was, after all, chairman of a bank which taxpayers had just bailed out signalled not just that FitzPatrick had lost touch but also that his stress levels were high.

No wonder. It would soon emerge that the Anglo accounts were sham for more reasons than the Irish Life & Permanent transactions.

There was also the matter of Anglo's secret loans of €87 million to FitzPatrick. These clandestine borrowings rocked the foundations of the financial system. They caused a crisis of confidence for shareholders: if the bank lied about the loans, what else had it lied about? The loans raised a series of questions about how Anglo Irish Bank operated. And they resulted in investigations by the Financial Regulator and the Office of the Director of Corporate Enforcement, headed by former civil servant Paul Appleby.

The scandal became known as the Irish Enron, after the

US energy company that went bankrupt in 2001. But white-collar criminals had done the 'perp walk' there, paraded in handcuffs before cameras. In Ireland, by comparison, no concrete action appeared to be taken, beyond references to slow-moving investigations. Public concerns ratcheted up. The perception took hold that once someone progressed high enough up the food chain, the law no longer seemed to apply.

Later, it was revealed that FitzPatrick actually had loans of €122 million in 2007 – three times that of other directors' loans put together – but he had managed to pay off some of them. Presumably he was hoping that his investments would come good and that he could clear everything with no one being any the wiser.

However Anglo buffed up its books, the word had been out internationally for some weeks that Ireland was a cowboy republic without banking regulation. One Irish banker was in New York in December 2008, trying to raise money ahead of government recapitalisation, as news spread about Anglo's nefarious activities. The Irish banker's mobile rang, with the chairman of the financial institution he was due to meet on the line. With New York directness, the chairman told him, 'Your banks are corrupt and your government is useless. The meeting is off.'

Seán FitzPatrick resigned as Anglo chairman on 18 December 2008. He was replaced by board member Donal O'Connor, who was left to apologise to shareholders for the bank's fall from grace. FitzPatrick's position was untenable elsewhere within Irish business, and he also resigned from his non-executive roles in Smurfit Kappa Group, Greencore Group and Aer Lingus, as well as from information supplier Experian and investment fund Gartmore.

There was residual defiance and not much in the way of contrition in his resignation statement. He admitted the surreptitious loans but called them only 'inappropriate and unacceptable' from a transparency viewpoint. Presumably on legal advice, he said they were not illegal. If they had come off, these concealed loans for a range of investments would have enhanced FitzPatrick's reputation as a serious contender. But he miscalculated gravely, and the gamble backfired. The taxpayer would be called upon to honour FitzPatrick's wagers.

Even more extreme behaviour, however, was to emerge about FitzPatrick's bank. This was the Golden Circle scandal. Ireland's wealthiest man, businessman Seán Quinn, needed to offload 10 per cent of his 25 per cent stake in Anglo quickly. (See Chapter 6.) So a scheme was devised whereby ten of the bank's biggest customers were extended €451 million in loans to purchase the shares. This was a mechanism for preventing a drop in shares, as would normally occur if 10 per cent of a company's stock arrived on the market at one time. However, the deal orchestrated for the Golden Circle amounted to market manipulation.

'It is ironic, in a way, that its property business is not necessarily its worst exposure. Its biggest exposure is Seán Quinn and his companies,' said the former Anglo executive.

As Anglo was scrabbling to find buyers for 10 per cent of the bank, entrepreneur Ulick McEvaddy was among those approached. But he was in California at the time and missed the call. He confirmed: 'Seán FitzPatrick rang my mobile. It was in the middle of the night.' McEvaddy did not participate in the shares' purchase.

'Deciding what to do would have been a hard judgement call,' he said. 'The people who bought the shares were brave and foolhardy. But there was a need to support the Anglo guys because once there is a run on a bank it is very hard to stop.'

McEvaddy said his loyalty to FitzPatrick was as a result of Anglo's willingness to back people instead of companies through the years. 'Anglo created the Celtic Tiger in many ways,' he claimed.

Those who did participate in the Golden Circle include Gerry Gannon, founder of Gannon Homes; Seamus Ross, who runs Menolly Homes; Joe O'Reilly, developer of the Dundrum Shopping Centre; Paddy McKillen, owner of the Jervis Street Shopping Centre; and landowner Jerry Conlan.

Details about where FitzPatrick spent the millions he borrowed began to emerge. 'We are merely acting today as stewards of wealth created elsewhere. We must be the creators of wealth,' he told UCD School of Business in 2008. Obviously he was hoping to strike it rich himself with one of his ventures.

FitzPatrick cast his net wide. He invested in shares in Anglo and in other publicly quoted companies. He put money into private companies which had plans to grow quickly. His cash was poured into film finance deals with attractive tax relief, into pension investments and into property.

A number of the ventures he invested in were with his close associate and friend Lar Bradshaw, former chairman of the Dublin Docklands Development Authority (DDDA) and a non-executive director of Anglo. FitzPatrick, in turn, was on the board of the DDDA. He and Bradshaw were 'bosom buddies' who sat on a number of the same boards, according to a businessman who dealt with both. One of their biggest investments was a Nigerian oil project. The pair owned close to one-fifth of Movido Exploration and Production, a Lagos-based firm that had started operations in 2003 when it acquired an offshore oil field. By late 2006, they had invested more than €20 million in the project.

FitzPatrick and Bradshaw were introduced to the company by Jim O'Driscoll, an engineer and old schoolfriend of FitzPatrick, who had sought backing for Movido from Anglo Irish Bank. O'Driscoll had a small stake in the firm, which was 60 per cent owned by a Nigerian group. An exploration consultancy firm, DWC, owned the remaining 20 per cent.

Bradshaw had also borrowed money from Anglo which was not disclosed in the bank's annual report. FitzPatrick said he had organised for Bradshaw's loans to be hidden too, although without Bradshaw's knowledge. Bradshaw quit the Anglo board when FitzPatrick went – his position was also now untenable.

FitzPatrick's replacement as chairman, Donal O'Connor, is a former director of the DDDA, where both FitzPatrick and Bradshaw were directors. So many choice jobs for such a limited group of people.

The Anglo Irish Bank scandal was responsible for a flurry of casualties over and above the downfall of FitzPatrick and his inner coterie. The most high-profile scalp belonged to Financial Regulator Patrick Neary. He was brought down in January 2009 by a damning report into his handling of the secret loans to Anglo Irish Bank directors. He said he was unaware that Anglo chairman Seán FitzPatrick had concealed loans – even though the Financial Regulator's staff knew since January 2008, a year earlier. At best, his defence was ineptitude. If he did not know, he should have known, if he did know, he ought to have acted on it. His officials maintained he was told verbally.

FitzPatrick's successor as chief executive, David Drumm, and his finance director Willie McAteer, also stepped down. (See Chapter 8.)

Within Anglo's board, non-executive directors were required to resign. Inappropriate practices at the bank made their positions difficult in other aspects of their careers.

Anglo director Anne Heraty left not just the bank's board but also the board of the Irish Stock Exchange. It would have been inappropriate for her to remain on the Stock Exchange board when it was conducting an investigation into Anglo share trading. She also left Bord na Móna and Forfás but remained as head of CPL Resources – the only female chief executive of a publicly quoted company in Ireland. Heraty made no statement on stepping down from the Stock Exchange. This came as no surprise, given the likelihood of assorted legal actions involving Anglo.

Heraty had been appointed to the Anglo board in 2006, and in 2008 she earned €110,000 in that role. In addition, Anglo's annual report, published in February 2009, showed her recruitment company received €78,000 in fees from Anglo Irish Bank in 2008, along with €263,000 the previous year. She was in receipt of a further €14,000 in annual fees from both Bord na Móna and Forfás.

In the Dáil, Brian Cowen insisted that people should not presume non-executive members of Anglo's board were 'informed, or in all circumstances, au fait with any inappropriate or unacceptable conduct brought to their attention'. However, directors were meant to keep abreast of a bank's operations – their fees were not just money for jam. Failure to protect shareholders' interests amounted to negligence.

The directors, in turn, have argued that it was unfair to expect them to pick up on such exceptionally devious behaviour as FitzPatrick displayed. Every year they signed off on the loans they borrowed from the bank. These were compiled in the annual report, which directors also signed off. But the report lumped all the loans into one figure without specifying borrowers or amounts.

'In order for us to spot it, we would have had to attend a committee meeting and ask if anyone had been temporarily warehousing loans,' said a source on the board. 'But we never imagined anything like that was going on so the thought of asking that question was preposterous.' The source insisted that other people within the bank must have known about the clandestine loans.

The Taoiseach's intervention in Leinster House made no

difference: directors continued to fall away. Hours after Brian Cowen spoke up for them, Gary McGann was also gone. Not only did he leave the Anglo board, he also had to resign as chairman of Dublin Airport Authority (DAA). As had been the case with Anne Heraty, his position on a State board was now untenable.

McGann issued a statement that highlighted the reason why he had stepped down: he did not want to attract adverse publicity to Smurfit Kappa, where he was remaining as chief executive. 'At all times I acted with honesty and integrity in this role [at Anglo], but given recent commentary about events at the bank my decision today is made in the best interests of the DAA and of Smurfit Kappa Group,' he said.

As chairman of the DAA, McGann was directly answerable to Minister for Transport Noel Dempsey, who had made a number of hard-hitting statements about board members of Anglo Irish Bank. Under the circumstances, he could not stay on.

There were five non-executive directors of Anglo (excluding FitzPatrick and Donal O'Connor, who filled the vacancy left by FitzPatrick as chairman, escaping accusations of negligence because he had only been on the board since the summer). All five stood aside just before the bank was brought into public ownership. Lar Bradshaw went at the same time as FitzPatrick. The other three, Ned Sullivan, Michael Jacob and Noël Harwerth, remained on the other boards of which they had membership. But shortly after, Jacob did not seek re-election to publicly listed food company Reox.

Non-executive directorships of banks were once prized positions in Irish society. They generated a useful strand of income and good contacts, and they enhanced one's reputation. But a downside has emerged: non-executive directors are among those responsible should there be evidence of irregularities and inappropriate behaviour within an institution. Heraty, McGann and the other Anglo directors were left holding poisoned chalices – their reputations far from enhanced by the fallout. Those part-time positions on the boards of banks suddenly looked less alluring – and banks would struggle to fill them with people of calibre.

The external auditor, Ernst & Young, which failed to spot FitzPatrick's 'revolving credit facility' as his successor Donal O'Connor referred to it, also found itself with a black cloud hovering above it. Legal action seems inevitable – from Anglo's disinherited shareholders, among others.

FitzPatrick lay low as the furore erupted – anti-banker sentiments mounting – flying to South Africa with his wife and daughter in January 2009 to escape attention. On his return, he declined to appear before an Oireachtas committee with questions to put to him about Anglo, although it was a forum for answering directly to the Irish people about his actions. And the Irish people had been left with a huge bill for his swashbuckling ways, after the government was obliged to nationalise Anglo Irish Bank. The legendary communicator had run out of words.

One businessman involved with FitzPatrick described him as a 'small guy with a big ego'. He said, 'Don't let the charm fool you: underneath it, he has always been breathtakingly arrogant. He has a tendency to start sentences with "in my humble opinion". People who say that generally mean the reverse.'

Even people fond of FitzPatrick accept that he is egotistical. A businessman who worked with FitzPatrick on a project said, 'His fall from grace has created enormous stress for him. He was considered one of the top five business people in the country. Now he is considered the number one crook. That is a big drop, and he is finding it very difficult to cope with that. I think he simply hid the loans because he did not want his own business in the public domain.'

* * *

Nobody can be reduced to two-dimensional villain status, and FitzPatrick is no exception. He had a charitable side and gave readily – not just of his money but of his time. While many of his efforts have gone unreported, he has worked with the Niall Mellon Township Trust in South Africa, which builds homes for people living in poverty. Over six years, the trust has completed 11,000 homes. FitzPatrick even spent time in South Africa, mucking in on the ground, working twelve-hour shifts in the searing heat and doing whatever was needed, including driving a van.

His social conscience also saw him take part in the Ready for Work Programme, along with other members of the business community, aimed at getting the homeless back to work in 2006.

On 27 March 2004, eighteen-year-old Leaving Cert student Geoff Harte was playing rugby for Belvedere College when he broke his neck in an accident and was rendered quadriplegic. Geoff's father Maurice, well known in banking circles, was a former head of Treasury Holdings. FitzPatrick led a fundraising drive for the teenager, including a golf outing and a dinner, and chaired a committee that accumulated €4 million. Maurice Harte said, 'Seán was very good to our family. An awful lot of effort went into it. It is very hard to see what is happening to him now.'

This is not the only instance of FitzPatrick's generosity. He was a major donor to the Special Olympics and was involved with Concern, with whom he travelled to Ethiopia. A friend said, 'He is the most generous person I ever met. He never said no to raising funds. I could not speak highly enough of him. He was the same to everyone, whether you were Mary the cleaner or Bill Clinton.'

Another friend added, 'When Seán gave money, you could see it was his own money, it came from the joint account he shared with his wife. Seán never asked "What's in it for me?".'

Such behaviour illustrates how mistaken it would be to view FitzPatrick in monochrome: his character has many tones.

His bank lent to companies which may have struggled otherwise, and some heavy-hitters have taken pains to acknowledge that. In March 2009, renewable energy entrepreneur Eddie O'Connor paid tribute to Anglo as the only bank willing to lend to his fledgling company. 'I'm going to say something quite unpopular,' admitted the Airtricity founder, before praising the bank for being 'great at lending'. Airtricity was sold in 2008 for around €2.6 billion.

O'Connor's comments were made before a business gathering at the O'Reilly Hall in University College Dublin. They followed a defence of FitzPatrick by telecoms entrepreneur Denis O'Brien at a private lunch in Milltown Golf Club in Dublin the previous month. 'What has been forgotten is that Anglo Irish also lent to a lot of entrepreneurs and business people who created thousands of jobs. And most of these jobs will survive the downturn. Anglo Irish backed people when others wouldn't. It backed me when I wanted to start a radio station and nobody else would,' said O'Brien. 'Seán FitzPatrick has been a friend of mine for quite a number of years. He has made mistakes but he continues to be my friend. Anglo Irish has been blamed for absolutely everything that has gone wrong in Irish banking. This is both wrong and unfair.'

Whether he was a wealth creator or a wealth stripper, FitzPatrick moved in moneyed circles. A business associate of the banker said, 'Seánie was responsible for making a lot of big names very wealthy, including builders Bernard McNamara, the Bailey brothers [Tom and Mick – he is very close to Mick] and Seán Mulryan of Ballymore Homes.'

These were among the colossus figures in Irish construction. In 2006, Mick and Tom Bailey agreed the biggest tax-evasion settlement with the Revenue Commissioners in the history of the State, at €22 million. Immediately afterwards, Mick Bailey was welcomed into Fianna Fáil's fund-raising vehicle, the Galway tent.

The Baileys and other developers made huge sums at the height of the boom. But when the crash came, taxpayers shouldered the burden while a spate of leading developers continued in business.

During 2008, people working in the banking community kept speculating about problems within Anglo – after all, it was the property bank, and property was vulnerable. But Anglo continued to insist that it had everything collateralised and that there was no danger. One businessman observed, 'There is a saying that nobody would eat something the chef would not eat himself. We watched what was happening, and all the staff were investing in Anglo: they believed the spin, too. It would be more sinister if the bank blew up and the bankers walked away, having nothing invested there themselves. But everyone had invested. Even Seánie. He is one of the big losers.'

Staff at Anglo, as in other banks and public companies, were able to avail of a 'Save as You Earn' arrangement. This is a Revenue-approved share-option scheme that allows employees to save up to €320 a month over a five-year period. At the end of the five years, an employee can buy shares at the price quoted on the scheme's start date. The company can also offer a discount of up to 20 per cent on the share price from five years ago. The Revenue-approved aspect of the scheme means that an employee is not liable to income tax (at up to 41 per cent) when the share option is exercised. Rather, he or she pays capital-gains tax at 20 per cent on the date the shares are ultimately sold. Naturally, bank staff were keen to sign up – and encouraged to hold on to their shares after exercising the option.

So anonymous members of the public were not the only ones left swimming naked when the tide went out, to paraphrase US billionaire Warren Buffet. FitzPatrick's own employees lost heavily.

But FitzPatrick was enamoured of the notion that he had spread the wealth. He used to repeat stories of people stopping him on the street to shake his hand and thank him for holiday homes abroad – bought after cashing in shares that had experienced phenomenal growth. He was less quick to tell anecdotes about small investors waking up at night in a cold sweat after entrusting their nest eggs in his bank and ending up covered in yolk.

At an extraordinary general meeting in January 2009 in Dublin's Mansion House, one shareholder complained that most of them were dished up gruel while a select few were served steak. It was a reference to Seán Quinn and the notorious Golden Circle.

Inherently affable, FitzPatrick liked being approached. During an evening of corporate entertainment in grand surroundings in August 2007, a Vanessa Redgrave lookalike in eye-catching jewellery tapped his shoulder. 'I just want to thank you for all those houses you're building in South Africa for the needy – you're doing great work,' she cooed. Genial as always, he listened as she heaped praise on him. But as soon as she was finished he was back at work, networking with his trademark, twinkly eyed charm. 'Buy Bank of Ireland and AIB shares, you can't lose,' he tipped guests at the dinner, before melting away to mingle elsewhere. Naturally, insider-information regulations meant that he could not discuss share prospects in his own bank – even in a social situation.

The timing of his pointer was crucial. Bank share prices had just started their seepage. He saw this as an opportunity for profit until prices rallied; instead, an utter collapse happened. Presumably he was taking his own advice, in which case, millions would have evaporated from his portfolio.

Was FitzPatrick aware of the risks his bank was running? It seems unlikely, because his own money went up in a puff of smoke as well as the bank's. He was by far the biggest loser among Ireland's bank bosses: at the top of the market in early 2007, his 4.5 million Anglo shares were valued at almost €80 million. The banker's confidence in bank shares proved to be misplaced. When the recession came, his Anglo holding was worthless.

FitzPatrick is currently waiting to learn if any charges will be pressed against him. As the storm rages, he spends his time on the golf course, although people have spoken of seeing him wander the links like a zombie. He has also been spotted pottering about in his garden shed drinking cups of tea brought out on a tray. He has made several golfing trips to Spain, where presumably he feels less exposed to public censure.

The man who bloomed under the spotlight has learned to keep his head down, although he did describe Anglo's nationalisation as 'a very sad day' and said that he had 'great sympathy' for the shareholders in it and all Irish banks. This sympathy is not a two-way street. No doubt he broods on the ifs and mights of it all. Even his deep reservoir of self-belief must sometimes fail him.

A friend of FitzPatrick's commented, 'Seán is being blamed for everything. But there were others. People might be surprised with what comes out at the end of the investigations. Everyone is prejudging the situation, and people seem to have forgotten that this is a human being. How could anyone's family deal with somebody being blamed for having destroyed the whole Irish banking system? His wife can't answer the door any more because she never knows who might be there.

'Seán has helped a lot of people down through the years; he did a lot of good. Some of these people are there for him. Many have walked away from him too. But the way he is dealing with the situation is admirable. Seán is making no plans to leave the country. He is not a fugitive.'

Public opinion has swung against the former poster boy for the banking sector. 'Heaven has no rage like love to hatred turn'd,' as Congreve observed. 'Seán now feels as if he is under siege. There are guys popping out of trees taking photographs of him,' said a former Anglo figure.

The outcry he has generated must be difficult for the banker, but worse could lie ahead. A criminal prosecution has been indicated, although whether a case can be constructed against him is unclear because the legislation is not cut and dried. He insists he did not breach company law by hiding the loans, although this is being reviewed by the Irish Stock Exchange, the Financial Regulator and the Office of the Director of Corporate Enforcement. Section 31 of the Companies Act 1990 forbids loans by companies to directors (including their family and corporate interests) where the loan is 10 per cent or more of net assets. There is a question mark over whether this applies to banks, however. FitzPatrick's debt was worth about a third of Anglo's entire market value. Anglo Irish Bank, and, initially, the regulator, were in agreement that the issue was a resigning offence but also that nothing illegal had been done. This deserves further scrutiny. If FitzPatrick's activities were legal, then surely substantial questions must be raised regarding the legislation in this area. Is a radical overhaul in order?

The government insists that FitzPatrick's loans will not be written off, and it expects them to be repaid – it has to say that, of course. But the reality is that stock and property markets around the world have imploded, so the security attached to these borrowings is impaired.

Anglo staff still find it all hard to believe. 'I would have said Seán FitzPatrick was capable of bending a rule but not of breaking one. No way,' said the former senior figure at the bank. 'He generated huge loyalty. He was regarded as a great banker, and the bank's ethos came from Seán FitzPatrick personally. He was idolised by his staff because he built the bank up from literally nothing.

'The staff are shattered, really bruised. And they are tarnished along with him. The funny stuff is all around Seánie and the top tier, but the staff are damaged too. Everyone in Anglo is dumbfounded at what happened. Many of them are good guys, and they feel as if they have been hit by a tsunami. There is an awful lot of human fallout from this.'

The directors are also smarting. One source within the board discussed what happened at Anglo with his adult children. He sat them down to explain the sequence of events, apprehensive they may be mocked in college about their father's association with the bank. He stressed he had always been honest. One of his children said, 'Dad, you don't need to tell us you are honest. We know that already.' He replied, 'That is probably what Seán FitzPatrick's children said to him too.' The contact insisted there was complete amazement among non-executive directors when details of the secret loans to directors emerged.

FitzPatrick, in conversations with those directors, has continued to maintain he did nothing dishonest. The boardroom source said that FitzPatrick is 'clinging to the legal advice' he received from the bank's legal advisers Matheson Ormsby Prentice, which told him that what he did was not illegal. This advice has still to be tested. 'But was it honest?' continued the source. 'Absolutely no way. Seán said it was going on for eight years, it may have been longer. I was in complete shock when I heard he had deceived everyone. It was dishonest. Relations with Seán are difficult now.'

The former non-executive directors were particularly surprised at the secret loans because FitzPatrick continually repeated the need to protect the interests of shareholders at board meetings. 'He said it again and again and again. He was saying it as if we never heard it before,' said the source.

But the board of Anglo did campaign to allow FitzPatrick to stay on as chairman. As his retirement date from the chief executive's post approached, they consulted with the Irish Association of Investment Managers. This body represents investors with major shareholdings in banks, such as pension funds. The association was initially reluctant because FitzPatrick's appointment would breach the Combined Code on Corporate Governance. However, when Anglo directors lobbied, arguing FitzPatrick would be 'an asset' as chairman, the association agreed to make an exception. This decision, by a cosy coterie within Dublin's interconnected business circles, kept FitzPatrick inside the bank at the head of its board. It was a monumental error of judgement.

'It's buried sores that fester – that eventually burst upon us in a worse fashion than they would have if they had been addressed earlier. I don't think I need to labour the point about the lessons in Irish society we have learned in recent years about the folly of attempting to cover things up.' Philosophical words. Perhaps even statesmanlike words. Above all, words to be read as a rallying cry for transparency and accountability. How odd, then, to realise that these remarks were made as recently as March 2008 at that UCD business alumni conference by Seán FitzPatrick – who created a lair of conspiracy within Anglo Irish Bank, a bank so compromised by dishonesty, mismanagement, furtive transactions and scandal that it had to be nationalised or go under.

Within months, his own secrets would be yanked into the light of day. By preaching the polar opposite of what he practised, FitzPatrick demonstrated an infinite capacity for self-delusion.

He had always been outspoken. But in the year or two before he destroyed himself, FitzPatrick showed a proclivity for spouting amateur philosophy, not to mention volunteering advice to the government and finger-wagging at the electorate. He wanted to be accepted as a great man – perhaps he imagined this was how to achieve it.

'The world hasn't stopped turning,' he was moved to remark on a radio show a few months later, even as his bank – at that stage toppling on the brink of collapse – was thrown a lifeline by the State guarantee. His intention may have been to offer reassurance amid the instability of global economic turmoil. But, in truth, the world *had* stopped turning for some people. Their savings were wiped out, their pensions were gone, their futures were in jeopardy. The State's credentials may have been harnessed in the nick of time to prop up FitzPatrick's bank, but the little people had been left to fend for themselves.

FitzPatrick   whose behaviour had helped put Anglo Irish Bank in jeopardy – clearly imagined he had made a clean getaway as he burbled on with that pop philosophy. But it was only a temporary reprieve. His world was about to stop turning too. The man with the gift for honeyed words was on the brink of being exposed as a pedlar of tall tales.

So much damage caused by such an amiable man. Not just because the once-insignificant bank he raised high had wound up nationalised, but because his behaviour damaged Ireland abroad – in terms of its reputation, which was grave, but also in terms of its finances, which was more critical again. FitzPatrick's bank lied to the international investment community – and all Irish banks were tainted by association.

Ireland Inc pays higher interest on borrowings to run the

country partly because of FitzPatrick's ducking and diving. Why was there no whistleblower for this and for other transgressions? At Anglo, the organisers played their cards so close to their chests that only a tiny number of people were aware of what was happening. Those who knew were already implicated in the transaction. It was a case of honour among thieves – they would sink or swim together.

FitzPatrick trampled across ethics and flattened legalities. He created a polluted bank that smeared all Irish banks internationally. He is not a victim of global forces, as he would have people believe, but of his own greed, recklessness and hubris – no sacrificial lamb, then, but a wolf in sheep's clothing. Some say FitzPatrick's would be a token scalp – that he has been scapegoated for a systemic failure. Yet, now more than ever, should Ireland not signal to the world that it refuses to tolerate corporate corruption? Should the State not show it is no banana republic but that it observes due process in which justice is served? Furthermore, how damaging to a nation's morale is it to tolerate a coterie that acted outside good governance? People have been jailed for failure to pay a television licence. Is deception on a towering scale somehow exempt?

FitzPatrick was not unlucky, he was dishonest. He was not imprudent, but unscrupulous; not a victim of global forces, but the instigator of his own and others' downfall. Even as he schmoozed, politicked and lied, his bank was corrupt on three counts.

- His concealment of up to €122 million of personal loans he received from Anglo Irish Bank over an eight-year period.
- The Irish Life & Permanent scam, an attempt to dupe the markets that Anglo was in good health when it was haemorrhaging deposits.

–The Golden Circle arrangement which manipulated the bank's share price.

The mystery is why. A business associate of FitzPatrick's observed, 'Seánie fancied himself as an entrepreneur, not as a banker. In the end, his ego got control of him. Seán built up Anglo from a bank with a tiny loan book until it had lending of over €70 billion. He saw it as his right to access some of that.'

Over the years, rumours surfaced occasionally about Anglo's ethics but FitzPatrick always hotly denied them. 'My mother always brought me up with good ethics. You always have to be able to look people in the eye and sleep soundly at night,' he said. Right to the end, he persisted with the illusion that he was an honourable man, as though repetition could make it true. Even in his resignation statement, he insisted that he was upright but for this single lapse regarding the loans.

The facts suggest otherwise.

6

Just an Ordinary Billionaire

'My life is a simple thing that would interest no one. It is a known fact that I was born, and that is all that is necessary.'
Albert Einstein

Seán Quinn has made both a virtue and a career from simplicity. Ireland's richest man started out in businesses he understood thoroughly. In his salad days, he supplied building materials and manufacturing; even after diversifying, he abided by the rule of keeping everything as straightforward as possible.

He will often tell a homespun yarn to explain why he moved into a particular area. Take his anecdote about his entry into the hospitality trade. 'Every time I used to come to Dublin, the pubs were always full, so I said to myself, "This has to be a simple business because they're charging a ransom for the beer. They get paid for the beer before they pay Guinness, so this seems to be a good business."' It was a cinch in Ireland, with its drinking culture, but a different case entirely in Germany. Quinn opened a €5 million super-pub in a Berlin suburb only to shut it down because, he observed ruefully, customers shared a bottle of mineral water and made it last three hours.

That lesson was less expensive – and less painful – than the one he took from the Anglo affair. For the first time, simplicity was left at the door, and the consequences almost proved fatal for Quinn's insurance business and for its employees.

Quinn used complex financial instruments called contracts for difference (CFDs) to bet on a highly volatile share price in Anglo Irish Bank, at a time when Ireland was staring down the barrel of a property collapse. He has never offered an explanation for why he gambled so heavily on Anglo, other than saying that he admired the bank. But, reading between the lines, even of his formal statements posted on the Quinn Group website, a sense of remorse is palpable. 'These equity investments were clearly ill timed, costly and are very much regretted,' he said in January 2009.

Commenting on mistakes with the benefit of hindsight makes a sage of everyone. Yet Quinn's investment in Anglo Irish Bank bewildered onlookers from the moment the scale of his holding became apparent 25 per cent at its peak. In acquiring such a large stake as other investors dived for cover, Quinn acted on instinct. It was a policy that had served him well in the past. As stockbrokers urged clients to sell Anglo shares, Quinn went on a buying spree.

He could have made a fortune: instead, he allowed one to slip through his fingers. It happened because Seán Quinn broke three basic rules of investing.

–Don't put all your eggs in one basket.

–Don't borrow money to buy shares.

–Don't think you are right and the rest of the stock market is wrong.

When an investor builds up a position in shares through CFDs, they pay a deposit of, for example, 10 per cent of the shares' value. If the shares fall by 10 per cent, the investor gets a phone call from stockbrokers asking them to put in more money. This is called a cash call. The authors of this book have established that Quinn received cash calls as a result of his Anglo investment in the third and fourth quarters of 2007. At that point, the shares were falling from their record high. If reports were accurate that Quinn held 5 per cent of Anglo at the beginning of 2007 and built up his stake from that point, it indicates that he was buying Anglo shares at an average of €16 per share. He owned a quarter of a bank worth €12 billion, so his stake was worth €3 billion. If that was the case, when the bank was nationalised, Quinn would have lost a total of €2.6 billion. He raised €400 million by selling 10 per cent of his position in 2008.

However, Quinn sources say he did not pay an average of €16 per share. It seems as if his total loss was in the region of €2 billion. Sources close to him say he first bought shares in Anglo in the mid-1990s, although at a smaller volume than his later splurge. There is also the possibility that Quinn was not simply speculating on shares in Anglo. He could have been planning to take over the bank as a complementary business to Quinn Insurance. 'Strength through diversity' is the Quinn Group's logo, after all. Sources close to Quinn denied this and say that he always viewed the stake as an investment.

This was a punishing loss by anyone's standards. However, the Anglo affair called to account not just Seán Quinn's business acumen, but also his integrity. More damaging than the financial hit was the sabotage to his reputation. Quinn's gamble on the stock market culminated in his name being bracketed with a Golden Circle of Ireland's elite – a team of ten men enlisted to help manipulate Anglo Irish Bank's share price.

Quinn insists he is blameless. Only the outcome of an independent investigation can establish his guilt or innocence.

* * *

Quinn once said he planned to 'live poor and die rich' – the polar opposite of most people's aspirations. Such an endorsement of the simple life is typical of Quinn. No imperial trappings for him. He has never been one to show off the vast wealth amassed over thirty-six years in business; he does not even like showing his hand.

There is little about his appearance to indicate the self-made billionaire or the exceptional entrepreneur. Quinn has the look of a reasonably prosperous farmer – if a slightly dour and reticent one. While not a recluse, he is no lover of the limelight, and few people would spare him a second glance if they passed him on the street. His innate reserve makes him one of the most private members of Ireland's unofficial Croesus Club.

Perhaps he plays his ace a little too frequently – the unassuming man impervious to wealth, who enjoys a hand of cards with old friends in modest surroundings. There is considerably less heard about him flying around in his twin-engine jet helicopter, which operates from Enniskillen Airport. A certain amount of hocus-pocus is woven through the son-of-the-soil legend.

In the eyes of many before the crash the Mighty Quinn could do no wrong. In the first instance, the narrative of his life was appealing: phenomenal success from modest beginnings. His dominance of Irish business is all the more remarkable in view of its genesis in the economically underdeveloped border area. Then there is his reputation as a devoted family man, with a wife and five children carefully provided for and protected. He seems incapable of forming a sentence without some reference to his family in it.

By and large, Irish people have been positively disposed towards Quinn, who stayed close to his roots and embraced a comparatively humble lifestyle. His way of life gave him the smack of authenticity in a plastic age. Public statements in his softly spoken voice have acquired significance because of their rarity as well as for his unrehearsed awkwardness, which lends them a bona-fide ring. He repeatedly insists that the simple things in life are what count, focusing on the importance of home life and old friends.

'I'm not overly shy, but I much prefer to just sit back and enjoy what I'm doing, with my two dogs, the Wellington boots on, and dodging about the mountain. It gives my brain much more time to do what it's best at doing,' he said. It was light years away from hobnobbing with the glitterati in VIP enclosures – the natural habitat of entrepreneurs and billionaires. Instead, here was a practical man who gave the impression he knew one end of a shovel from another and would not be afraid to use it.

Quinn's reputation is that of a man who would let nothing turn his head, and Irish people approved of such unpretentiousness. Even as Celtic Tiger excesses proved irresistible across the social spectrum, there was a realisation that level-headedness remained a valuable commodity. Someone who preferred a holiday in Sligo to the Seychelles was an antidote to the culture of bling.

Plus there was the added bonus that Quinn stayed and paid his dues in Ireland, unlike the rash of tax exiles at the upper echelons of the business milieu. He and Michael O'Leary from Ryanair helped to keep the Exchequer's engine purring.

Quinn's manner is somewhat gruff, but what he lacks in presence is counterbalanced by grit. He is accustomed to winning – as the extent and span of his business interests testify. The Quinn Group is the most important family-owned conglomerate in Ireland, employing 5,500 people across a range of businesses plus 2,500 staff in twelve other countries.

By 2008, this understated man had climbed to number one on the *Sunday Times* 'Rich List' for Ireland, propelled there by the soaring profits from his Quinn Direct financial-products subsidiary. His personal wealth was estimated then at €4.7 billion, although it has been nibbled away by the credit crunch. He was listed by *Forbes* magazine as the 164th richest man in the world and was ranked twelfth among Britain's richest. Not bad for a fellow who left school in his teens to work the family farm.

That upgrade to number one on the Rich List was not evidence of Quinn's unstoppable upward trajectory, as might be supposed. On the contrary, he had already hit a complication – more than a complication: an obstacle. Its name was Anglo Irish Bank. And his dealings there showed the man with the Midas touch for business had feet of clay. While he was still identified as the wealthiest man in Ireland in the 2009 *Sunday Times* 'Rich List', his Anglo losses could be more punitive than the newspaper has estimated. This may well have pushed him at least one place down in the pecking order, below Denis O'Brien.

There are three elements which no account of Quinn's career omits. One is his rags-to-riches transformation, complete with his rejection of the trappings of success. Another is that he can read financial statements more adeptly than any accountant, despite having left school at the age of fifteen. Both contribute to the image of a David who challenged the Goliaths of business – and trumped them. The third factor is the land.

Quinn is a farmer's son. He was born in 1947 in Teemore in County Fermanagh, on the main road between Enniskillen and Cavan town and just over the border into the North of Ireland. A future spent scratching out a living on a 23-acre farm seemed to be his portion. He had failed to sit his Eleven Plus grammar-school exam, to the annoyance of his mother, who prized education. (He must have thought of her when he was awarded honorary doctorates from NUI Maynooth and Queen's University Belfast.) According to Quinn, his father told his wife, 'He'll be fine. He'll help me with the farm. He'll be all right.'

And the land did see him right, although perhaps not in the way his father envisaged. He may not have had the advantage of a flush background or a smart education, but Quinn had one stroke of fortune in life: there was gravel under the family's farm. In 1973, he borrowed £100 and started extracting the gravel, washing it and selling it to local builders. The international tycoon was on his way.

No business prospers without a system of contacts, and Quinn's came courtesy of his boyhood fondness for Gaelic football. Connections he developed with the GAA (Gaelic Athletic Association), with which his family was involved, helped him network on both sides of the border. In time, he would repay his debt by sponsoring the sport, and he was delighted when his son Seán lined out for the Fermanagh minors.

As his quarrying business grew, he expanded into the cement market. The sector was dominated by a few large players led by the inescapable profit-making machine of CRH. It was a tricky market to break into, and the might of the competition made it no easier. But Quinn was tough. His success demonstrated a dogged capacity to take on both established players and a market others perceived as impregnable. In the 1980s, he began to supply all of Ireland with cement and concrete blocks. He opened a roof-tile factory, followed by a pre-stressed concrete plant. By the next decade he was making tar and polystyrene insulation. Then he expanded into glass manufacturing in Derrylin in Fermanagh, taking on Ardagh's Irish Glass Bottle Company in Dublin's Ringsend. Not one to rest on his laurels, he branched out into a wide variety of manufacturing, including plastics, radiators, chemicals and packaging.

During the 1990s, newspaper headlines were dominated by

complaints from businesses and consumers alike about the exorbitant cost of insurance. Right on cue, in 1996, Seán Quinn opened Quinn Direct and started selling insurance cover, cutting out the middleman by marketing directly to the public. He says he founded his insurance arm because he had had enough of paying excessive insurance on his lorries. That feeling of being ripped off – and the drive to do something about it – prompted the foundation of the most successful insurance business in Ireland. By the early years of the twenty-first century, Quinn led the field in motor insurance and cover for homes and businesses. In January 2007, he took over Bupa's health-insurance operation for €150 million.

True to that guiding force of 'strength through diversity', Quinn's business domain expanded well beyond Ireland. His finger is in every pie from offices and warehousing in India to DIY hypermarkets and retail in Russia, and property in Eastern Europe. He spent €230 million buying the famous De Vere Belfry hotel and golf course in the West Midlands of England, four times host to the Ryder Cup, after expanding into the UK's motor- and commercial-insurance market in 2004. Back home in Ireland, he started his own wind farms in Fermanagh and Cavan and plans a gas-fired power plant to make electricity in Louth.

His approach to big business is deceptively fuss-free. In 2007, he shared his philosophy with 400 delegates at a lunch organised by Cavan County Enterprise Board: 'I'm not a very good speaker, so I'll just run through some bits of stuff that we have found handy . . . A lot of people are rushing to phones – they're rushing to meetings backwards and forwards, and they're always in a panic, but really they're not thinking. That's not a way to run a business.' It sounds suspiciously close to the Forrest Gump philosophy, but this is not to trivialise what he shared. He was urging a back-to-basics approach and explaining why it worked. He went on, 'If there is somebody that wants me, we have secretaries and great support teams. If whoever wants me can't take a return call from me in thirty or forty minutes, then there's something wrong. You should be slowing the whole thing down, getting the view right.'

Through all the expansion, Quinn has remained close to his origins. Many of his businesses are based around counties Cavan and Fermanagh, with his headquarters in Derrylin in Fermanagh. His home in Cavan's Ballyconnell is a comfortable but not particularly ostentatious seven-bedroom granite-clad building with Spanish arches and leisure area. It stands just 500 metres away from the Slieve Russell Hotel, which he owns, and a few miles from where he was born. Quinn uses the hotel gym on his way into work. He believes in the importance of keeping in shape, and some of his ideas occur to him while he is using the machines.

He is married to Patricia, a Galway woman he met at a dance. They have four daughters and a son: Seán, Colette, Ciara, Aoife and Brenda. The children are all in their twenties and early thirties, and the elder ones hold senior positions in the Quinn Group. Between them, Quinn, his wife and five children own a majority of the Quinn Group. The board is quite small, which allows for greater control from the top. Seán Quinn is a director of all the companies. Colette is on the board of the hotel division; Patricia and brother Peter are on the board of Quinn Group RoI.

He is close to his brother Peter, a major figure in the GAA and its president from 1991 to 1994. A chartered accountant and financial adviser based in Enniskillen, Peter shares his brother's bluntness and has attacked the 'non-risk-taking dead hands' in Ireland.

In an April 2007 interview with the *Irish Independent*, Peter Quinn used the example of the Roman Empire and said no organisation was unassailable or should let itself become complacent. When the Quinn Group takes over a business, its first priority is to study existing structures. 'If we have to destroy them and start with a clean sheet, we do it straight away,' said Peter Quinn. He is credited as the brains behind the commercialisation of Croke Park and, indeed, the GAA itself. A significant shareholder in the Quinn Group, he once described his brother Seán as 'an eternal optimist, which is necessary in business'.

If self-belief and an optimistic nature chipped in towards Seán Quinn's meteoric success, they have also contributed to his blind spot. As the first tremors of the banking crisis began to shake share prices in 2007, Quinn was speculating vast sums in Anglo Irish Bank stock – at a time when others wondered if bank shares were such a sound investment. Quinn had no such qualms. And this rosy conviction highlighted a previously unsuspected weakness.

CFDs allow investors to borrow money from a stockbroker, who purchases shares on their behalf. If the shares rise, the investor benefits greatly – despite having put only minor sums up front. This share purchase route attracts less tax. But it has a third benefit which would not have escaped Quinn's attention: investors do not have to disclose their shareholdings to the stock market. This is a critical issue for large investors. When they own more than 3 per cent of a company, they are legally obliged to issue a statement to the Irish Stock Exchange revealing the full extent of their shareholding.

Such a mechanism of investing suited Quinn. If the shares rose, as he believed they would, he stood to make a handsome profit. At the same time, he was under no onus to declare his shareholding to the stock market, a situation almost unique to Ireland. As Quinn was building up his Anglo stake, Financial Regulator Patrick Neary had indicated he would close the loophole allowing holders of CFDs to remain anonymous. He wrote to the government requesting a change in legislation, but no action was taken.

During 2007, media reports noted that Quinn had begun to amass an enormous position in Anglo Irish Bank. In his address to the Cavan County Enterprise Board in March of that year, Quinn said that two-thirds of his personal investments and those of family would go outside the Quinn Group in the next five years. He was not specific about where the money would be directed. At that time, he already had 5 per cent of Anglo Irish Bank shares. By August 2007, he owned 11 per cent of the bank. Quinn bought shares as they traded near their peak. The shares hit a record price of €17.85 in May 2007. At that price, the bank was worth more than €13 billion.

But stockbrokers outside Ireland were increasingly nervous about the amazing upward arc of Anglo over recent years, considering property prices were already beginning to fall. The bank was a specialist lender to property developers. There was considerable worry because Anglo's lending levels had shot up to €72 billion, as property prices were reaching their zenith. A hair-raising prospect dangled: developers might be unable to sell or complete projects, or they could go bust. And the bank would be left holding the baby. Soon after their May apex, Anglo shares started falling, and by the autumn they were on a steady slide. To the amazement of Dublin stockbrokers, Quinn was undeterred. Timing is everything in life. He continued buying overpriced Anglo shares in prodigious quantities. He was a gift horse for traders, a willing purchaser for shares other people were busily offloading. The bulk of the Anglo share-buying was conducted by NCB Stockbrokers, 25 per cent owned by Quinn.

Investors did not share Quinn's confidence, and their worries about the bank multiplied. By December 2007, the Anglo share price had dipped below €11. The following month, the London operation of Swiss investment bank UBS told its clients to sell their shares in both AIB and Anglo Irish

Bank. UBS analyst Ross Curran said there was a danger that commercial property values in Ireland could fall by 30 per cent, which would represent a 'significant risk to earnings' over the next two years for Irish banks. The foreign brokers were making their views crystal clear – unusually so, in an industry that relies on jargon.

Unfortunately, Irish stockbrokers still believed the story from Seán FitzPatrick and David Drumm that everything was hunky-dory at Anglo – even though it was fast becoming a case of wishful thinking. Some brokers even privately expressed the view that the London-based traders were engaged in 'Paddy bashing'.

As Quinn watched Anglo's share price plummet, rather than heed warning bells he regarded it as an opportunity to buy cheap shares. It was at this point that his reputed shrewdness deserted him. By the summer of 2008, Quinn had upped his stake in Anglo to 25 per cent – although he had never officially disclosed owning a single share.

Anglo's board knew that Quinn held this massive position. They were in the dark about his motives – but anxious. Consequently, the bank's management was in contact with the Financial Regulator about the situation. Quinn decided to clean up the situation following discussions with Anglo and after taking advice from within the Quinn Group. He moved quickly to unwind his 25 per cent holding. Ten per cent would be disposed of, while his wife and five children would retain 15 per cent in the form of ordinary shares rather than CFDs.

In August 2008, he confirmed that he had converted his position. By this stage, Anglo shares had dropped to €5. Many of his shares had been acquired when Anglo was trading at two or three times that price. Quinn had suffered a significant loss – buying high and selling low.

In an August 2008 statement, Quinn said, 'The family regards these shareholdings in Anglo Irish Bank as long-term holdings with significant opportunity for capital growth over such a period.' The optimism mentioned by his brother was apparent, as he added, 'In recent years, we have been highly impressed with Anglo's ability to outperform the banking sector in terms of profit growth, and we are confident this trend can be maintained over the longer term, notwithstanding the current difficulties being experienced in international banking.'

The family's faith in Anglo was soon to be dented. On the surface, the deal looked like a tidying-up process. Behind the scenes, it meant the remaining 10 per cent of Quinn's position would have to be sold off quickly. Senior figures in Anglo were disturbed. If a large volume of shares were to flood the stock market, the already damaged share price would be crushed. So, a plan was devised within Anglo to manipulate the share price. Those responsible ensured that Quinn's shares were bought by other investors without going through the normal route of the stock market. This led to a sweetheart deal involving ten major clients of the bank.

These men, mainly developers, became known as the Golden Circle and were lent €451 million to purchase the shares. Three-quarters of the borrowings were secured on the shares and only one-quarter on the personal assets of the borrowers. It meant if the shares collapsed and the developers could not pay, the bank would be liable for three-quarters of the loans. More serious again was the plan to manipulate the share price – a version of insider trading. If a case can be proven, it falls within the ambit of market-abuse legislation and carries a maximum ten-year jail sentence and a fine of up to €10 million.

But Quinn had another headache. In order to purchase the 15 per cent of Anglo for which he now had to make full payment, he needed to dig deep. Part of the money came from Quinn Insurance, in the form of a €288 million loan to the

Quinn family investment vehicle. However, those millions were legally supposed to remain in the insurance company. They were reserves to pay for claims against accidents. When the Financial Regulator's office became aware of the loan, it decided to investigate. A separate issue was that Quinn borrowed some of the money to purchase the 15 per cent stake in Anglo from the bank itself.

This probe resulted in a stinging slap for Quinn. In October 2008 he was forced by the Financial Regulator to stand down as chairman of Quinn Insurance. The company was also fined €3.2 million, the highest penalty of its kind. In addition, Seán Quinn was personally fined €200,000.

'We will pay the fines and move on,' he said. That undemonstrative sentence could not camouflage Quinn's rage at the reprimand. It bubbled through in a statement on the matter in which he insisted taxpayers were not left exposed by his actions. 'These loans breached insurance regulations and as a result of this the Financial Regulator has sanctioned Quinn Insurance and myself. I accept complete responsibility for this breach of regulation. While I accept that I made mistakes, I feel that the levels of fines do not reflect the fact that there was no risk to policyholders or the taxpayer, but are a result of the pressures existing in the current environment.'

The Quinn Group had to take an exceptional charge of €829 million to its 2007 accounts. This was a once-off hit to the accounts because of its exposure to the Anglo Irish Bank shares. It meant that instead of recording a profit for that year of just over €400 million, the group suffered a loss of €425 million. The company said that the maximum negative impact for its 2008 accounts would be €130 million. Put another way, Quinn was officially acknowledging that he and his family had lost almost €1 billion gambling on Anglo Irish Bank – and that was before the bank's shares underwent an utter collapse and Anglo was nationalised.

As Quinn affirmed in the aftermath of the share losses, the group is still lucrative – even after a pounding. If ever a family could withstand shockwaves, that family is the Quinns. But nobody likes losing money, irrespective of how much they have.

Seán Quinn had other problems. Something else had happened during those months in which the Quinn family lined up the purchase of that 15 per cent stake in Anglo. Quinn Insurance had pulled out of Moody's credit-rating system. Agencies such as Moody's provide an independent financial health check of a company, with Triple A the desirable top rating. Ostensibly, Quinn's withdrawal seemed relatively unimportant. There was no hue and cry at the time. But it was a source of some concern to brokers in the insurance industry. This rating matters to insurance companies because they invest sizeable amounts of their premiums in the stock market – that money is then used to pay claims when people have accidents. The rating agencies give outsiders a picture of how those investments are performing.

In July 2008, it was reported that Quinn Insurance had been given a Baa2 rating, which meant that the company offered 'adequate financial security; however, certain protective elements may be lacking or may be characteristically unreliable over any great length of time'. A Quinn spokesperson said that the company stopped using the credit-rating agencies because it did not need to borrow money. Others were sceptical. The withdrawal from the credit-rating system did not necessarily mean anything ominous, but it did not bolster confidence either.

At least one major Irish stock-market-quoted group decided not to do business with Quinn Insurance, concerned that the insurance arm would either not pay or would delay settling a major claim. For the company in question, that outcome could be so punitive that it preferred to deal with a more expensive insurer.

Quinn's reputation was not helped by a legal dispute

between Quinn Direct and John Reynolds, owner of the POD nightclub in Dublin. Reynolds, a nephew of former Taoiseach Albert Reynolds, suffered damage to his fashionable club when it was flooded in August and September of 2006. Reynolds lodged a claim for €120,000 for repairs and renovations. Quinn Direct offered €9,000. Reynolds said that the damage had been caused by a series of flash floods, while Quinn argued that Sisk, a construction group working on the adjoining building, was responsible. The dispute reached the High Court, and Mr Justice Bryan McMahon came down firmly on the side of Reynolds. He criticised the insurance company for failing to deal with the claim in a fair and prompt manner.

Reynolds was awarded €105,000 plus costs in August 2008, and Mr Justice McMahon said, 'It is incumbent on insurance companies to deal expeditiously and fairly with claims – it is not appropriate for insurance companies to be urging the insured to chase third parties.' The judge also applied interest of 8.1 per cent on the award from February 2007 to take account of the delay.

Afterwards, Reynolds said, 'This should never have gone to court. The legal costs in this case are more than the amount of money that was at stake. I am very annoyed that we had to go through all this to get our rightful claim, and the first offer of €9,000 was a joke. I have now taken all my properties off Quinn Direct insurance.'

The publicity was harmful to the reputation of the Quinn business. There were other cases in which Quinn disputed claims and lost. Another High Court judge said he found the insurer's behaviour 'disturbing' in a case involving Murray Timbers of Galway. Mr Justice Peter Kelly even threatened to hold a Quinn Direct manager in contempt and to send papers to the Director of Public Prosecutions.

Then there was the case of John Deegan, left a paraplegic

in a car accident: Quinn Direct alleged fraud, saying he had sustained his injuries in a fall from a balcony. The judge said there was no evidence of fraud, the allegation was withdrawn, and a settlement of €1.75 million made.

As with banking, insurance is about trust. Any perception of being slow to pay up can create a problem for an insurance company.

In the early weeks of 2009, rumours began to circulate in Leinster House that Quinn's insurance operation was facing large, unspecified issues. This was sparked by the collapse in Anglo Irish Bank's share price. To counter the gossip, Quinn decided on a public-relations exercise. This can be a risky strategy, but he pulled it off. In January 2009, the idea came to him in the gym to give RTÉ's northern editor Tommie Gorman a rare television interview. An undemonstrative man, he allowed an occasional flash of emotion to disturb the gravity of his face when discussing the debacle. At one point he barked out a wry laugh as he admitted to losing 'more than a billion' on the Anglo affair, although he refused to specify the amount. 'We feel the media frenzy around the Quinn Group is totally outlandish – outrageous. We have no idea why this agenda is to get Quinn,' he said, betraying no grasp of public concerns about a gilt-edged junto privately arranging matters to suit themselves.

Gorman first interviewed Quinn in the 1980s. Just before the interview began, he suggested that Quinn close the top button on his shirt – it would look tidier. Quinn laughed. The button was missing. This latest interview was less relaxed, with Quinn edgy at being associated with high rollers and their hedonistic lifestyles. He wanted to counter what he regarded as a misleading impression of him as a big shot. The session took place in Quinn's office in Derrylin, Fermanagh – headquarters of the group. Opening up about his business did not come readily to him, while answering questions about its balance sheet seemed particularly unwelcome.

'We are writing everything off, we are not counting anything on the Anglo shares,' he said. Matter-of-fact rather than blustering, he went on, 'We will survive without the Anglo shares. We are very well off.' Rather disingenuously, since it was he who had brewed up the deal, he said, 'It is the five kids and the wife that owns the shares in Anglo Irish Bank. So we are not discussing their losses but they are substantial.'

Anglo Irish Bank had just been nationalised at this stage, and the government had taken ownership of the shares. They had collapsed from a high of €17.85 to a miserable 21 cent. Under the Irish Constitution, the State cannot take ownership of something held by citizens without paying compensation. An assessor has been hired to establish how much money – if any – is due to former Anglo shareholders.

But none of the Quinns were expecting a handsome cheque in the post. Quinn shrugged off his mighty hit. 'Our company makes €400 million or €500 million profits per year. It would probably be making six or seven only we're in a recession right now. But our company is extremely profitable. The money we lost: it's hurtful, and we don't like it. I am not trying to dismiss it, I'm not trying to downsize it. But at the end of the day, a lot of people in Ireland today – individuals and companies – have lost a lot more in share dealing and their value than we have. I believe that there are companies with a fraction of our profits and they are losing a greater multiple than we are losing.'

He spoke of the company in terms of 'we' – identifying it clearly as a family endeavour. But he does not see the Quinn Group as part of the establishment. When it was suggested that there was a corporate culture of powerful people convinced they could invent their own rules, he insisted, 'We never perceived ourselves in that light. I finished school at fifteen, I've never seen myself as some high-flier. I just live a very simple life with my wife and five kids and that is what is important to me.

'As regards what institutions have done, did they fly too high? Yes, they did. Did we all fly too high? Did we all get carried away in the last few years, in the last five to seven years? I think most people over-extended themselves. They built bigger houses, better houses, they had second and third cars and holiday homes outside of Ireland.'

He spoke of a new sense of realism in Ireland and said young people needed a 'settling-down period and to know life is not always Golden Circle'. He took pains to disassociate his own company from any wrongdoing. Indeed, this was the core message he wanted to convey. Over and over again, he insisted that the Quinn Group had made a mistake and had been penalised. But it had not acted dishonestly.

'There are two things that can be said. We are totally innocent. Anything we did, we paid the price for it. We were not involved in anything, no impropriety at all, at no stage, in anything. We paid a price for it – a heavy price. We did not see the stocks continuing to go down as much as they did.'

Any issue of impropriety is not for Quinn to decide. It is, as he admits, the task of a formal investigation. Quinn's insistence on propriety implies he was not complicit with the Golden Circle arrangement. But a clean bill of health will depend on the various ongoing inquiries into that deal.

Leaving that to one side, he did benefit from the Golden Circle's purchase of his shares. It meant he was paid something for them, covering some of his losses – and he probably received a better price than if the shares were sold on the open market. Ultimately, there is a danger that the taxpayer will be presented with a bill for some, if not all, of that 10 per cent stake.

A shadow overhangs Quinn because of his forced resignation as chairman of his insurance company and the fines he received. But the Anglo affair, while damaging, has not finished off his career by any means.

What was striking about Quinn's interview was his determination to address the issue head on rather than to send out a rehearsed spokesperson. Quinn's public appearances over the previous decade could be counted on the fingers of one hand. But his name is on the group logo, and he was purposeful about defending it himself. He spoke diffidently but without resorting to corporate buzzwords, and his intervention made a positive impression.

One month after Quinn's television interview, telecoms entrepreneur Denis O'Brien launched a blistering attack on him. He accused Quinn of 'destabilising the entire banking system – not just Anglo Irish Bank' with his secret stake. 'The €300 million in Anglo Irish investor losses should be left at the door of Seán Quinn in Cavan and should be repaid by him,' the *Sunday Times* quoted O'Brien as saying at a private function in February 2009. O'Brien went on to speak up for his old friend at Anglo, who had financed 98FM, O'Brien's first radio station. Perhaps he believed Seán FitzPatrick had been vilified unjustly – although to diminish the banker's conduct with an anodyne 'he has made mistakes' was inappropriate. O'Brien's logic in defending FitzPatrick while taking a swipe at Quinn was hard to fathom. Insiders say more damaging material about the Golden Circle deal and Quinn's shares may come into the public domain, however, which could throw light on why O'Brien's hackles were raised.

The Anglo episode has been immensely damaging to Quinn. But the mechanism whereby 10 per cent of his shareholding was purchased by the ten Golden Circle investors does not appear to have been orchestrated by Quinn himself, according to his TV interview.

Speculation has hummed about his motivation in building up his stake in Anglo Irish Bank to 25 per cent. In his rationale for buying the shares, he indicated a belief in the bank as a star performer: he judged the shares good value and thought they would rise in price. He never asked for a seat on the board, despite his extensive shareholding, which points to a money-making strategy rather than a grand plan to take over the bank. But dipping into his insurance company to help pay for a potty investment created a perilous situation for himself and the Quinn Group. His reputation as a businessman suffered.

Despite the Anglo catastrophe, Quinn's efforts to bring competition to the markets of insurance, building materials and hospitality have benefited a great number of people. More than 5,000 people in Ireland owe their livelihoods to him, and many of those jobs are in the long-neglected border area.

This region was avoided by multinationals for decades because of the Troubles. Quinn inspires respect from many who believe he has helped deliver confidence and prosperity to a stretch of the country insufficiently assisted by the State. Without him, the border area might never have shared in the boom.

Some see Quinn as a business genius, others as a champion of consumers, while in the border counties he is a local hero. They describe him as laid back and allude to his generosity to local charities, always given on condition of silence. RTÉ's Tommie Gorman said that Quinn seemed very much the same, plain person he met twenty years earlier, who was 'grounded in his family, his community and the GAA'.

Even in its diminished form, his wealth sits uneasily on those slightly hunched shoulders. Perhaps when his children get their hands on the loot there might be more flamboyance in the Quinn camp. On the other hand, they have consistently avoided the gossip columns. When his daughter Ciara married Dublin-based solicitor Niall McPartland in November 2007, the wedding was strictly private. Heavy security surrounded the church in Staghill, Cavan – even people trying to visit the graves of relatives were stopped at the gates. Onlookers strained for a glimpse of the nuptials but had to content themselves with admiring the white roses tied to the church railings and arched over the doorway and the miniature pine trees in pots brought in to line the avenue. The only hint of extravagance was a pair of new Rolls-Royce Phantoms which carried the bridal party to the door.

Quinn did pose for a few photographs with his daughter and her new husband, although there was no sign of the rest of the family. Afterwards, everyone was whisked away for a reception at – where else? – the family's four-star Slieve Russell hotel. Like father, like daughter: the bride stayed on home turf and saw no need for ostentation, even on her wedding day. The understated dignity of the event contrasted with some of the more lavish displays of affectation in Irish society in recent years.

Seán Quinn's self-image is of an uncomplicated quarry man. Perhaps, at this stage, he has said it so often he believes it. He insists job creation is his priority, but that has to be the cherry on the cake. It cannot have been the driving force behind his rise. Job creation is only one of the many benefits of success. Still, there have been no redundancies within the group due to the downturn, although staff members have been shifted around as necessary. Nor are any redundancies expected, he has reiterated. He has had to temporarily shut down a plant, however. In that RTÉ interview, he said the only people he owed an apology to were his employees, if the group had overreached itself and become tarnished in the process. He knows a fair number of his staff by name, and they call him Seán rather than Mr Quinn. He stressed that he would have the same number of employees this year as last year, despite the losses on Anglo, and pointed out it was the family's money rather than that of customers which had gone.

Perhaps his bizarre gamble in relation to Anglo Irish Bank

can be understood within the framework of his best-known leisure activity. This is a Tuesday night hand of poker with a group of old friends in Ballyconnell. Quinn enjoys a flutter – sizing up how lucky he feels and taking a chance. But in a card game he keeps risk-taking under control. Bets are restricted to 50 cent for ten games so nobody can lose more than a fiver or win more than €10. 'That's fine with me,' he has said. The subtext: what would he spend it on anyway? Maybe not bank shares any more. Applying the Ballyconnell poker-school philosophy to Anglo dealings would certainly have contained his losses there.

The Anglo affair is bound to smart. Losing so much money probably hurts less than the chastening realisation that he made a mammoth – and avoidable – mistake, however. His association with his namesake, Seán FitzPatrick, led to Quinn overreaching himself. Was it greed? Ambition? Bull-headed self-belief? Maybe his excess can be traced to the gambler's fire – that addictive desire to chance your luck just one step further.

He put it best himself once, in his characteristic no-frills fashion: 'The more you have the more you want and the more you expect.' Winning had become so commonplace to Quinn, he never expected to lose.

In March 2007, at that conference held by the Cavan County Enterprise Board in Quinn's own Slieve Russell Hotel, he replayed his philosophy: 'We came from a very simple background and we tried to make business very simple. We don't believe in too much fuss. We never had a feasibility study done in our lives. I don't use a mobile phone. I live a very simple life, and that's the way I want to continue.'

Over and over, that word 'simple' is brandished – at once self-definition and guiding star. How paradoxical, then, for Quinn to be seduced by a mechanism as convoluted as a CFD.

7

A Minister for Good Times – another for Bad Times

'And anything that happened to me afterwards, I never felt the same about again.'
From 'Guests of the Nation' by Frank O'Connor

Champagne Charlie

During the good times, Charlie McCreevy developed a reputation as 'Champagne Charlie'. After Ireland Inc fell prey to a thumping hangover, however, it was Brian Lenihan who had to administer the cure.

McCreevy is admired and abhorred in equal measure. When Ireland's economy skidded off the tracks in 2008, radio presenter and newspaper columnist Matt Cooper suggested he should be recalled from his post as European Commissioner to help manage the crisis. By comparison, commentator Fintan O'Toole remarked, 'It is true that a return of Charlie McCreevy from Brussels would be good for someone. The European Commission would be greatly enhanced by his absence.'

McCreevy, a horseflesh aficionado often spotted at race meetings, has a pronounced Kildare accent and a habit of using folksy analogies. The latter endears and obfuscates in equal measure. After being appointed to the Commission, he faced questions from MEPs about his policies at an introductory session. In the Parliament, contributions are translated into the language of each member state. During one answer, he began describing a financial scenario by comparing the odds on horses at an imaginary race. One journalist tuned into the Spanish translation, eager to hear how the translators were faring with the bookie babble. The silence was absolute.

Born in 1949 in Sallins, County Kildare, McCreevy was first elected to Dáil Éireann as a Fianna Fáil TD in 1977 and held the seat in Kildare (and later Kildare North) until 2004, when he became European Commissioner for Internal Markets. In successive governments he served in a number of ministries before becoming Minister for Finance. His closest political ally at the Cabinet table was Mary Harney, a fellow proponent of the free market and low income tax. He was an opponent of Charlie Haughey and lingered on the backbenches under his leadership of Fianna Fáil.

McCreevy's family had been lock keepers on the Grand Canal since the late 1700s, a job carried on by his mother after his father's death when he was four. A bright schoolboy, he was educated at Naas Christian Brothers School, and won scholarships. He studied commerce at UCD around the same time as Seán FitzPatrick and after graduating became a chartered accountant. He is married to his second wife Noeleen, a former personal secretary in the Department of Finance.

McCreevy was the longest serving Minister for Finance during the boom, holding the office for seven years between 1997 and 2004. Economist Jim Power said, 'We are now paying the price for a lot of the policies he set up. I admired one thing about him. He implemented a lot of pension reforms and he reduced taxes. He did leave an imprint on the Department of Finance, but he was blinded by free-market ideology. While McCreevy made the snowball, Brian Cowen then took over and continued to push the snowball down the hill.' In his *Irish Times* newspaper column in January 2009, former Taoiseach Garret FitzGerald said the country had lost competitiveness during the McCreevy years because of escalating pay demands. Three months later he was back on McCreevy's case, describing his handling of the economy as 'appalling'.

One of McCreevy's most contentious measures was the allocation of €2 billion in a range of tax incentives to encourage investment in property – a move that was just plain unnecessary. It was like hosing down flames with petrol instead of water. They did have a purpose: to bring development to many areas of Ireland. Frequently, however, they resulted in properties springing up where there was no natural demand. In reality, many landlords were buying a tax shelter on rental income – with the fringe benefit of an apartment attached. In places where there was demand, houses and apartments would have been built anyway. In areas where there was no demand, such as Leitrim, swarms of empty apartments and houses now overlook the Shannon as a monument to ultimately foolish policies.

It was not just homes: the number of hotels grew rapidly, partly as a result of tax incentives. Hotel bedroom numbers jumped from 26,000 in 1996 to 64,000 in 2008. That was an increase of 150 per cent, but the number of tourists coming to Ireland only rose by 70 per cent over the same period. Hoteliers were left fighting for customers and drastically discounting prices in an attempt to stay in business. But the lessons from tax incentives were the same: Ireland built lots of things it did not really need. People invested because they did not like paying tax rather than because Ireland was short of hotels or apartments.

During the Celtic Tiger years there was a misapprehension that property would rise in value irrespective of location. When the intoxicating haze of spiralling prices was wafted away by the credit crunch, rural Ireland was left with senseless developments bought by people who only wanted the tax relief. Many are unoccupied and create a ghost-town image.

Perhaps one of the initiatives that will make McCreevy unpopular for years to come was his ill-fated decentralisation of the civil and public service. This stuttered along before being watered down and eventually stalling. Another idea to draw criticism was tax individualisation, intended to make it more attractive for women to work outside the home. Families with a stay-at-home spouse objected. Other controversial decisions include €1 billion of public money spent on bailing out religious orders from the consequences of child sexual abuse by clerics, and cutting taxes while increasing spending as the economy boomed, storing up problems for future administrations. But there were welcome reforms, too. Among them were:

–His imaginative SSIA deposit scheme, which did focus the minds of consumers and financial institutions on saving for the future, notionally at least;

–the successful changeover to the euro in 2002;

–the fall in unemployment from 10 per cent to 4 per cent during his term of office;

–the National Pension Reserve Fund, which is intended to meet the cost of Ireland's public and social-welfare pensions from 2025 onwards.

McCreevy glowed with utter self-belief and frequently ignored the views of those around him. He never worried about treading on toes and said that Britain's banking regulations meant it only had itself to blame for the Northern Rock crisis.

The Irish people's first rejection of the Nice Treaty was 'a sign of a healthy democracy,' he remarked. There were calls in Europe to have him removed from his post as commissioner after he admitted he had not read the Lisbon Treaty and did not expect any 'ordinary decent' Irish person to pore over it.

When, as Minister for Finance, he announced medical cards for everyone over the age of seventy, he did so on the basis of a back-of-the-envelope calculation. He estimated it would cover 39,000 people at a cost of €19 million. But in the first year alone, 63,000 received cards, and the bill was €126 million. It was not the only one of his measures that went askew. Decentralisation proved costly rather than cost-effective and has been put under review. And better-off senior citizens over the age of seventy were required to hand back medical cards at the start of 2009. This caused consternation among those who felt they had earned the perk by paying crippling taxes to help Ireland out of recession in the 1980s.

Any analysis of McCreevy's career has to conclude that he was a lively politician who showed ingenuity. Rather than play it safe, he championed big-picture ideas. But his legacy of boosting public spending by 48 per cent, while slashing taxes, has left Ireland limping along the road to recovery. He was replaced by Brian Cowen who held the ministry until becoming Taoiseach in 2008.

Budget Blues Brian

The banking crisis was a test of Brian Lenihan's nerve and resolve. He was pitched into the Department of Finance in May 2008, following the reshuffle that accompanied Brian Cowen's accession to replace Bertie Ahern. Ahern had been forced to step down as Taoiseach after eleven years amid controversy over his personal finances.

Lenihan was a surprise choice. Before his appointment he

expressed no overt interest in an economic ministry, unlike his Cabinet colleague Dermot Ahern. Lenihan had been in the justice ministry, an appropriate position for a former senior counsel. When Lenihan was offered finance, Dermot Ahern replaced him as Minister for Justice.

Lenihan has a sharp legal mind and approached his new job in a lawyerly fashion. He absorbed information readily and could argue his case adroitly. While he had a deficit of financial experience, he had lectured in banking law for eight years – experience that helped him handle bespoke-suited bankers flexing their muscles and threatening legal action.

Born in 1959, Brian Joseph Lenihan spent his early life in Athlone before moving to Dublin's Castleknock as a boy. He was educated in Belvedere College, the Jesuit-run rugby school in Dublin city centre, where he distinguished himself from an early age and became head prefect. He studied law at Trinity College – his father had been a barrister before entering politics – and was awarded first-class honours. At Trinity, Lenihan is remembered as well dressed and handsome. He was a prominent member of 'The Hist' or the College Historical Society, the oldest debating society in the world, founded by philosopher Edmund Burke in 1747. It was a breeding ground for barristers, solicitors, diplomats and politicians. Lenihan fitted in without a crease.

Next, he studied for a Master's degree in law at Cambridge before being admitted to the Bar. Immediately afterwards, in 1984, he began lecturing in law at Trinity. But politics were always in the background, especially when Brian Lenihan Senior became ill and he helped with his constituency work. The father died in 1995, and the son won the Dublin West seat held by him in a 1996 by-election. He also became a senior counsel a year later.

After years of pushing for a meaty job in government – Bertie Ahern was singularly reluctant to elevate him and left him kicking his heels on the backbenches for more than a decade – he was offered a junior ministry. That lengthy delay on his leader's part could explain why he told a Dublin Castle conference, during an interval in Ahern's appearances at the Mahon Tribunal, that the venue was where Ireland tried corrupt politicians.

When he became Minister for Justice in 2007, it was the first time a son had taken a Cabinet post previously held by his father. Brian Lenihan Senior had held Justice and a host of ministries, including Tánaiste to Charlie Haughey, for a quarter of a century. Brian Lenihan Junior's political pedigree is peerless, although he denies – implausibly – that he is part of the political establishment. He is a third-generation TD: his aunt Mary O'Rourke served as a TD for twenty-four years and also held a series of Cabinet posts, including deputy leader to Bertie Ahern; his grandfather Patrick was a TD; and his younger brother Conor is currently a junior minister with responsibility for integration.

Brian Lenihan wanted to show his mettle in Finance, but his appointment to the ministry was a baptism by fire. It coincided with an enormous slide in the public finances, a banking crisis and the inevitable splat of a property bubble connecting with the sharp edge of the credit crunch. It took him a while to understand the figures, despite his academic dexterity in other areas – he barely scraped a pass in Leaving Cert mathematics. One avoidable faux pas was when someone in his department got their sums wrong over the amount to be generated by the pension levy on public servants' incomes. It left a hole of half a billion euro in the estimate.

His critics frequently carped that he was under-qualified for the job, and there is no doubt he made some serious mistakes. His first budget in October 2008, rushed forward from the usual December date, was a disaster. In part, the government failed to sell the need for cutbacks – and then criticised the electorate for its inability to 'internalise precisely the lightning-rod issue in the way which respects the broad parameters of the budget arithmetic'. The scale of the communication problem between leaders and reluctant-to-be-leds was apparent from that gem alone, courtesy of Brian Cowen. Another error was Lenihan's repeatedly ruling out another budget to mop up after his failed introductory one. But he had to flip-flop and introduce emergency measures with a second budget in April 2009 after all.

Lenihan's policies were behind the curve. Some of the solutions he proposed had merit at the time but kept being overtaken by events. It was as if the problems had Miracle-Gro sprinkled on them and expanded before his eyes. His situation was not helped by over-laden civil servants in the Department of Finance. Pressure from the crisis foisted a hefty additional burden on the department's banking section. Simultaneously, the entire department was trying to cope with the deficit in the public finances. This was caused by the government spending considerably more than it was receiving in taxes.

When Lenihan wrapped himself in the tricolour, citing patriotism as a reason not to shop in the North of Ireland before Christmas 2008, it backfired on him. He made a snippy remark about paying VAT to Her Majesty's government, but financially pinched shoppers ignored the subtext of his suggestion, which was to carry on paying rip-off prices for Mother Ireland's sake. And the North's Deputy First Minister, Martin McGuinness, accused him of a partitionist mentality.

But the minister showed resolve, and an appropriate application of patriotism, when he faced down Britain's Chancellor of the Exchequer. This was during the attempt by Alistair Darling to steer Lenihan away from his bank-guarantee strategy. Darling protested it was anti-competitive, but Lenihan insisted it was essential to Ireland's interest.

And he also spotted the discrepancies in the directors' loan figures that exposed Seán FitzPatrick at Anglo Irish Bank.

Often Lenihan looked haunted, eyes hollow with exhaustion. As a night owl, however, he appeared able to survive on a couple of hours' sleep. He worked incredibly hard – early mornings, late nights and weekends for months on end. Here was a man doing his best with an almighty mess that changed shape by the hour.

Lenihan is excellent company. Away from the microphones, his conversation is peppered with anecdotes and witty remarks. A gifted impersonator, he would sometimes mimic the bankers with whom he spent long hours. He did a particularly adroit impression of one who addressed meetings with the government as if he was in a court of law.

A francophile, Lenihan enjoys holidays in France, travelling by ferry with his wife, Circuit Court judge Patricia Ryan, and their two children. Traditionally, wives pose for pre-Budget photographs with their finance-minister husbands holding the all-important document case, but Ryan has not taken part.

He is viewed as an honourable man and as someone with integrity. During Bertiegate, the contentious whip-round proceeds for Ahern, Lenihan was the only Cabinet member to slate his leader for taking the money. Ahern was furious and regarded it as rank disloyalty.

In a casual conversation with one of the authors of this book in a Brussels hotel before meeting European finance ministers, Lenihan put his finger on the central question dogging policy-makers across the globe. 'Where has all the money gone?' he asked laughingly, a rhetorical question. It had obviously been put to him on a number of occasions. As Lenihan knew full well, the money was never there in the first place. It was paper money – notional wealth. That was the crux of the problem.

He was not alone in under-estimating the scale of the evolving crisis. Many political leaders and business people made the same mistake. Even the best brains in business miscalculated. The world's richest man in 2008, Warren Buffett, lost almost half his wealth. Former US Treasury Secretary Hank Paulson, considered a demigod in the world of finance, allowed Lehman Brothers to collapse, with disastrous effects.

Some of the negative appraisal of Lenihan has been unjustified, such as an over-reliance on his civil servants. All ministers are supposed to canvass advice and depend on their civil servants, especially during a once-in-a-century financial catastrophe. He would be a lightning rod for more deserved criticism if he tried to tinker with solutions on his own.

In March 2009, Lenihan appointed as an adviser Alan Ahearne, a lecturer in economics at the National University of Ireland in Galway. Previously, Ahearne had worked for the US Federal Reserve and had consistently warned about the dangers of the property bubble. The *Irish Times* profiled him under the headline, 'The Economist Who Told You So'. Lenihan also takes advice from a broad range of people inside and outside the department. Among them is David Doyle, Secretary General of the Department of Finance.

One legitimate critique of Lenihan was that he procrastinated. Dithering went on in the corridors of power. Dealing with the banks dragged on interminably and damaged the economy. The decision to introduce the bank guarantee at the end of September was the single convincing action the government took – only to undermine it by failing to implement the necessary steps at each subsequent stage of the crisis.

Would it have helped if Lenihan was an economic guru or a whizz on the capital markets? Probably not. Just about everyone called it wrong.

8

The Straw Man

'But rules cannot substitute for character.'
Former chairman of the US Federal Reserve Board,
Alan Greenspan

3 December 2008

Anglo Irish Bank's logo features an arrow pointing upwards: a simple illustration that reflects the bank's impatient ambition. This symbol is conspicuously displayed at the bank's headquarters on St Stephen's Green in Dublin. Here, the centre of operations shares an idiosyncrasy with the Tardis. It is not quite what it seems.

Pedestrians and motorists pass a modern five-storey office block with tinted windows, somewhat at odds with the Georgian buildings that form the parameters of the Green. It is, after all, just a few doors down from the landmark Shelbourne Hotel. But a number of interlinking buildings feed into the headquarters. Adjacent to the pillared, brown-brick office block is an impressive Georgian redbrick edifice called Heritage House. Corridors connect it to the main structure of Anglo so that visitors enter through a modern doorway and find themselves ushered into a lofty, rather dark reception room with stucco plaster ceilings.

On the morning of 3 December 2008, Anglo Irish Bank held a press conference in this olive-green room on the ground floor of Heritage House. The occasion was its annual results. The business journalists milling around, drinking coffee and checking their watches were oblivious to their historic surroundings. They were anxious to hear what the bank's senior executives had to say. More media representatives than usual turned up because of the bank's vulnerable position over preceding months. Its share price had been almost obliterated. It had reached a high of €17.85 in May 2007 but was now down to a miserable 49 cent. The stock market was brimming with alarm that this specialist property lender would be the first victim of the crash.

Attention levels stirred up when chief executive David Drumm strode purposefully into the room, dressed in the traditional banker's uniform of navy suit and striped tie. At his heels was finance director Willie McAteer. There was no sign of Seán FitzPatrick, the dynamo at Anglo's core, but the chairman was not normally present at a results meeting. As usual, cameras flashed while the pair posed with copies of their annual results for the year ended 30 September 2008. Journalists took their seats around a highly polished rectangular table. They switched on recorders, produced notebooks and laptops . . . and waited expectantly. Drumm sat in the middle of the media set, McAteer at his side, and launched into his presentation.

Just two months later, it would be revealed as a tissue of lies. Anglo Irish Bank accounts were as genuine as a piece of the true cross bought at Relics-R-Us.

In 2005, when Seán FitzPatrick retired and became chairman, David Drumm was an unexpected choice as the new chief executive of Anglo Irish Bank. Before his elevation, Drumm did not even have a seat at the board of directors – a sign he was not an obvious candidate. On the other hand, FitzPatrick was his mentor. Curiosity was rife about why he had been given the nod instead of Anglo's chief operations officer Tiarnan O'Mahoney, number two for the previous ten years; or why he had bypassed head of wealth management Tom Browne. Both were executive directors and tipped for the post.

Some suggested FitzPatrick was occupying a comfort zone with 'young Drumm' as CEO at the relatively tender age of thirty-eight, because he might be easier to control than a more experienced successor. 'Drumm was very bright, and he and Seánie got on well. There was surprise about his appointment, though,' recalled a former colleague. Another senior banker said, 'When they went for David Drumm they went for a customer-facing person as opposed to Tiarnan O'Mahoney who was more involved in the internal workings of the bank.' Although FitzPatrick was not on the committee that appointed Drumm, people close to the situation say his view was canvassed and proved influential. The general consensus was that the new kid on the block would be under Fitz-Patrick's patronage.

In becoming chairman, FitzPatrick ignored corporate governance guidelines. These stipulate a chief executive should not take over the chair because it prevents fresh per-spectives on previous decisions. But Anglo was not the only Irish company to disregard the protocol, which is a recomm-endation only and lacks bite. While it is considered best practice, politicians had never bothered to introduce legis-lation enforcing it. This could be interpreted as an early indicator of FitzPatrick's capacity to ride roughshod over ground rules when they proved inconvenient.

Drumm settled in the desirable seaside village of Malahide, just outside the capital – birthplace of U2's Adam

Clayton and The Edge. He lives with his wife Lorraine and their two daughters in an upmarket development of detached houses on a parcel of former farm land – at their peak they were selling at close to €4 million.

Chez Drumm is amongst the most overtly ostentatious of all the senior bankers' homes and can best be summed up in two words: nouveau riche. The development is ultra modern but the houses come with neo-Georgian façades and a wealth of period affectations. Close neighbours on the Abington estate include Bertie Ahern's daughter Georgina and her Westlife husband Nicky Byrne and Ronan Keating and his ex-model wife Yvonne. The rooms are what estate agents like to call generously proportioned, only in this case it is no exaggeration. The properties occupy a massive 4,500 square feet. The usual prerequisites of fine living apply: bathrooms made for hedonism and kitchens crammed with gadgets that could launch a rocket ship as well as cook a joint, plus handsome staircases, recessed lighting and half-acre land-scaped gardens to ensure privacy. Residents of this exclusive community are particularly concerned about protecting their retreat and in 2006 attempted to have a ten-feet-high wall built around the estate. Planning permission was refused.

Drumm has maintained his links with his hometown, where he has membership of Skerries Golf Club despite being a self-confessed 'high handicap' golfer. Bankers have always found it advantageous to play a round of golf. More than just a chance for some exercise, it is an ideal networking opportunity. Where Drumm differs from the standard-issue banker is in his zest for rock music. Typically he would arrive at his St Stephen's Green office with U2 or Bruce Springsteen blasting out from the car stereo and audible through the windows.

His schooldays were spent at the local De La Salle Christian Brothers School. He left in 1984 and four years later qualified as a chartered accountant with Deloitte & Touche. This triggered a relocation to Dundalk in 1988 to join Enterprise Equity, the venture-capital arm of the International Fund for Ireland. It proved invaluable experience in dealing with start-up companies north and south of the border.

Five years on, he moved back to Dublin and joined accountants Bastow Charleton, where he was regarded as a quick-fire operator who was going places – albeit not at Bastow Charleton. Audit work proved a drudge for someone accustomed to the stimulation of venture capital. He applied for a manager's job with the relatively insignificant Anglo Irish Bank and was offered an assistant managerial position instead. It meant a large pay cut, but he took it anyway. His timing was impeccable. It was 1993, and economic activity was picking up. In 1995, he made manager. Colleagues remember him for his quick decision-making capacity – a quality prized at Anglo. 'He was set aggressive targets, and he always beat them. He was always up for the next challenge. It would be wrong to describe him as aggressive, but he was very driven, very focused,' said a former colleague.

Drumm caught FitzPatrick's eye. He recognised someone pushing for success and sent him to the US two years later to build up Anglo's operation Stateside from scratch. It was a test of his mettle and he passed with flying colours. Moving to the US with his young family, Drumm reconnoitred various locations – from New York to Chicago to the West Coast – before recommending Boston. By the end of 2006, the US business had gross assets of more than €4.3 billion. This was an impressive record for a business started from Drumm's rented apartment.

In 2002, FitzPatrick recalled him to become head of lending. Now he was on the fast track and, once again, his timing was inspired, because the race for a successor to FitzPatrick would soon be under starter's orders. As it reached the home stretch in late 2004, four candidates were interviewed: Tom Browne, Tiarnan O'Mahoney, John Rowan – then head of Anglo's UK operation – and Drumm, the dark horse. All three rivals named him as their chief executive of choice should they be passed over.

They were.

Stockbrokers read his appointment as business as usual at the bank. The chief executive of one of the bailed-out lenders said of Drumm, 'He was cordial, he grew up in the Anglo culture. He thought the only way was up.' FitzPatrick described Drumm as being 'soaked in the ethos' of Anglo –a disturbing endorsement in view of subsequent events.

At first glance, Drumm tended to look older than his age because of premature hair loss. But there was a light-hearted streak in him that high finance had not suppressed. He seemed to march to a different beat to FitzPatrick: less showy, less gregarious and with no particular interest in lecturing politicians or expressing views beyond what was required of him as chief executive. That is not to suggest that he lacked opinions – indeed, workmates colleagues have described him as opinionated. 'He spoke his mind, he was a no-nonsense guy,' said one former colleague.

FitzPatrick's decision to remain at Anglo as an influential player must have put Drumm under pressure to prove himself – to make his own mark. He had to step out from his master's shadow. He did so by driving profits through the roof in a frenzy of lending: profit before tax was €615 million for the year ending September 2005 compared with €1.2 billion two years later.

The morning of the annual results, Drumm and McAteer each took a deep breath and steadied their nerves before setting in motion their plan to dupe the markets. No doubt they convinced themselves it was a matter of expediency: the

Machiavellian doctrine of the end justifying the means. Drumm was tense and jittery. But he remained witty, as always. He produced a thick book of figures, which, as usual, had been presented to stockbrokers earlier that morning. Brandishing this tome, he joked with journalists that he had no problem giving them the long, boring version of the accounts if they preferred.

It was gallows humour. Beneath his mask, Drumm was the proverbial cat on a hot tin roof. He was about to tell the assembled representatives of Irish and international media outlets a series of tall tales. He would follow this press conference with a succession of television, radio and newspaper interviews – and he would lie through his teeth in all of them. Not just sins of omission, not just putting the best possible spin on the results – out-and-out whoppers. Backed by McAteer, Drumm was embarking on a propaganda campaign to shore up the bank. What he held between his hands was a sexed-up dossier. Key elements of the results were a fabrication, while vital pieces of information had been deliberately omitted.

The accounts showed that Anglo Irish Bank had profit before tax of €784 million, down 37 per cent on a year earlier. One of the main reasons for the drop was because the bank had set aside half a billion euro to pay for future bad loans. Despite a property market that was grinding to a halt and an economy that was slowing, Anglo's lending had roared ahead by €9 billion to €73 billion. Remember, this was the property developers' bank. So it was continuing to lend – and lend heavily – on overvalued property.

On the plus side, the bank touted its increase in deposits, which had risen from €49 billion to €51 billion. In any bank, deposits are the bedrock of stability. In the climate of uncertainty after the government was forced to guarantee all loans and savings in Irish banks, it was critical for Anglo's deposits to grow. This would demonstrate solidity. But the deposit figure registered in the accounts was not the true one. It had been artificially boosted to give a deliberately misleading impression.

There was one tense moment. When the press conference began, Anglo shares were at 94 cent. Drumm referred to the price being under pressure. RTÉ reporter Emma McNamara corrected him: 'The shares are actually 66 cent now.' Drumm paused, before saying through gritted teeth, 'Thanks for that, Emma.' The shares closed that day at 67 cent, down by more than a third.

On that December morning, only a handful of people knew the reality. It seems implausible that Seán FitzPatrick was not among them. 'He admitted concealing loans, and I find it hard to believe he was not aware of the Irish Life & Permanent deposits and the Quinn share deal,' said the chief executive of one of the other bailed-out lenders. Whether this can be proven is another matter.

The chairman's statement in the results, dated the previous day, was resolutely upbeat. It said, 'Notwithstanding the environment, Anglo Irish Bank delivered a resilient performance in 2008 . . . we are confident that our business model and our stringent risk management process will continue to generate robust profits and capital for each of the next three years.' FitzPatrick was banging the gong just as energetically as Drumm and McAteer.

After being questioned by journalists, Drumm went upstairs to a room set aside for a prearranged interview with RTÉ's business correspondent – and co-author of this book – David Murphy. He was edgy, although good-humoured. As the camera rolled, he explained the reason for sidelining half a billion euro for future bad loans. 'Given the economic environment in Ireland and in the markets that we are in – the UK and US – it makes sense to be prudent. And it is an ultra-prudent move, really, to put aside rainy-day money to provide for potential future losses in a recessionary period.'

All this prudence – indeed, *ultra*-prudence. Drumm was waving around the bank's ostensible diligence to lend credence to those results. After the interview, Murphy asked Drumm to remain seated while cameraman Magnus Kelly filmed another shot for background purposes. Kelly asked Drumm to say something so he would be filmed talking, although his words would not be recorded. Drumm quipped to Murphy, 'So who did you bribe to get that business journalism award last week?' Everyone laughed, Drumm loudest of all.

Drumm's campaign of deception did not get airborne. Neither he nor McAteer could convince the people who mattered. The market believed neither them nor their bogus set of results.

On the front page of those results, the pair claimed that Anglo Irish Bank would make profits for the next three years. During the press conference, they limited their forecast to two years. Either way, it fell on deaf ears. By the end of the day, the share price had fallen 38 per cent – proof that their predictions were mistrusted. The following day, NCB Stockbrokers flatly contradicted the bank's senior executives by saying it expected Anglo to lose money over the next two years.

10 December 2008

Minister for Finance Brian Lenihan spied something odd about Anglo Irish Bank. It was peculiar enough for him to contact Financial Regulator Patrick Neary and to ask for an explanation. The minister was poring over a report compiled for the government by a firm of consultants, the accountants PricewaterhouseCoopers. This contained figures for the levels of directors' loans in all the Irish financial institutions covered by the State guarantee. Cross-referencing the columns to check his initial misgivings, Lenihan noticed the loans to directors at Anglo far exceeded those in other banks.

Rather limply, Neary admitted he did not have an explanation. He checked with his staff, whose response was startling. The banking supervision division of the Financial Regulator's office did know that Anglo's loans to directors were exceptionally high. It had spotted the issue as far back as January 2008 and was concerned enough to pursue the matter, holding two meetings about it with Anglo Irish Bank. But no further action was taken.

Neary reported back to Lenihan the full extent of Seán FitzPatrick's loans. During this account, he maintained he had known nothing about the loans previously – that his banking-supervision division had not informed him. This was a disturbing claim, but there were more pressing matters to contend with. Temporarily parking the inadequacies of information-sharing at the regulator's office, the minister focused on Anglo Irish Bank. Its directors, including FitzPatrick, were summoned to his office in the Department of Finance on Upper Merrion Street. FitzPatrick must have suspected, walking into that meeting with Lenihan, that his days as chairman were numbered.

18 December 2008

Lenihan deserves credit for his eagle eye. The issue of directors' loans had escaped everyone from Anglo's directors to the external auditors. In the two days preceding 18 December, FitzPatrick contacted any remaining members of the Anglo Irish board still in the dark to report his loans. A special board meeting would have to be convened to decide a course of action. The directors gathered on 18 December.

In the weeks following the results announcement on 3 December, the buzz swirling around Dublin's financial circles had persistently tipped that something was seriously wrong at Anglo Irish Bank. The shares had continued to collapse. By the day of the board meeting into directors' loans, the price was on the deck at 32 cent.

That day, the jungle drums were pounding into overdrive as stockbrokers across the city swapped rumours about Seán FitzPatrick and David Drumm quitting the bank. In a financial community as small as Dublin's, information-sharing is standard. As the day wore on, some stockbrokers rang well-placed journalists to see whether they could confirm stories that something was due to happen at Anglo Irish Bank before nightfall. Frantic calls from media organisations revealed that a board meeting was, indeed, being held at the bank. They were alerted to expect a significant announcement.

A few minutes before 9 p.m., a statement came from chairman Seán FitzPatrick. Its contents stunned Ireland and dealt immeasurable damage to its financial system. He had resigned with immediate effect, and non-executive director Donal O'Connor had taken over. The statement said the board accepted FitzPatrick's decision 'with great regret', which struck an off-key note in view of the reason he was leaving.

FitzPatrick's comments in the statement are worth dissection. The absolution which he generously awarded himself could not hide the way he played fast and loose with the rulebook. He said, 'My decision to tender my resignation has been prompted by the fact that at 30 September 2008 I had fully secured loans, on normal commercial terms, with the bank, totalling €87 million, which will be included in the annual report for 2008 in the note relating to directors' loans. This balance is substantially higher than in the 2007 report because, in prior years, I had temporarily transferred my loans to another bank before each year-end.

'I had done this on my own initiative over an eight-year period. The transfer of the loans between banks did not in any way breach banking or legal regulations. However, it is clear to me, on reflection, that it was inappropriate and unacceptable from a transparency point of view.' Rather unconvincingly, he made the case for a one-off lapse, insisting, 'I have always pursued high standards in my personal and professional life, and I failed to meet those standards in this instance.'

FitzPatrick was defiantly adamant that he had broken neither banking nor legal regulations. He had legal advice to back it up. Others would clamour to disagree. The only way to determine whether or not he had contravened the law would be via an investigation, which could lead to a court case. Inevitably, this would be some way off.

He could not stay on as chairman because he had concealed the bank's position from investors and share-holders. For years, he had produced annual reports which failed to reveal that he was borrowing large sums of money from the bank. At the end of each financial year, when the auditors took a snapshot of the accounts and reported it to shareholders, FitzPatrick moved the loans off Anglo's books. He did so by playing a money-go-round game. He borrowed an amount from Irish Nationwide equivalent to the sum he owed and paid off Anglo for a few days. Then he would re-borrow with Anglo and pay back the Irish Nationwide loan. Round and round the debt went. This caper allowed him to borrow enormous sums from Anglo without any disclosure in the annual report, as is required. Over a sustained period of time, he used this trick repeatedly to obscure his debts.

FitzPatrick's resignation statement, which bleated with a distinctly self-serving element, added, 'I have spent the last thirty-three years working hard to build a successful, respected bank. I reached this decision of my own volition and without pressure from any quarter. I have done so because my remaining ambition for Anglo is that it would continue to progress with determination.'

By the time that statement had been drafted, terms such as 'respected' and 'successful' could no longer be applied to his bank. It had become a synonym for corruption.

Within five minutes of the statement being circulated, Minister for Finance Brian Lenihan issued his own press release, in which he expressed 'disappointment' with the circumstances surrounding FitzPatrick's departure but insisted government plans to inject money to recapitalise the banks remained on course. He followed it up with a barrage of phone calls designed to reassure the markets and the public that, despite the bombshell, it would be business as usual at Anglo Irish Bank.

The statements were coming thick and fast in the wake of FitzPatrick's admission. Next up was one from the Financial Regulator. Its contents initiated a sequence of events that spelled out how Official Ireland was utterly unprepared for the whirlwind of chaos generated by the banking fiasco.

For years, the light-touch regulation of the banking system had oiled the wheels of the financial-services sector. International banks arrived on Ireland's shores knowing they would encounter few obstacles. In fact, nobody would bother them at all. But when it was tested, the regulatory system was woeful. It was Keystone Cops territory. Not only did regulators have no grasp of what was happening in the banks and building societies, they did not have a clue about what was going on in their own organisation.

The man in the eye of the storm was regulator Patrick Neary. From the outset he was no match for smooth operators such as FitzPatrick and Drumm. Here was a civil servant from tip to toe. His working life had passed within the stress-free ambience of the Central Bank and its regulatory arm, the Financial Regulator.

Neary, known as Pat, grew up in Ballyragget near Castlecomer in County Kilkenny. He joined the Central Bank in 1971, after a year studying Greek and Latin at UCD, answering a newspaper advertisement for the job. Married, with three adult sons, he left the Central Bank in 2003 to join the newly established Financial Regulator's office as prudential director. Three years later he became chief executive.

Polite, impeccably turned out and trusting to a fault, he had the whiff of a figure from another age – as old-fashioned as the moustache that lent him a Second World War military appearance. A keen golfer, he is a member of South County Golf Club in Brittas, County Dublin.

The Financial Regulator's office was not a challenging environment: characterised by inertia rather than action. Staff took their tea breaks as regularly as clockwork, and long-serving employees were automatically promoted when their turn came. The ethos was never to say or do anything to displease government, trade unions or banks. At a time when bank profits were humongous and public concern flared about bankers' earnings, sources within the regulator's office suggest that a move was afoot to push for increasing tax on bank profits. Nothing came of this. The regulator self-censored, feeling that the government would consider it heresy.

'If you take two normal people sitting at a table and one asks the other to pass them the milk, normally it is just handed over,' said Brendan Burgess, former director of the consumer panel at the Financial Regulator. 'If you ask someone for milk in the Financial Regulator's office, he would have to go off and see if milk is in this year's budget, have a planning meeting to discuss it, and then get the chief executive to sign off on it.'

Burgess said he left because progress was impossible. 'There was a consumer panel of twenty great people, but the

Financial Regulator saw us as a problem. If the regulators could find reasons not to take action on any of our suggestions, they would do so. Every communication to the panel had to be signed off by the chief executive of the Financial Regulator.'

A retired senior banker said, 'The Financial Regulator did not have enough quality people. That was its biggest deficiency. In the US, there would have been regulatory auditing people in the banks checking things 365 days a year. In the UK, it would have been something similar. The Irish Regulator never seemed to be resourced to do those audits. The ground below the regulator was thinly populated on quality.'

Another banker said, 'The Financial Regulator is a policy-maker, not a deal-maker, but we needed experienced bankers checking through the loan books. Such an undertaking requires not just manpower but brainpower – and plenty of experience at the banking coalface. Liabilities are cloaked in devious ways.'

Neary was such an innocent that people almost felt sorry for him. When he was interviewed during the banking crisis, a journalist asked if he wanted to be referred to as 'Pat' or 'Patrick'. He had to turn to his press officer for the answer. If he was incapable of deciding something as simple as his name without advice, how on earth was he going to manage the financial maelstrom?

On an earlier occasion in 2007, before the crash, he was questioned about the possibility of banks over-lending. Naively, he used the purchase of his own home in Dublin's Ballinteer in the 1970s and compared that price with its current value. This was supposed to reassure people that property values heightened nicely – no cause for the heebie-jeebies. But the world was a different place in the 1970s, relatively free of the calibre of financial chicanery in Anglo's books.

When the Financial Regulator issued his statement on the night of 18 December 2008, it was greeted by a stunned response. In it, he said, 'The Financial Regulator became aware, following an inspection earlier this year, of matters surrounding loans from Anglo Irish Bank to Seán FitzPatrick.' It was an admission that the regulator's office knew about the issue of FitzPatrick's hidden loans for almost a year – and did nothing.

It was wrong not to share this important information with investors. But keeping it quiet from the government was a greater mishandling. Less than three months earlier, the State had guaranteed Anglo Irish Bank along with the other financial institutions. It might not have been so willing to underwrite Anglo with a true picture of its footing. The Financial Regulator's office, with its remit to protect the public interest, had done the exact opposite.

One source within the Anglo board said the regulator would have received reports every three months revealing the full extent of loans to FitzPatrick. In 2007, these quarterly reports would have shown FitzPatrick's loans stood at €122 million. The annual report claimed the total loans to directors were just €46 million. If the quarterlies had been cross-checked against the annual report for that year, the discrepancy would have been glaring. Even in a culture of light regulation, this betrays an atrocious level of sloppiness in the Financial Regulator's office.

Privately, Brian Lenihan was incensed. It was galling enough to be hoodwinked by FitzPatrick but more indigestible again to learn that the Financial Regulator's office had known about the ruse for almost a year.

19 December 2008

Just after 1 a.m., following his resignation four hours earlier,

Seán FitzPatrick makes a rare public appearance in Dublin city centre in January 2009, a month after his resignation as chairman of Anglo.

Willie McAteer (left) and David Drumm of Anglo Irish Bank at their December 2008 annual results meeting, later exposed as a tissue of lies.

Anglo Irish Bank directors at an extraordinary general meeting, January 2009. From left to right: Government appointee Frank Daly, former chairman of the Revenue Commissioners; Gary McGann, non-executive director; Matt Moran, finance director; Noël Harwerth, non-executive director; Government appointee Alan Dukes, former Fine Gael leader; Anne Heraty, non-executive director.

Shareholders vent their anger at the Anglo Irish Bank extraordinary general meeting in Dublin's Mansion House, January 2009.

Seán Quinn, a self-made billionaire who prefers the simple life.

Top: Michael 'Fingers' Fingleton of Irish Nationwide in his trademark black hat and, above, listening to criticism from members at an annual general meeting.

Never slow to express his feelings: Brian Goggin, former chief executive of Bank of Ireland.

AIB chief executive Eugene Sheehy (left) chats with chairman Dermot Gleeson at AIB's annual general meeting, April 2008.

In happier days: former Irish Life & Permanent chief executive Denis Casey with chairwoman Gillian Bowler outside the bank's headquarters in Dublin.

Top: Patrick Neary, retired Financial Regulator.
Above: John Hurley, governor of the Central Bank.

Minister for Finance Brian Lenihan shows the strain as he answers questions from RTÉ radio listeners on the morning after the emergency budget, April 2009. Below: speaking to reporters outside the Department of Finance, February 2009, as he welcomes Denis Casey's resignation from Irish Life & Permanent.

FitzPatrick rang a journalist. He sounded garbled – perhaps even a little the worse for wear. He made a number of statements that made no sense, but he kept repeating one fact. He claimed the loans he had taken out from Anglo Irish Bank were on behalf of a tax partnership of seven people. He was one of a group – the loans were held in his name only. However, this was never subsequently confirmed.

That morning's newspaper and radio headlines were dominated by FitzPatrick's sudden departure. The banking crisis, which had already caused uncertainty, trepidation and anger, was deteriorating yet further. And now it had a face. FitzPatrick had been a charismatic ambassador for corporate Ireland. Suddenly, smiling, obliging Seánie – a hero – turned out to be conniving, false FitzPatrick – the villain. Were there other maggots in the woodpile? Who else would be exposed?

Attention was drawn to a television interview FitzPatrick gave RTÉ's *One to One* programme in December 2007. In it, he criticised too much regulation of business: 'We don't have the Enrons or the scandals that happened elsewhere. We don't need over-regulation – what we need is appropriate regulation.' At the time, his opinion had been listened to deferentially. He was an Irish success story, and his accomplishments invited respect. 'Appropriate regulation' – weasel words, it was now apparent. He was making an overture for zero regulation.

FitzPatrick's activities raised questions about Anglo Irish Bank. Who else knew about the loans?

Just after noon, Drumm bowed to the inevitable and announced he had resigned after fifteen years with the bank. One colleague revealed that a visibly shell-shocked Drumm said privately, 'I've had enough of living a lie.' In a statement to the Irish Stock Exchange, Drumm said, 'It is appropriate for me to step down today, given last evening's announcement in relation to the resignation of Seán FitzPatrick.' He referred to the 'the strong statement of support for the bank and its recapitalisation programme by the Minister for Finance'. By doing so, he suggested that because new funding would be provided for Anglo it was an opportune time to stand aside. Nobody believed that.

The Financial Regulator's incompetence was now on the table. The political temperature escalated at the implications of Neary's bungling, which had left taxpayers exposed to FitzPatrick's orgy of loans to himself. Word rippled through Leinster House that Neary was finished. Nobody saw any justification for allowing him to remain in a role he had demonstrated he was incapable of filling, a role which needed to be handled with strength and authority as the financial sector continued to split at the seams.

That evening, the body which ran the Financial Regulator met. They did not view the situation through the same prism as politicians and the country at large. Following a late-night meeting, the board defiantly delayed a decision on what should happen to Neary, saying it would launch an investigation.

4 January 2009

Drumm had given specific assurances that directors at Anglo Irish Bank would not be paid bonuses. He did not include senior managers in this moratorium. As a result, *Sunday Independent* readers choked on their toast and marmalade as they read a front-page story that revealed, 'The ailing bank, which is on the verge of collapse, confirmed last night that "performance-related" bonuses were paid to "middle managers" at the bank.' It added that the bank had racked up colossal bad debts, with loans running into billions of euro.

One staff member was quoted as saying, 'If we are going to lose our jobs, we will need the money.' With Anglo's performance attracting a volley of censure, and the taxpayer in line to pick up the bill for the bank's buccaneering, these bonus payments proved highly controversial.

Meanwhile, Drumm subsequently started dividing his time between the US and Ireland. His career was unsalvageable in Ireland, and he presumably hoped to tap into contacts from his time as head of Anglo's US operation.

7 January 2009

Anglo's finance director Willie McAteer, who was born in 1950 and lived in Dublin's Rathgar, 'gave the appearance of being part of an über-race: bankers set apart from the herd by dint of their own brilliance'. That's how another banker described him. But his brilliance had deserted him.

As the situation degenerated during the month of December, McAteer, who was also head of risk management, had been on an investor roadshow abroad – with a set of dishonest results under his arm. He was using these results to try and convince international investors to inject €1 billion into Anglo Irish Bank. The roadshow involved meeting big financial institutions which invested money on behalf of pensions. Such meetings usually gave investors an overview of a company's performance in its most recent results. But if a company needed money, it was also an opportunity to raise funds.

McAteer was adept at this wheeling and dealing. So adept, in fact, that he had collected an award from *Investor Relations Magazine* in 2008 for having 'Best Overall Investor Relations'. That, of course, was before it emerged how Anglo had been deceiving investors for years.

By lying to potential investors, McAteer inflicted immeasurable damage on the reputation of Irish banking. The capacity of any Irish bank to turn to international investors again was compromised.

From the moment the story about Seán FitzPatrick's secret loans broke, McAteer was on borrowed time. As finance director, he had prepared and signed off on annual reports that concealed FitzPatrick's loans. It was impossible to have him act in a senior capacity in Anglo – or, indeed, in any other bank.

After seventeen years with the bank, McAteer resigned on 7 January. Anglo announced that the board had decided to split his two roles. It named the bank's chief financial officer, Matt Moran, as finance director, and a new chief risk officer would be appointed to the board. In an admission that fresh blood was needed, the Anglo statement said, 'This appointment will be filled by an external candidate with international best-practice experience in the function.'

No real explanation was given for McAteer's departure. None was needed. He was tainted. FitzPatrick had now taken the two most senior executives in Anglo down with him.

9 January 2009

Anglo Irish Bank shares had collapsed from a high of €17.85 to a miserable 21 cent, and the value of the bank caved in: from €13 billion to just €164 million. Against this combat zone, the board of the Financial Regulator finally delivered its report, and Neary took early retirement. Mary O'Dea, formerly its consumer director, was appointed acting regulator.

The man charged with policing the banks instead pointed the finger at his staff as he left. 'There has been no oral, written or email escalation of these issues [FitzPatrick's loans] to me, or to the authority, over the period until the matter was raised with me by the minister on 10 December 2008,' he said in his resignation statement.

It was not one but two slingshots that finished Neary in the end. The fatal blow was the secret loans to directors. But he had already been compromised by an appearance on RTÉ's *Prime Time* in September 2008. The television interview was an attempt to reassure the public that there was no run on the banks; in it, he fostered the impression that the banking system was solvent. Crisis, what crisis? Eleven days later, the government was obliged to provide a blanket guarantee for all the banks.

After the interview, Fine Gael's finance spokesperson Richard Bruton had cast doubt on the regulator: 'I found it astonishing to hear Patrick Neary say that the risky lending of banks and the property market collapse had nothing to do with the current crisis our banking sector is facing.

'I also found it incredible that he thought bad lending practices from Irish banks was not part of the problem. His insistence that liquidity was the only issue, rather than including bad lending and levels of capitalisation, suggests that the regulator thinks we are largely dealing with a business-as-usual situation.' A man out of his depth, in other words.

Neary's already damaged reputation was incapable of withstanding the Anglo directors' loans debacle. He was seen as a poodle doing a rottweiler's job.

The report to the authority running the Financial Regulator's office did little to reassure either investors or consumers. It spelled out that the regulator's office was not on top of its brief – despite having 380 people on the payroll. The report noted that the banking supervision division had persistent concerns about Seán FitzPatrick's loans from January 2008. But it said, 'The matter was not pursued, partly because a letter from Anglo went missing, and partly because of the pressure on officials from the unfolding of liquidity problems in financial markets.'

This was regulation Irish-style: an important letter was

lost, and regulators were too busy with other matters to chase it up. The chairman of the State's third largest bank had been lying to investors and shareholders for eight years, but this was overlooked because regulators had a lot on their plates.

Officials in the regulator's office said they had passed the issue up the line, but Neary claimed he was never told. Either way, Neary was sitting on thorns. The government had provided a State guarantee to Anglo and other banks in September 2008 without being told about the secret directors' loans – but officials in Neary's office knew. He had to go.

Neary, already a controversial figure, became a locus for resentment when it emerged that he had secured a golden parachute of €630,000. He received a lump sum of €428,000 plus €202,000 in respect of the two years left on his contract. He was also entitled to an annual, bulletproof pension of €142,670 or €2,750 a week. The deal caused disbelief at a time when private-sector pensions were devastated by the collapse in Irish bank shares – due, in part, to Neary's inability to do his job. Meanwhile, the regulator's public-service pension insulated him against those falling share prices. As with the banking guarantee, failure appeared to be rewarded by the State. Some suggested that since the regulator did not regulate, the country should be suing him for breach of contract.

Minister for Finance Brian Lenihan was not told in advance about Neary's generous pay-off. Nor did he have any role in approving the settlement, which was made by the board of the Financial Regulator, an independent State body. The decision to award it was made following independent legal advice, according to the board.

There was a sense of dismay in the Cabinet at the scale of this deal and discussion about whether it could be reversed. The Green Party's Minister for the Environment, John Gormley, called on Neary to return part of the 'mind-boggling' €630,000. Neary did not step up to the plate. At the end of his career as Financial Regulator, just as he had done throughout it, he kept his head down.

'Patrick Neary came from the system – he had forty years of good work, but he did not have the strength of character to deal with things going wrong on his watch,' said Brendan Burgess, former director of the consumer panel at the Financial Regulator. The bankers had no trouble running rings round him. 'Neary was slightly in awe of Seán FitzPatrick,' recalled one businessman who saw them together.

When Neary left, in effect he took the blame for everything that was wrong with an entire system of regulation. But the Central Bank has 600 employees and the Financial Regulator has a staff of 380: there was more than one person at fault. It was the principle-based system of regulation that was in the wrong – a notion predicated on trust. This did not work. It is too simplistic to lay all the blame at Neary's door.

However, the financial cocoon of his and others' severance packages infuriated the public, who saw it as the elite protecting their own.

15 January 2009

15 January was supposed to be the calm before the storm. An extraordinary general meeting of shareholders in Anglo Irish Bank was scheduled for the following morning in the Lord Mayor's Mansion House. The venue was hired because a sea of shareholders was expected to arrive with opinions to offload.

The purpose of the meeting was to approve a €1.5 billion injection of taxpayers' money into the stuttering bank. Its attempts to raise funds on the financial market had failed miserably. This was no surprise. If FitzPatrick had been playing fast and loose with the rules on disclosing loans to directors, who knew what other horrors were lurking within the bank? Investors gave it a wide berth. If the State did not capitalise it, the bank would be finished.

But at mid-afternoon on 15 January, everything changed. Newly appointed Anglo Irish Bank chairman Donal O'Connor, a tall, thin and impeccably turned-out former partner in the PricewaterhouseCoopers accountancy practice, was summoned to the Department of Finance. Lenihan informed him of a change in plan. The government was going to nationalise Anglo.

At 7 p.m., the media was alerted to a press conference, which the Minister for Finance would hold in his department at 8 p.m. It began at 8.25 p.m., and Lenihan did not mince his words. 'The funding position of the bank has weakened, and unacceptable practices that took place within it have caused serious reputational damage to the bank at a time when overall market sentiment towards it was negative. Accordingly, the government believes that the recapitalisation is not now the appropriate and effective means to secure its continued viability. Therefore, the government must move to the final and decisive step of public ownership.'

Lenihan's demeanour was suitably grave and his tone commanding – but he looked absolutely exhausted. He had been coasting on too few hours of sleep a night. Since the Dáil had resumed in October 2008 after the summer recess, the amount of time he was able to spend at home with his wife and their two children was diminishing exponentially. It was hard to gauge what class of Minister for Finance Lenihan was, because circumstances forced him to become a fire fighter. No matter how much water he poured on the inferno, it never went out. Each day threw up another crisis. And many of them originated in the same place: Anglo Irish Bank.

The press conference was cut short so that Lenihan could

do a quick television interview with RTÉ's *Nine O'Clock News* and speak directly to the public. In a room dominated by photographs of every Minister for Finance since the foundation of the State, he told viewers, 'The unacceptable behaviour of the former chairman has done immense damage to this institution.' It was an epic U-turn less than twenty-four hours before the extraordinary general meeting to approve recapitalisation. Lenihan denied there had been a run on the bank. But, plainly, huge sums had been lost from deposits if the government had to take the bank into public ownership.

Why not let the wretched bank go wallop? After all, who cared about a bunch of high-rolling property developers whose borrowing days had been cut short? There might be sympathy for bank staff, but workers were losing jobs around the country, sometimes at a rate of 1,000 a day. Lenihan's explanation was uncharacteristically concise: 'Anglo Irish Bank is a major financial institution whose viability is of systemic importance to Ireland.'

Anglo had borrowed so much money from other banks that should it go bust, international investors would lose heavily. If they did not get their money back, no other Irish bank would be able to borrow so much as a euro from the international markets. In such a doomsday scenario, Ireland would end up nationalising all the banks. Failure was not an option, in the government's view.

Not everyone shared that opinion. Alan Ahearne, a former economist with the US Federal Reserve and lecturer at NUI Galway, told the *Sunday Independent* in January 2009, two months before becoming adviser to Lenihan, 'The markets quite clearly don't believe in the future of Anglo, and yet the government is saying it's too important to let go. I'm not convinced by this. There needs to be a much greater transparency about what is going on at the bank.'

16 January 2009

By this stage, checking the news updates to discover what new calamity had surfaced overnight was becoming a hazardous start to the day. The news went downhill daily, but 16 January was the nadir for shareholders in Anglo Irish, who had been hoping for the best since shares began to fall more than eighteen months earlier. Now, the shares were delisted from the Dublin and London Stock Exchanges, which meant that shareholders could not sell them, even for the few cent they were worth. The shares were only worth 21 cent each when delisted. After they were suspended, bookmaker Paddy Power offered odds of just one to three that people would receive between 1 cent and 10 cent per share from the State by way of compensation.

The only action left for shareholders was to attend the meeting called to approve the recapitalisation of the bank – a proposal superseded by events of the night before when the bank was nationalised.

Extraordinary general meetings are usually dull affairs. But this one lived up to its name. The deeply unhappy shareholders began to gather at the Mansion House at 9.30 a.m. Despite the perception that many of the bank's share-holders were Bentley-driving property tycoons, hundreds of ordinary Irish people saw their nest eggs shattered. Each had their own story. John O'Leary, aged eighty-five, from West Cork, voiced the bewilderment of the majority when he said, 'We don't even know if we will get anything out of our shares.'

The full extent of Seán FitzPatrick's mischief at Anglo Irish Bank staggered investors. Confusion, frustration and disgust distinguished the meeting, which started at 10 a.m. Newly appointed chairman Donal O'Connor had prepared an extensive presentation and caught the mood of the room, if not its wrath, when he described recent events as 'traumatic and painful'.

He outlined where FitzPatrick had spent his loans, and perhaps the most shocking aspect to this unbridled spending spree was that Anglo had lent him money to buy shares in the bank itself. The former chairman's investments were made at the top of the cycle in the stock market and property sectors. Considering the shares were almost worth nothing when the bank was nationalised, a bad situation had just become worse. FitzPatrick could not even sell his shares to recoup some of the losses.

O'Connor offered an explanation of sorts as to why FitzPatrick's activities were never detected. 'Temporary refinancing of directors' loans was not identified as a risk area,' he admitted, calling it 'a weakness in the system' – an observation that was blindingly obvious to everyone in the room. He said the external auditor, Ernst & Young, was unaware of the transactions that hid FitzPatrick's loans. The accountancy saying, 'if you can't do it – audit' had clearly never been applied with any rigour to Anglo.

But it was not just FitzPatrick who had borrowed massive sums from the bank. Other directors had taken out €95 million in total. One non-executive director who, in the event of an inquiry, may face more questions than others about his knowledge of the secret loans is Lar Bradshaw. He co-invested with FitzPatrick in a number of projects. He would, therefore, have been more informed than fellow board members about the scale of investments and the extent of FitzPatrick's borrowings.

Shareholders fumed as they left the meeting. Their rage was directed at both watchdogs and bankers. A retired man with a peaked cap said, 'The people responsible have just resigned and walked away. They should not be allowed.' A woman echoed this, 'I am angry because the people who really let us down were the watchdogs and the auditors.' The consensus was that heads should roll. But there was no mob storming the Bastille – just a group of dispirited shareholders whose investments had evaporated, many of them pensioners facing into a less secure old age than they had bargained for.

24 February 2009

It is not every day that the Fraud Squad raids the headquarters of a bank. But at 9 a.m. on 24 February, a team of sixteen gardaí and officials from the Office of the Director of Corporate Enforcement turned up at Anglo Irish Bank's headquarters on St Stephen's Green. They spent all day examining computer hard drives, files and records of emails. A day earlier, the Garda Bureau of Fraud Investigation had been granted search warrants by the Dublin Circuit Court, allowing the team to seize documents that might show crimes were committed contrary to Section 20 of the Companies Act 1990.

This was not a 'kick the door down' investigation: Anglo remained a working bank – although how much work was done by staff that day, knowing the Fraud Squad was in the building, is anyone's guess. Police officers and officials were given prearranged spaces in the underground car park and spent eleven hours sifting through files for evidence. Just before 8 p.m., a white van, a Mercedes and two unmarked garda Ford Mondeos sped away from Anglo. They were far from finished and spent three more days on site searching for material that could build a prosecution case.

The various tentacles of the Anglo affair under investigation are as follows:

–Anglo's secret loans to directors refinanced by Irish Nationwide. These are being examined by the Financial

Regulator, the Irish Stock Exchange and the Director of Corporate Enforcement, Paul Appleby.

–The Golden Circle's purchase of shares from Seán Quinn. This is being probed by the gardaí and Paul Appleby and will examine the role of Anglo and advisers who set up scheme.

–Back-to-back deposits involving Anglo and Irish Life & Permanent. This has been referred to the gardaí by the Financial Regulator.

–The roles of ex-Anglo directors Seán FitzPatrick, David Drumm and Willie McAteer, Irish Life & Permanent's ex-finance director Peter Fitzpatrick and accountancy group Ernst & Young. These are being scrutinised by the Institute of Chartered Accountants in Ireland.

The most serious aspect of the multiple investigations relates to the Anglo and Irish Life & Permanent deposits and the Golden Circle deal. These scandals may involve potential breaches of market-abuse regulation, which carry penalties of up to €10 million in fines or ten years in prison or both.

One senior executive with a stock-market-listed company said, 'People in the business had doubts about Anglo but buried them. What happened to the bank was a good lesson to remember the old saying, "If it walks like a duck and quacks like a duck – it's a duck."'

PART III

The Game

9

The Green Jersey Agenda

'Patriotism is an arbitrary veneration of real estate above principles.'
American drama critic George Jean Nathan

Ireland's senior bankers are a dapper clique: none of them ever appears to have a crease in his shirt, a gravy stain on his tie, dandruff on his shoulders. Double cuffed shirts are part of the uniform, lending that trace of sophisticated formality to the workplace and allowing them to showcase their cufflink collection. Double cuffs and cufflinks are their peacock trait. Even bankers like a hint of swagger.

The cultivated behaviour of these financiers betrayed a driving sense of entitlement. These were alpha males – although not in the overt, Russian oligarch style. Their sense of power was understated. They were gentlemen, after all. However, their ambitions to grow their banks' profits and to earn impressive bonuses were anything but muted. The culture had become performance-related, for all the suave veneer of its mandarins. Behind the navy or grey suits, white shirts and discreetly striped ties, their hearts beat a goal-driven tattoo.

At a lunch between bankers and banking authorities,

during a pause in the polite chit-chat, one of the diners looked across the starched linen weighed down with silverware and crystal glasses. She recalls being struck by the fact that she was surrounded on all sides by men earning an average of €3 million a head – 100 times the industrial wage. But the thrust of the conversation left her wondering if these executives ever bothered talking to their customers. They seemed as remote from their customers as a prince from a plasterer.

January–March 2008

A taut atmosphere pervaded the usually sedate corridors of the Central Bank. The tension emanated from a man in Austin Powers-style glasses, who was watching world events and fretting as he tried to second-guess them. This was the bank's governor John Hurley.

With his grey hair parted to the side and just a trace of creamy Munster vowels after decades in Dublin, Hurley was the duplicate of a cloistered academic. He seemed to emerge, blinking and mole-like, into daylight. He was inherently cautious, rarely did live interviews and kept broadcasts to a minimum. In one recorded interview for television, he stopped halfway through the first answer and turned to his press officer. 'I can't really say that, it will drive the trade unions mad,' he announced, before asking to start again.

As an intellectual, his understanding of banking and economics was never in question. But Mallow-born John Hurley failed to put a halt to the unbalanced lending policies of Irish banks. And he neglected to take adequate measures to ensure that the banks had enough money on reserve to deal with bad debts. Being clever enough to grasp ramifications was one thing; being bold enough to call a halt to Ireland's credit binge, conveniently filling tax coffers year after year, was another.

He blamed that failure to rein in the banks on legislation

that set up the Central Bank, pointing out, 'Time and again we said debt levels are growing too fast and too strongly. Time and again we said we can't go on building 80,000 or 70,000 houses per year.' But his public comments about the banks were never direct. He sounded like a palaeontologist describing fossils. Hurley and his Central Bank appeared disengaged from events, as if the bank bore no responsibility for anything that happened in the financial world.

Loyal to his civil-service roots, Hurley never ruffled government feathers. No minister, no builder, no bank was ever stung by his words. That suited the politicians. It explains why senior civil servants ran the Central Bank.

Although he qualified as a barrister, Hurley joined the civil service in 1963, beckoned by more attractive salaries than the Law Library. He was conscientious, meticulous and, above all, conservative. After working his way up to Secretary General at the Department of Finance, he was promoted to head the Central Bank in 2002. This was in keeping with the department's famously close association with the bank – some would say too close.

Hurley was paid the princely salary of €345,000. It dwarfed the pay of Ben Bernanke, chairman of the US Federal Reserve, whose pay has been set at $191,300 for superintending one of the most important financial institutions in the world.

There was another anomaly in Hurley's outsize pay packet. His mantra was a complaint about unsustainable salary levels: 'Wages in Ireland have risen too quickly over recent years and our economy has become uncompetitive,' he told an Oireachtas committee in March 2009. It might almost be droll but for the detachment it conveys. In any case, there is scant amusement in the Central Bank, one of the most orthodox institutions in the State, whose inhabitants take themselves extremely seriously; apart, that is, from the incongruity of its location in one of the most controversial buildings in Dublin's trendy Temple Bar district.

The Central Bank was built on Dame Street with blatant disregard for the planning authorities. The office block was the creation of the *enfant terrible* of Irish architecture, Sam Stephenson. Although structurally ground-breaking, the design was criticised for its height in the heart of the low-rise old city. In 1973, when the bank was under construction, the roof was discovered to be 29 feet higher than authorised by Dublin Corporation. Stephenson railed against 'noisy lynch mobs baying around the drawing board'. Although it was eventually completed in 1978 after a testy public inquiry, followed by a series of planning applications and appeals, the building still evokes mixed emotions.

Hurley may not have been chief executive of a bank, but he was top banana at the Central Bank. This could mean only one thing: a room with a view. He had a top-floor office – naturally – on the seventh storey. From pedestrians crossing the Ha'penny Bridge to trucks inching along the quays, all street life was laid out beneath his gaze. No wonder Ireland's senior bankers had a tendency to appear removed from the cut and thrust: geographically they generally were.

But in January 2008, as Hurley sat in his plush, tranquil office with its floor-to-ceiling windows, he was preoccupied. His coal-black eyebrows met in a frown as the daily gush of news from around the world pointed towards a formidable reckoning.

In the US, the sub-prime stew was bubbling over. One of its biggest mortgage lenders, Countrywide, had to be bailed out by Bank of America. US banks Citigroup and Bear Sterns were facing huge losses. The British government was in the process of nationalising Northern Rock after its chaotic collapse, and UK banks were one step short of a high-noon showdown. Around the world, stock markets were tumbling. To add insult to injury, a young Frenchman named Jérôme Kerviel had turned rogue trader and cost Société Générale €4.9 billion.

Apart from a disturbing fall in bank shares, Ireland was managing to dodge the worst of the banking crisis. So far. But its economic machine was slowing after years of breakneck growth. Ireland is a small, open economy: if the worldwide banking sector was in tumult, the effects would be felt before long.

Action was required. In the first three months of 2008, Hurley liaised with the chief executive of the Financial Regulator, Patrick Neary. The regulator's office shares a building with the Central Bank, in addition to staff and information. Like Hurley, Neary was inclined to pussyfoot. But the two decided they should hold a round of pre-emptive meetings with Irish banks and building societies.

The executive washroom on the seventh floor of the Central Bank would put a deluxe hotel's facilities in the shade. No paper towels here: a stack of pristine white cotton towels are supplied daily, with a laundry bin for disposal after a single use. Inspiration sometimes springs to mind in the bathroom. Perhaps this was the birthplace of the idea they were keen to impress on the bankers at these meetings. Its driving force was to ensure the banks would support one another if the Wall Street contagion spread across the Atlantic. This idea was called, informally, the Green Jersey Agenda.

11 March 2008

Jim Cramer, financial expert and TV-show host on American channel CNBC, stood before the cameras with a viewer's letter in his hand. The viewer had contacted the *Mad Money* programme to ask if he should sell his shares in investment bank Bear Stearns. With his sleeves rolled up, arms flailing like a windmill, Cramer worked himself into a berserker: 'Bear Stearns is going be fine! Bear Stearns is not in trouble! Don't move your money from Bear! That's just silly! Don't be silly!' he blasted him. Bear Stearns' shares had fallen to $60, from

$171 a year earlier. But there were no caveats from Cramer: sit tight on those shares.

16 March 2008

Within five days, an emergency fire sale took place. Madison Avenue-based Bear Stearns was taken over by JPMorgan Chase & Co. The price was a low $10 a share in a deal assisted by finance from the Federal Reserve central bank. Aside from a salutary lesson in the quality of CNBC's personal-finance advice, the collapse of one of Wall Street's most respected institutions peeled away the façade. A shambles was revealed in the investment bank run by legendary hard man Jimmy Cayne. He was a card-playing banking salesman who had elbowed his way to pole position and remained a dominant figure on Wall Street for fifteen years.

With problems in the US housing market mounting in 2006 and 2007, Bear Stearns – 'the Bear' – bought up mortgage-backed securities. This meant it was purchasing investments composed of bank debt. Normally, as customers repay borrowings, groups such as Bear Stearns make a profit over time. Or they can sell off the securities to other financial institutions. But when the sub-prime storm blew up and thousands of US homeowners were unable to meet their mortgage payments, the value of those securities plummeted. Bear Stearns was mortally wounded. To cap it all, the Bear had also snapped up a huge assortment of exotic securities which were rapidly turning sour.

An even graver problem loomed. Once Bear Stearns collapsed, others would inevitably follow. Watching the scalps pile up on Wall Street, Dublin banks began to circle the wagons.

31 March 2008

Denis Casey was chief executive of Irish Life & Permanent, an organisation with an unblemished track record during decades when other banks had floundered from one scandal to another. Casey has short silver hair and bright blue eyes which give him an intense stare. Enterprising, able and confident, he offered his views readily and was in no way reticent, unlike colleagues in the banking industry.

This image was backed by the company's advertisement for its bank, Permanent TSB, which featured screen mobster Frank Vincent of *The Sopranos* and *Goodfellas*. It was direct, informal and rather daring within the financial orbit. It showed Vincent standing in a bathroom while customer Jim showered behind a curtain. Jim was 'stuck in a rut' in his current bank, said Vincent. It was time for a wake-up call to the virtues of a Permanent TSB current account. Cue close-up of Vincent's hand turning a tap from hot to cold and a freeze frame of Jim's pained expression. That advertisement spoke volumes about the left-of-field image the bank was seeking to convey: it was out to shake up the industry and to build its customer base.

Casey, who lives in the Dublin suburb of Castleknock with his wife and three children, was born in October 1959. He left school at sixteen, and his first job was as an office post boy, before training to become an accountant. He joined AIB in 1976 and four years later moved to Irish Life. He was central to the major reorganisation of that business during the 1990s. This led to promotion, and he was made chief executive of the life company when Irish Life merged with Irish Permanent in 1999, forming Irish Life & Permanent. Casey operated the life company, Ireland's largest, for six years until he was shifted to run the bank, renamed Permanent TSB following the takeover of TSB Bank. But a senior banker made a damning assessment of his appointment: 'Denis Casey had a sales and marketing background – he would not have had a deep understanding, or long experience, of lending.'

Casey's transfer to the bank had dual purposes. Permanent

TSB's share of mortgage new business was slipping, and he was viewed as the powerhouse to return the bank to its former growth path. He succeeded. The second reason was to groom him for the front-seat job across the group's two divisions by extending his expertise to both.

With less than two years' experience as head of Permanent TSB, Casey took up the post of chief executive of Irish Life & Permanent in 2007. The life-assurance division is tremendously important and accounts for the majority of Irish Life & Permanent's profits. But Casey also had to run a bank, which is a highly technical job. Senior bankers, sizing up what went wrong at Irish Life & Permanent, identify this as its handicap. It meant Casey was relatively inexperienced when he came eyeball to eyeball with blitz conditions in the high finance and property domains.

During the housing boom, Permanent TSB was at the forefront of the rapid growth in home loans – it was speculating on the residential property upswing. Ireland's largest mortgage lender gambled even more royally by marketing 100 per cent mortgages, where homebuyers were not required to put down a deposit. Obviously this was appealing to customers, and business spurted. But there was a drawback. Without a deposit, there would be no equity in these houses and apartments. Britain had seen how 100 per cent mortgages were instruments of the Devil less than twenty years earlier, when its property downturn pitched the yuppie generation into the negative-equity trap. But Ireland did not learn from its nearest neighbour's difficulties.

First Active was first off the blocks in Ireland to lend 100 per cent mortgages, in July 2005. Days later, Permanent TSB dived into the market, intent on growing profits at any cost. When the crash came, these homebuyers were sitting ducks for negative equity.

Casey was among those who oiled the property boom by

supplying easy credit. Equally, he had a hand in increasing the casualties of the recession, with many homeowners devastated to discover their loans were worth more than their properties. Factor in rising unemployment and the potential was in place for a property massacre.

A senior banker with AIB said, 'When First Active came out with 100 per cent mortgages, we were beaten up by our shareholders for not introducing the same thing. It was really the wrong product, and the regulatory system allowed a free for all.'

Over at Bank of Ireland, there was equal dismay. 'We were stunned when 100 per cent mortgages were introduced by Bank of Ireland. I remember seeing the ad on a double-decker bus one day,' said Adam McNulty, a middle-ranking executive then employed in Bank of Ireland's asset management division, who resigned in 2008.

'I used to work in Japanese equities and was familiar with what went on in the lost decade of Japanese banking, the 1980s. They did everything they could to increase affordability during a boom. They introduced inter-generational mortgages – you inherited a mortgage. We were on that road when we introduced thirty-five-year mortgages.

'If the Financial Regulator was going to allow thirty-five-year mortgages he should have allocated more capital against them. He should have made it more onerous for the banks. Every experience in every economy which has ever gone down this road has ended in tears. People did not even have to put any money down. Banks said these loans were not widely available and only for top creditors. But it was loose lending.'

Unlike the headquarters of the other five Irish major lenders located south of the Liffey, Casey's office was on Dublin's north side in the Irish Life Centre. The complex was developed in 1974 as an innovative architectural concept incorporating offices, apartments, underground car parking and a shopping centre. Irish Life & Permanent's headquarters is the centrepiece of the complex.

The institution had two advantages over the other five Irish lenders. It was a big life-assurance company that owned a bank: this left it less exposed to the banking collapse. And it concentrated on residential mortgages rather than lending to developers – the sector which was causing banks the most trauma as builders either went belly up or reneged on their loans and had to have a percentage written off.

But Irish Life & Permanent had a chink in its armour with the Permanent TSB bank. Instead of relying on customers' savings to finance mortgages, it borrowed from other banks. When the credit crunch began its war of attrition on the banking system, Permanent TSB had a problem. It was more dependent on funds from other banks for mortgages than any other Irish lender.

The Central Bank did not want a repeat of the Northern Rock episode six months earlier, when the British lender experienced a run on the bank and had to seek liquidity support from the Bank of England. The Central Bank pointed out that banks such as Permanent TSB could borrow short-term funds from the European Central Bank. That provided enormous support for Irish lenders, argued the Central Bank. But for many analysts, this reliance on Frankfurt was a sign of weakness. Stockbrokers in London disparagingly referred to the bank as Permanent ECB because it looked to Europe for so much money.

There were certainly challenges ahead in 2008 for Casey's Irish Life & Permanent. However, regulators and investors were most spooked about Anglo Irish Bank. This was the acutely vulnerable lender. And if one bank fell overboard, it could easily cause a ripple effect and capsize the entire system.

Casey's institution was already helping Anglo to lie to shareholders. But much, much worse was in store.

May 2008

Financial Regulator Patrick Neary and his officials met Denis Casey, along with finance director Peter Fitzpatrick, chairwoman Gillian Bowler and non-executive directors from Irish Life & Permanent. It was one in a chain of meetings the regulator set up with banks to check their liquidity.

The financial institution 'set out the challenges it was facing in relation to funding and options were discussed', according to a spokesperson for the regulator's office. Neary said the industry 'might wish to consider formulating proposals which would be appropriate in times of liquidity crisis to assist each other'. He was making sure the banks could place inter-bank deposits with each other to continue working properly during the financial crisis. It was a reprise of the Green Jersey Agenda: everyone pulling together.

The regulator quoted Bowler as saying the board she chaired was very active and experienced and met regularly to discuss these issues.

Best known as the founder of Budget Travel, Bowler became the first woman to chair an Irish public limited company when she was appointed to the chair of Irish Life & Permanent in 2004. With her trademark sunglasses perched on top of her head, Bowler was the face of cheap sun holidays. She had set up the Budget Travel agency in 1975 and made an estimated €10 million from its staged sale between 1987 and 1995. At the end of 1999, Bowler and her husband Harry Sydner severed their ties with Budget Travel, and she was much sought after as a corporate director.

Bowler cut her teeth in business as a teenager, organising dances on the Isle of Wight where she worked in local council offices. She progressed to Greek Island Holidays in London before transplanting its affordable travel culture to Ireland. Bowler was paid €300,000 for her services as Irish Life & Permanent chairwoman in 2007.

5 September 2008

If there was one moment when panic had Irish banks and regulators alike by the throat, before the walls came tumbling down, it happened at 6.15 p.m. on 5 September 2008. A report flashed up on the international newswire service Reuters. It claimed Irish Nationwide Building Society was in 'talks with their lenders to avoid insolvency'. At 8.15 p.m., the story reappeared with a strenuous denial from Irish Nationwide. At 10.45 p.m., the report was removed and replaced by a retraction, stating there would be no substitute story.

Irish Nationwide's captain, Michael Fingleton, fulminated. What he probably said privately would not be printable. What he said publicly was as follows, 'In the present highly sensitive economic, financial and commercial climate, the putting out of such statements is tantamount to commercial sabotage by people who are trying to undermine Irish Nationwide Building Society.' Reuters stated the error had occurred because a reporter misinterpreted a source.

While preparing to appear on *The Late Late Show* (broadcast from the Wexford Opera Festival), Taoiseach Brian Cowen was briefed on the situation. He commented, 'Rumours and unfounded rumours are not good at all.'

7 September 2008

The effect of a major news agency running a story, albeit inaccurate, about Irish Nationwide going bust terrified the Central Bank and the Financial Regulator. They called bankers into Dame Street for another succession of crisis talks.

As these discussions were under way, Brian Lenihan took to the airwaves to calm strung-out nerves. In a round-table discussion, he rejected economist David McWilliams' charge that Irish banks had engaged in 'explicit and delinquent policies' in lending to people 'who couldn't afford the houses they bought'. Lenihan responded, 'I don't accept this, and I think this is very dangerous.' It was his favourite tactic: warning about the effects of commentary, a version of the US War Office slogan 'Loose Lips Sink Ships'. The Minister for Finance went on, 'Irish banks are not exposed to the sub-prime problem which US banks are exposed to.' Referring to the bad debts faced by Irish banks from a despondent property sector, he said, 'There is an exposure in the Irish banks, but they made it clear they can accommodate it. The analysts of the different firms that look at bank shares and bank performances have said the Irish banks can weather this crisis.'

So Lenihan was on the record as saying he believed the banks. But what if the banks were lying?

12 September 2008

It was Friday evening, the end of another hairy week on the markets. Wall Street giant Lehman Brothers was looking shaky. Once the New York Stock Exchange closed for business, Hank Paulson, head of the US Treasury, knuckled down to dealing with Lehman. It had to be done before the markets reopened on Monday. Alongside him, in the Federal Reserve's ornate boardroom at Liberty Street in New York, he gathered the most powerful figures in capitalism. Chief executives and their senior staff from Lehman, Goldman Sachs, Merrill Lynch, Morgan Stanley, JPMorgan Chase, Citigroup and Credit Suisse were arranged round a table. The future of Lehman, a 158-year-old firm with origins as a dry-goods store and cotton trader in Montgomery, Alabama rested with these people.

A bombshell was dropped on Richard Fuld, chief executive of Lehman Brothers – commonly known as Dick and even more commonly known as 'the Gorilla'. Fuld was a Master of the Universe, paid $34 million in 2007 and $40 million in 2006. He was used to calling the shots. Not any more. The message from the Treasury was uncompromising: come up with a private-market plan in forty-eight hours to save yourself from insolvency – or you're toast.

The answer was for a major bank to take over Lehman. In what soon came to be viewed as a monumental blunder, the Bush administration indicated it was prepared to let Lehman go under, even though it would mean a catastrophic unwinding of Wall Street's complex financial relationships.

13 September 2008

Bank of America was the obvious candidate to buy the venerable Lehman Brothers. But by Saturday morning, it was clear that Bank of America's head man Ken Lewis was not going to bite. The next plan was to encourage British bank Barclays to make an offer. Barclays' bankers pored over the books, growing ever more aghast at the spectrum of problems confronting Lehman.

John Thain, king pin at Merrill Lynch, realised that his bank would be the next to fall. Fuld could have struck a deal a month earlier, but he had delayed. Thain learned from his example and acted quickly. Knowing Bank of America was not interested in Lehman, Thain contacted Lewis with a pitch for him to buy Merrill Lynch instead.

14 September 2008

After an exhaustive overnight discu sion, Barclays said it would buy Lehman – with a list of conditions attached. Bankers assembled at the offices of the Federal Reserve in New York at 9 a.m. Paulson telephoned the British Chancellor of the Exchequer, Alistair Darling. At 9.45 a.m., Paulson told the bankers, 'The deal is off.' The Financial Services Authority in Britain had recoiled at the exposure for Barclays and was concerned the British bank might not be in sound enough shape to handle it. The Lehman team was devastated. Paulson repeated that he was not going to allow the US government to bail out the bank.

Scrappy to the end, Fuld mounted a one-man telethon as he worked his way through the phone book that Sunday afternoon, in a frenzy to save the bank – he even tried Merrill Lynch. Paulson told him to file for bankruptcy before 7 p.m. But Fuld continued scrabbling for a last-minute solution. He later told a congressional hearing that he did not know why Lehman failed. 'I do not know why we were the only one. We walked into that weekend firmly believing that we were going to do a transaction. I believe that Lehman and Merrill Lynch were in the same position on Friday night. That transaction [with Barclays], though awfully close, never got consummated.'

In a voice thick with emotion, he added, 'My employees, my shareholders, my clients, have taken a huge amount of pain. I wake up every single night thinking, "What could I have done differently? What could I have said? What should I have done?" And I have searched myself every single night. This is a pain that will stay with me the rest of my life.'

15 September 2008

The Lehman collapse would have been unthinkable a week earlier, but the world order had overturned. Masters of the Universe were sovereign no more. The disintegration of Lehman Brothers – a bank which pre-dated the Great Famine – loosened the cornerstone, and the financial edifice was no longer structurally sound. Once the fourth largest investment bank in the US, Lehman had succumbed to the sub-prime mortgage crisis it helped to create. This was the biggest bankruptcy in history.

Employees with no jobs to go to turned up at its New York headquarters on 745 Seventh Avenue to clear their desks. A graffiti portrait of Fuld was signed with venomous messages – among them, 'I hope your villa is safe.'

Lehman owed other banks $613 billion and had $155 billion in bond debt. Its assets were worth $639 billion, but its liabilities outstripped them: it was insolvent. The banks and bondholders which had lent Lehman billions of dollars were burned. Barclays and others bought some stripped-down assets.

Bankers across the globe began to digest the new reality that if Lehman could crumble, their lenders could also fold. In the blink of an eye, three of the big Wall Street names had vanished: Lehman Brothers was gone, and both Merrill Lynch and Bear Stearns had been gobbled up by larger operators. This was no ordinary catastrophe, and it would not be confined to the world of high finance. It was going to affect ordinary people – legions of them. Predictably, bank shares everywhere began to sink.

16 September 2008

Not only were share prices in free fall, but also, behind the scenes, a ruinous problem was rearing its head. With banks now petrified to lend to each other, the credit market seized up entirely. To prevent a complete collapse, the European Central Bank, headed by Frenchman Jean-Claude Trichet, machine-gunned €70 billion into the system so banks could lend to each other again. In the US, the Federal Reserve pumped in similar sums.

17 September 2008

The US Federal Reserve was forced to bail out insurance giant American International Group (AIG), and the markets trembled once again. AIG was no ordinary insurance company. It insured banks against a drop in value of risky financial instruments, known as CDOs (collateralised debt obligations), which were plummeting in the wake of Lehman.

The Federal Reserve gave AIG access to $85 billion in credit, in return for a stake of 79.9 per cent.

In Ireland, shares sagged 5 per cent as Bank of Ireland cut its dividend in half and warned about mortgage arrears. But Financial Regulator Patrick Neary told the Institute of Directors, 'Irish banks are resilient and have good shock absorption capacity to cope with the current situation.'

So, that was all right, then.

In Britain, the share price of Halifax Bank of Scotland was fluctuating wildly. It, too, had been stung by the sub-prime debacle. That day, the BBC reported it was in talks which could lead to the bank being taken over by Lloyds TSB to create a super-bank with 38 million customers. The talks were confirmed, and the British government waived normal competition rules to permit the deal.

18 September 2008

The spectre of banks going bust and looking for bailouts was terrifying ordinary depositors. On RTÉ's *Liveline* radio programme, callers agonised about the security of their savings. One caller with some €150,000 on deposit, the proceeds of a house sale, said, 'The banks aren't exactly reassuring people, they are not saying anything – that makes people nervous. I don't know whether I should put the money in the Post Office.' Another caller named Michael, who said he worked for the Post Office, had noticed 'a large increase of people taking money out of various financial institutions and putting it in the Post Office'. An estimated €50 million was reportedly lodged to An Post's State-assured savings scheme in a single twenty-four-hour period.

The cat was out of the bag. The radio show precipitated a flurry of withdrawals by consumers as people realised others were taking out their savings. Nobody wanted to miss the boat. Brian Lenihan rang Cathal Goan, director general of RTÉ, to express his outrage at the programme for provoking unprecedented consumer panic. But RTÉ stressed it was the authorities' job to reassure the public. Financial regulator Patrick Neary then appeared on the nine o'clock TV news and said, 'People can have full confidence that their deposits in Irish institutions are safe.'

Whatever about a radio show's responsibilities – it had almost caused a run on the banks – the issue exposed a glaring inadequacy: there was a State guarantee for bank deposits, but it was too limited. Only 90 per cent of the first €20,000 of any deposit was secured. Many people had savings in excess of that entrusted to the banks. And trust was no longer enough.

20 September 2008

It was a beautiful Indian summer Saturday. With the banks closed for the weekend, the government could change the rules. Lenihan called a news conference and announced the deposit guarantee had been raised to €100,000. He pointed out the previous guarantee had been in place since 1999. This new guarantee for Irish banks was among the highest in Europe.

22 September 2008

The markets remained jittery, although the Bush administration was working on a €700 billion bailout for the banks. Billionaire Warren Buffett told the CNBC network that the US economy had 'fallen off a cliff'. The bailout was an attempt to throw it a lifeline, and Wall Street was anxiously watching that space.

By this stage, the Irish stock market had lost 60 per cent of its value since its peak a year earlier.

24 September 2008

The trading floors of stockbrokers were swamped with rumours about Anglo Irish Bank after the Financial Regulator held a meeting with the bank. Anglo's own account of that exchange claimed Patrick Neary raised no objection to it bolstering deposits as year-end approached, using money from Irish Life & Permanent. In fact, he encouraged it, according to the version of events contained in a report from that day's meeting prepared by the audit department of Anglo.

Its internal documentation shows Anglo's chief executive David Drumm and finance director Willie McAteer met Neary to discuss liquidity issues. McAteer told Neary the bank would 'patch up' Anglo's balance sheet after the 30 September year-end – to which Neary responded, 'Fair play to you, Willie, you boy you.'

26–28 September 2008

As the Irish banking crisis deteriorated, Anglo Irish Bank's share price dropped and investors were terrified the bank would go under. Depositors rushed to withdraw around €4 billion from Anglo. Chairman Seán FitzPatrick denied significant sums had been taken out, 'No, not dramatically,' he said soon after. This was not economy with the truth. This was a barefaced lie.

The critical day in Anglo's calendar was 30 September – the end of its financial year. It was the day on which the amount of money deposited in the bank was recorded and used to demonstrate that the bank was in sound financial health. For Anglo chief executive David Drumm, it was critical for the bank to pull in deposits. If its results showed a significant drop, the bank would almost certainly face failure.

In this feverish atmosphere, Denis Casey gave a helping hand. He instructed finance director Peter Fitzpatrick (no relation to Seán FitzPatrick) and his head of treasury David Gantly to support Anglo. Certain Irish Life & Permanent executives knew Anglo would dress up the transfers when they made large deposits through their Irish Life Assurance division. They understood Anglo could disguise them as customer funds. But this was a fight for survival. The rules were suspended to preserve the system.

A source in Irish Life & Permanent has suggested that the detail of how Anglo was to be buttressed was left to Peter Fitzpatrick and David Gantly – both considered to be honest, decent bankers, according to a former colleague. The source says that Casey was aware of the arrangement but not of the finer points of the transfers. However, this stretches credulity and smacks of plausible deniability. It seems improbable that Casey did not know what was going on.

Irish Life & Permanent made five deposits totalling €3.45 billion to Anglo between 26 September and 29 September. In return, it received €3.45 billion from Anglo. These were back-to-back deposits. The same money was going round in a circle: from Anglo to Irish Life & Permanent and back to Anglo – in a false guise in the final phase.

Other banks elsewhere in the world were also battling to survive the liquidity crisis. In the two days between 28 and 30 September, four major European banks had to be bailed out.

A run on Belgium's biggest bank, Fortis, led to the Belgian, Dutch and Luxembourg authorities investing €11.2 billion in the bank. Fortis also had a joint venture with An Post, called Postbank, which offered saving and insurance in post offices around Ireland. While the joint venture was not affected by the global carnage, Postbank opted to join the Irish government's State guarantee scheme.

The German government had to orchestrate a €35 billion bailout of its lender Hypo Real Estate, which was unable to get refinancing after the collapse of Lehman Brothers. Hypo blamed its problems on its subsidiary Depfa, the Dublin-based bank at the IFSC. It said it was forced to seek credit from the German authorities after Depfa encountered problems securing short-term funding. The German government stepped in because it believed Hypo was too large to be allowed to fail. Days later, Hypo admitted it actually needed €52 billion, and a livid German finance minister stumped up the extra money. The episode did little to enhance Ireland's reputation in Europe, or the reputation of the IFSC in general and Financial Regulator Patrick Neary in particular. However, reports showed Germany had known Depfa was sailing in choppy waters six months earlier.

And in the US, trouble showed no sign of taking a day off. Washington Mutual Inc, the holding company for Washington Mutual Bank, filed for voluntary bankruptcy. Washington Mutual Bank, the sixth largest in the US, had been placed in receivership. America's Office of Thrift Supervision had taken the action due to the withdrawal of $16.4 billion in deposits during a ten-day run on the bank. The banking subsidiaries were sold to JPMorgan Chase for $1.9 billion.

29 September 2008

In Britain, several days of frantic action culminated in the government taking Bradford and Bingley, its biggest buy-to-let mortgage lender, into State ownership. The bank was split into two parts: its mortgage book was nationalised, while its branch network was sold to Abbey, owned by Spanish bank Santander. 'Clearly we're disappointed,' one leading shareholder said. 'But given we're losing a bank a day in the Western world, it's not very surprising.'

Chancellor of the Exchequer Alistair Darling said the government had 'acted immediately to maintain financial stability and protect depositors, while minimising the exposure to taxpayers'. Taxpayers, however, were exposed to £150 billion of potentially toxic mortgage debt.

Meanwhile, concerted European action was taken again. Dexia, a Belgo-French municipal lender skating on thin ice, became the fourth European bank to be saved within forty-eight hours. Governments and shareholders from Belgium, France and Luxembourg injected €6.4 billion to keep it buoyant. It suffered from exposure to the US mortgage market.

In Ireland, bank shares had been nose-diving all day. At a meeting to discuss the situation held in the Central Bank with Governor John Hurley, Irish Life & Permanent executives aired the possibility of Bank of Ireland making a €5 billion deposit in Anglo, according to one account. But this is disputed by Bank of Ireland and the Central Bank. None of the internal notes from the banks are specific about exactly what sort of transfers were suggested by the Financial Regulator or the Central Bank.

In a subsequent statement, the authority which runs the Financial Regulator said that the regulator met regularly with banks to discuss funding. It said the focal point of these meetings was to ensure that the banks could use 'normal inter-bank funding arrangements at a time when international inter-bank funding had effectively dried up'. It added, 'The meetings did not at any time focus on other types of deposit arrangements, such as those engaged in by Anglo Irish Bank and Irish Life & Permanent. This was a very different type of transaction to a normal inter-bank arrangement and by its nature had no beneficial effect in terms of providing liquidity.' It viewed the transactions involving these institutions as 'completely unacceptable'.

Without an accurate note of what happened during those meetings, none of the banks can argue convincingly that the Anglo and Irish Life & Permanent transfers were sanctioned by the authorities. A source close to the regulator's office points out it was the job of the banks to ensure they complied with legislation. The notion of a nod and a wink to waive the rules was ludicrous, according to the source: 'If the regulator and the Central Bank gave their imprimatur to what happened, it would have turned Ireland into a banana republic.'

Some might argue it was already one: welcome to Irelandistan. 'Investors can be confident in the rule of law in Ireland,' a leading industry figure had said at a recent conference. But the speaker was Seán FitzPatrick, at that talk to UCD business alumni back in March 2008.

Despite the vast sums of money involved, Anglo was still desperate for more deposits to compensate for a cascade of withdrawals. On 29 September, its executives contacted Casey's senior staff three more times looking for further deposits on top of the €3.45 billion already transferred to Anglo. Their panic was palpable. Casey and his team turned down their requests because Anglo no longer had the cash to deposit in Irish Life & Permanent before the money went back to Anglo. If Anglo collapsed, Irish Life & Permanent would lose billions. The Green Jersey Agenda did not stretch that far.

That night, as Casey sat in his office looking at the city lights, he wondered if the group he had joined twenty-eight years earlier would open for business the following day. This had been a day like no other. The entire Irish banking system was hanging by a thread. Thousands of jobs – the Irish economy itself – hinged on what the coming hours would bring.

30 September 2008

At 6.50 a.m., the government announced it had guaranteed the deposits and loans of the Irish banks and building societies. This changed everything. If Casey's team provided further support for Anglo and it went bust, the government would make good any losses. Irish Life & Permanent again gave

Anglo a dig-out. A second series of transactions in four tranches, totalling €4 billion, went from Anglo to Irish Life & Permanent and back to Anglo – the final stage again tricked out as customer deposits. Over a four-day period, Irish Life & Permanent deposited €7.45 billion in Anglo. The money would all be paid back by 3 October.

This was on top of that earlier €750 million short-term deposit, made in a single transaction in March, to coincide with Anglo's result for the first six months of the year. Irish Life & Permanent had already assisted Anglo when it misled the markets six months earlier – smaller scale, same principle. To put the scope of these exchanges into context, at that time Irish Life & Permanent was worth €1.3 billion. It had transferred five and a half times more than the entire company's worth.

But the Financial Regulator's cultivation of the Green Jersey Agenda justified these transactions. Or did it?

A senior banker commented, 'Irish Life & Permanent would have a policy of how much you can normally deposit in another bank. The sums involved in these transactions were simply enormous. They were far too big. Normally banks set a limit on these kinds of deposits, so they do not deposit more than a certain percentage of assets. Then how much they can deposit in another bank is limited as well, depending on how big that institution is in size. Even then the deposit has to be approved at credit committee.

'If Irish Life & Permanent felt the regulator had given the all-clear, the bank's law officer would have been all over it. Something like this would have to be examined upside down if it was to go through the official channels.' But the indications are that the transactions did not follow normal procedures.

1 October 2008

A section of a document prepared by Anglo's audit department in early 2009, to defend its actions in relation to the deposits, refers to a number of calls from regulatory staff in October about these transactions, which were disclosed in Irish Life & Permanent's returns. Significant among them was a call on 24 October from Mary Burke, head of banking supervision with the Financial Regulator, to Peter Fitzpatrick, finance director at Irish Life & Permanent.

She asked if Irish Life & Permanent had given Anglo a significant level of support on 30 September. He said yes and asked if there was an issue with the deposits. She said no, according to the note of their conversation made by Anglo – she was simply clarifying something. But the document notes that following Mary O'Dea's appointment as acting chief executive at the Financial Regulator's office, there was a 'seismic shift' in attitude to the transactions.

The defence document from Anglo shows that the bank was subsequently called by the regulator's office on 1 October, asking about the deposit figures on 30 September. The call was recorded by Anglo. An official from Anglo clearly said that the bank took money which was supposed to be classified as an inter-bank deposit and described it as a corporate customer deposit. The Anglo official also said that this was done to improve the appearance of the year-end accounts due to be published in December.

In the transcript of that call, the unnamed individual from the regulator's office says, 'I just want to ask about . . . the corporate figure, the €8 billion, it that still a net figure there?'

Anglo: 'Yes, that's still a net figure, that's correct. Do you want me to continue? It's trying to manipulate our balance sheet for our financial year-end last night.'

Regulator: 'Yes.'

Anglo: '. . . We boosted our customer funding number . . .

191

so when our snapshot is produced at the beginning of December it will look as good as possible.'

So, the bank official was effectively divulging to the regulator's office that the Irish Life & Permanent money was a ruse, intended to enhance the appearance of Anglo's accounts.

The Anglo official continued by saying that the customer deposit was 'not a real number'. 'If you look at the other side of the balance sheet you will see an inter-bank placement of €8 billion,' said the banker. Anglo was admitting that a corporate customer deposit, something expected to remain in the bank for a long period, was actually an inter-bank deposit – and only likely to stay for a matter of days or hours.

The conversation ended with the official from the regulator's office saying, 'OK, that's grand, right, I think that's everything.' Neither the Anglo employee nor the official from the regulator's office seemed fully conscious of the significance of their exchange. While the banks later tried to suggest such conversations showed the regulator's office gave its imprimatur to the transactions, the dialogue suggests the office was checking facts – not bestowing approval.

3 October 2008

The US was in a febrile condition, leading to the Bush administration's $700 billion emergency bailout for bankers finally becoming law. This followed a week of horse-trading which persuaded Congress to reverse its opposition to the plan. It allowed the US Treasury to clean up banks' balance sheets by dealing with the toxic assets causing so many problems.

As the banking legislation was being finalised, the Wachovia Corporation – one of America's largest financial institutions through a series of aggressive acquisitions – was forced to sell itself to rival bank Wells Fargo. Bad mortgage loans had led to it becoming mired in losses. It was yet more evidence of financial volatility.

9 October 2008

Iceland went bankrupt, and a shudder rippled through Ireland. But for eurozone protection, it could easily have happened to the Irish. Iceland's government had to shut down the stock market and seize control of its last major independent bank. This meant its entire banking system was nationalised. Trading in the country's currency was brought to a halt, with foreign banks no longer willing to take Icelandic krona, even at fire-sale rates. With the krona valueless to the rest of the world, Iceland could not meet its debts.

Preceding these exceptional circumstances had been a decade-long, debt-fuelled binge. The banks, while avoiding the toxic mortgage securities that humbled Wall Street, had expanded pugnaciously at home and abroad. When credit tightened and the krona fell, they were unable to finance their debts.

Icesave, a subsidiary of Iceland's Landsbanki, which operated in Britain and Holland, was declared insolvent, putting the savings of thousands of British and Dutch customers at risk. More than seventy local authorities in the UK had £550 million plus of funds in Icelandic banks. When Iceland's government said that these deposits would not be guaranteed, the British government seized Icesave's assets, controversially using anti-terror legislation.

Landsbanki had an 84 per cent stake in Dublin stockbrokers Merrion Capital. Management at the Irish operation, led by John Conroy, moved hastily to buy the stake back at a €60 million discount.

There was an extraordinary reversal in Iceland's fortunes, and many people were in distress. Some homeowners had taken out mortgages in Japanese yen. The idea was that as the yen dropped in value against the krona their mortgage payments would fall. This seemed a cracking idea during a time of economic expansion – but when the krona imploded, payments on home loans escalated with terrifying speed at the same time as property prices collapsed. Bankers were spat on in Iceland's streets, as a nation (ranked most developed country in the world by the United Nations' Human Development Index in 2007) struggled to comprehend its lunge into recession.

As the crisis in Iceland's financial system quickened, its government powerless to prevent meltdown, only one realistic option remained. A bailout by the IMF. 'Iceland is bankrupt,' said Arsaell Valfells, a professor at the University of Iceland. 'The Icelandic krona is history. The IMF has to come and rescue us.'

With Iceland on life support, emergency funding of $4.6 billion to restore fiscal stability was to be supplied by the IMF and a range of European countries in November 2008. Germany, Britain and Holland would also give a joint loan of €5 billion in relation to the deposit insurance dispute.

Within a few months, Iceland's Prime Minister was to be caught by an angry mob and rescued by Special Forces police using tear gas. And in an unequivocal break with the recent past, early in 2009 Iceland voted for Jóhanna Sigurðardóttir as its first female and first openly gay Prime Minster.

10 February 2009

In February 2009, it emerged that acting Financial Regulator Mary O'Dea – replacement for Patrick Neary who had to resign in January – was investigating Anglo's deposits. A report on RTÉ's *Six One News* revealed that Irish Life & Permanent money had been used to artificially prop up Anglo's end-of-year results. Within two hours, Irish Life & Permanent issued a statement saying it had offered 'exceptional' support to Anglo Irish Bank. It blustered, 'During a period of unprecedented turmoil in global financial markets, there was an acceptance that financial institutions would seek to provide each other with appropriate support where possible.' This was an attempt by Irish Life & Permanent to justify its actions by citing the common good. What the statement did not reveal was the dread among Irish Life & Permanent executives that if they did not intervene, Anglo might go under – and they could be next in line.

11 February 2009

The blame game of who knew what when juddered into overdrive as the issue exploded in the Dáil. Brian Lenihan admitted that, although he had read the Pricewaterhouse-Coopers report for the government on Anglo and the other banks, he skipped over the section about Irish Life & Permanent deposits. 'I did not read that particular passage in the report. My officials were concerned about the matter and referred it to the regulator,' he said. Labour's finance spokes-woman Joan Burton asked pointedly, 'Why was the Anglo report not red-letter reading, every word and comma? This was the bank everyone was worried about.'

12 February 2009

Public and political opinion was solidifying against the banks. Lenihan had been made to look foolish because of the actions of Irish Life & Permanent. Lenihan called in Denis Casey and Gillian Bowler. Later, Lenihan said, 'I shared my views with the chair, and I expect the board to face up to its responsibilities.' This was a call for officers to fall on their swords. The board of directors met through the night. Casey and two executives were expected to stand down while Bowler would remain as chairwoman. One source said the minister 'pointed a gun at the bank but stopped short of pulling the trigger – he left that to the bank itself'.

13 February 2009

At 3.17 a.m., Irish Life & Permanent issued a statement after an exhaustive eight-hour board meeting. There were only two resignations – the third was notable by its absence. Peter Fitzpatrick and David Gantly went, with the board paying predictable lip service to their 'integrity and professionalism'. This was followed by a single line saying that the board had declined Casey's offer of resignation. The board expressed its 'strong disapproval of and disappointment with some of the specific measures used to support Anglo Irish Bank'. But the implication was that two heads had rolled, and enough was enough.

RTÉ arranged a television interview with Bowler. Only one question mattered: why was Casey remaining at the helm? The interview was cancelled, as the bank was brought to realise how dumbfounded the government was at Casey's failure to clear his desk.

Lenihan was in his Dublin West constituency that morning. Before lunchtime, he had called Bowler and instructed her to present herself at the Department of Finance for a second meeting. By now, the situation had descended into farce. Lenihan was speaking for the taxpayer, who called the shots. The State guarantee meant that the taxpayer was underwriting all the debts and deposits of Irish banks, including those of Irish Life & Permanent. The minister had already appointed two directors to its board: former EU Commissioner Ray MacSharry and Margaret Hayes, previously Secretary General of the Department of Arts, Sport and Tourism.

Lenihan had made it clear he wanted the bank to take responsibility for its actions. By this, he meant it should sack the chief executive. However, the board was trying to hold on to Casey. It believed Casey could best plot the bank's course through the financial crisis. It was convinced Casey's two lieutenants – who had resigned – were more culpable, and that he was unaware of the details of their actions. The board was holding out in the hope that the government would tolerate Casey. Furthermore, his departure would come at an awkward time, with Irish Life & Permanent's annual results due out the following month. Who would present them, with their top three executives gone?

At 4.30 p.m., with the media camped outside the Department of Finance where Bowler was due to meet Lenihan, Irish Life & Permanent caved in. It issued a statement confirming Casey was gone. He had 'reflected on the situation with his wife and family overnight and again [that] morning' and had come to the decision that 'regardless of the board's support, his continued involvement with the group would only serve as a distraction from the group's efforts to successfully navigate the difficult challenges of today's market'. By standing down, Casey spared Bowler the humiliation of locking horns in a contest she was doomed to lose.

In their interaction with Anglo, Irish Life & Permanent's senior team had adopted an attitude of looking the other way. How Anglo dealt with the money in its accounts was the responsibility of David Drumm and his team, not theirs. But reality bites. And the reality was that Irish Life & Permanent, by using its life-assurance arm as a conduit for the money, was complicit in the deception. Innocence and ignorance are not interchangeable.

The conclusion of this episode was pivotal because it showed the dynamic between politicians and bankers had changed. The balance of power had now shifted. Irish Life & Permanent backed off under pressure from Lenihan – and the other banks were paying close attention.

10
Swimming with Sharks

'I am a nice shark, not a mindless eating machine.'
Bruce, *in* Finding Nemo

23 October 2008

'We would rather die than raise new equity.' AIB chief executive Eugene Sheehy was on feisty form at a conference of heavyweight investors at Goodbody Stockbrokers in Dublin. For Sheehy, new equity would mean giving new investors control of the bank. That could signal an abrupt end to Sheehy's job. This was about power and control – the never-ending game; only the players changed.

Despite the fighting talk from Sheehy, he was wearing blinkers. So were the other bank bosses. They were in denial about the dire straits of their own institutions and they were in denial that Ireland's property prices were on the cusp of a landslide. They did not want to accept it because they would be left with billions of euro of bad debts.

Raising new equity meant issuing and selling new shares. This would dilute the value of existing shares, and their already apoplectic shareholders would suffer even more pain.

On the same day, Brian Lenihan said that injecting tax revenues into the banks was 'the very final option'. The government was still hoping the State guarantee alone would prevent their collapse. The Minister for Finance knew that after an austere budget only nine days earlier, which resulted in street protests, bailing out the banks would cause a political nightmare.

The budget was already being reversed more times than a family hatchback. If he handed over money to bankers, he might as well put it in a bag labelled 'swag'.

The Irish government's authority was weak, with the Taoiseach regarded as particularly feeble. In contrast, British Prime Minister Gordon Brown's speedy and vigorous reaction to the unfolding crisis appeared to resuscitate a flagging political career. Brown had seized the moment and had thrown every weapon in his armament at the situation – including a £37 billion bailout shared by Royal Bank of Scotland (owner of Ulster Bank) and Lloyds TSB, which was taking over Halifax Bank of Scotland.

His bold action to tackle banking meltdown transformed him into a phoenix, emerging gloriously from the ashes of his career. His Irish counterpart Brian Cowen looked drab by comparison. He appeared to believe leadership was the art of waiting until trouble came knocking before testing possible remedies.

Across Europe, as in Britain, governments accepted they had to sink money into their banks. The Irish solution – a guarantee alone – suggested political faith that the difficulties facing Irish banks were unique. They were not. But the Irish Government, like the Irish stockbrokers who gave no advice to clients to sell bank shares, still believed the bankers' insistence that they could handle the downturn. Nobody else believed them.

20 November 2008

Without warning, a sign appeared at the entrance to the Georgian mansion in the hands of the State: 'Farmleigh

House will be closed today, Thursday 20 November, due to official government business.' Visitors grumbled as they were turned away. They would have squawked a lot louder had they known why the stately home was off limits. Brian Lenihan was holding a round of emergency meetings with the captains of Irish banking.

Set in Dublin's Phoenix Park, the lungs of the city, Farmleigh was built by Edward Cecil Guinness, 1st Earl of Iveagh and the great-grandson of legendary brewer Arthur Guinness. The State acquired it in 1999 – an example of wise use of the boom-time tax receipts – and it accommodates visiting dignitaries there. Former US President Jimmy Carter and his wife Rosalynn, King Harald V and Queen Sonja of Norway, as well as King Albert II and Queen Paola of Belgium have all stayed in Farmleigh.

The stately home has all the trappings, from columns of Connemara marble in the entrance hall, to a marble-floored conservatory with exotic plants and flowers, to a galleried library with first editions including Swift's *Gulliver's Travels*. Farmleigh even has a ballroom, and the story goes that its oak floor was made from disused brewery barrels. For all their exposure to fine living, these well-heeled bankers arriving for their meeting with the Minister for Finance cannot fail to have been impressed.

But Lenihan had not summoned the chief executives and chairs of AIB, Bank of Ireland, Irish Life & Permanent, Anglo Irish Bank, Irish Nationwide and EBS to parade the grandeur of Farmleigh. He thought it was off the beaten track and would allow the meetings to be conducted in privacy.

The banks urgently needed a reality check. They were living in a parallel universe – utterly divorced from events around them.

Shares are often compared to the canaries which, for decades, were brought down mines to alert workers to toxic gases. When the canaries showed signs of distress, the miners knew it was time for a strategic retreat. Deluded though the bankers were, the dramatic disintegration of Irish bank shares told the real story. On 20 May 2007, the value of financial shares on the Irish Stock Exchange was €55 billion. Eighteen months later, on 20 November 2008, as bankers met in Farmleigh, the shares were worth €4 billion.

Large-scale investors who managed money on behalf of pension funds had voted with their feet and had sold off. The Irish banks were untouchables. They were over-exposed to property and in line to suffer crippling bad debts, and they ran the risk of going bust. No wonder investors were evacuating as quickly as a miner with a dead canary on his hands. Despite this blindingly obvious conclusion, the bankers persisted in peddling tall tales, saying they could muddle through – falling back on bluff about 'prudent lending' and 'strong capital positions'.

Lenihan was worried that if the banks conserved their cash to cover bad debts they would curtail lending. Such a move would stifle business and enflame the recession. He had a report codenamed 'Project Atlas' by consultants Pricewater-houseCoopers. Atlas was the Titan in Greek mythology who propped up the heavens on his shoulders, his punishment for being on the losing side in a war. This document, with its cautionary codename, outlined the risks faced by the banks – and, by default, the taxpayer, carrying their load courtesy of the State guarantee.

Lenihan brought in the banks individually to meet him in Farmleigh. Word of the location leaked out within three hours, however, and television cameras were camped outside Farmleigh before the talks concluded.

When bankers entered the meeting room, they were confronted by a phalanx including not just Lenihan but also the secretary general of the Department of Finance David Doyle, Padraig O'Riordan of Arthur Cox Solicitors, and the

Central Bank's Governor John Hurley. One senior banker said, 'It was full on – not what I was expecting at all. Lenihan did talk about consolidation. But he was not a great listener, he kept on interrupting us.' Senior bankers still expected to be treated with deference.

Speaking in general terms, Lenihan told the bankers he wanted to see major changes at their institutions. He outlined his vision of the future, but none of his comments were prescriptive: there were no specific instructions to the banks. He did not load, take aim and fire. One banker came away with the impression that Lenihan envisaged a smaller number of large players surviving rather than the existing six Irish financial institutions. And, instead of the State bailing out the banks with capital, as in Britain, bankers left thinking that private-equity investors would inject fresh supplies of cash.

Irish Life & Permanent's chief executive Denis Casey and chairwoman Gillian Bowler were angered by what they heard. They believed the government wanted them to merge with Bank of Ireland, with private-equity investors funding the merger. A banker said, 'We heard non-directive counselling. The government wants a major restructuring. They are obsessed with a two-bank solution anchored around AIB and Bank of Ireland. Everyone will be encouraged to merge with these two banks.'

Some bankers were numb with shock. They had to confront the prospect of working for somebody else instead of running their own empires – a calamity on this scale had never happened before in Ireland's cosy banking cartel. They had stumbled into *The Twilight Zone*. A politician with a plan was a truly daunting prospect.

21 November 2008

Within twelve hours of the Farmleigh meetings concluding, Irish Life & Permanent had a counteroffensive. It said it was in talks that could lead to a takeover of EBS. Casey and Bowler were proposing a solution that would leave three large banks standing – and theirs would be among the survivors. The talks with EBS had been ongoing for some time, but it was no coincidence that the merger negotiations leaked out immediately after the Farmleigh encounter.

24 November 2008

Barbarians at the Gate is a film starring James Garner, based on a non-fiction book of the same name about the mother of all takeover battles in 1988. The story concerns Ross Johnson, played by Garner, the boss of tobacco company RJR Nabisco. He decides to buy the company from shareholders. But other bidders enter the fray, notably the top guns of the private-equity firm, Kohlberg Kravis & Roberts. These two groups and others fight for control of the company for weeks, with ever-escalating bids and intrigues. Kohlberg Kravis & Roberts finally carry home the prize – at a cost of $25 billion. Johnson loses control but walks away with a fortune. The Irish banks were facing their own Barbarians at the Gate moment.

Two words make bankers' blood run cold: private equity. And so, with the Irish banks in a tailspin, the stock market in tatters and government leaders biting their nails and debating the next move, it was no surprise when the head honchos of the private-equity world came calling. Private-equity firms, including Kohlberg Kravis & Roberts themselves, booked out the ritziest hotel suites in Dublin.

Perhaps the most tenacious of these groups was a consortium called Mallabraca, named after the County Cork townland of GAA icon Sam Maguire. The group was headed by Nigel McDermott and Nick Corcoran. McDermott, born in 1958, has slightly greying hair offset by youthful features. He forged his career alongside deal-maker Dermot Desmond, as a founder director of Desmond's investment vehicle IIU (International Investment and Underwriting). He had also worked in NCB Stockbrokers, owned by Desmond, until 1994.

Corcoran, slightly built and red-haired, was ten years younger than McDermott and a founding director of Zurich Capital. Corcoran, from Dorset Street in Dublin, had already clocked up impressive deals. Fellow UCD students say he stood out as smarter and more ambitious than most of his peers. Corcoran loves to communicate by text, and his phone has a photograph of his daughter on its screen.

Both McDermott and Corcoran, who were based in London with their business Cardinal Asset Management, had a more realistic grasp on the banking situation than the flock of others offering opinions. They assembled an impressive cast of dramatis personae from the galaxy of private equity. Among them was Chris Flowers, founder of New York-based JC Flowers. Flowers is a chess-playing Harvard graduate who left Goldman Sachs to set up his own investment house. He had experience in turning around ailing banks after his purchase of Shinsei Bank in Japan in 2000, where he cut jobs and repaired its balance sheet. McDermott and Corcoran brought Flowers to Dublin, and he met Brian Lenihan in the Merrion Hotel to discuss a possible investment in the Irish banks.

At the meeting, Lenihan referred to the avalanche of speculation about who wanted to invest and said even billionaire investment guru Warren Buffett had been mentioned. Flowers pulled out his mobile phone and said, 'If you want Warren in, I'll get him in. We are friends. I have him on speed dial on my phone.' Flowers, who was prepared to invest €750 million in the deal, said the fact he was willing to put up money meant that Buffett was likely to invest as well. Lenihan laughed, 'Chris, your money is just fine.'

The Mallabraca consortium included the behemoth Carlyle Group, the world's largest private-equity group. Its portfolio of investments employs more than 400,000 people around the globe. Those who worked as advisers for the group include former US President George Bush Senior and former Secretary of State James Baker, while ex-British Prime Minister John Major was chairman of its European operation.

Many people first heard of Carlyle in *Fahrenheit 9/11* – a documentary by US film-maker Michael Moore. This highlighted Carlyle's links with the bin Laden family. As New York's World Trade Center came under attack, Carlyle was holding an investment conference in the Ritz Carlton Hotel in Washington. Among those in attendance was Shafiq bin Laden, one of Osama's platoon of half-brothers. Shafiq bin Laden's family were Carlyle investors. Although Shafiq disowned Osama and was a minor investor in Carlyle, the connection was reported in the film, along with ties to the Bush family, and spawned a blogosphere of conspiracy theories.

McDermott and Corcoran's discussions with Carlyle were held with Olivier Sarkozy, half-brother to French President Nicolas Sarkozy. Olivier, a French-American, was co-head of Carlyle's global financial services division. He was specifically hired to find investment opportunities among the banks for Carlyle. Nicolas and Olivier share the same father, Pál Sárközy de Nagy-Bócsa, who left his family when Nicolas was five and subsequently married Olivier's mother.

Corcoran brought Olivier Sarkozy to Dublin and noticed during his meetings that women were constantly trying to catch Olivier's eye. Olivier resembles Nicolas but is slightly taller. But Corcoran decided against setting up a meeting with Olivier and Lenihan. He feared media coverage would be linked to the French President's visit to Dublin three months earlier, when he pressed the Irish government to address the rejection of the Lisbon Treaty.

Also a member of the Mallabraca consortium was US investment bank Sandler O'Neill & Partners, whose co-

founder Herman Sandler died along with sixty-seven
employees in the 9/11 attacks. The bank had an office on Floor
104 of 2 World Trade Center. The other partner, Tom O'Neill,
met Lenihan in the Conrad Hotel during a trip to Dublin.

Irish businessman Bryan Turley and his group Sorrento
Asset Management were in the consortium too, along with an
investment from the royal family of Abu Dhabi.

Generally, private-equity investors have an image problem.
Critics say they smell money, like sharks to blood – circling,
waiting for weakness and pouncing. They take over a
company, frequently with borrowed money. This is added as a
hefty debt to the balance sheet of the company they purchase.
Then they slash costs and jobs, boost profits and flog off the
company at a vast return.

This is probably an unfair over-simplification. But the
critics only needed to point to the example of phone group
Eircom in the Irish context, which was taken over in 2001 by a
private-equity consortium led by Tony O'Reilly. Eircom was
blamed for delaying Ireland's broadband progress before
being sold in 2006 at a huge profit of €2.36 billion, even with
debts of €1.8 billion on its books. The O'Reilly consortium
had cut costs, introduced a redundancy programme and
grown profits as the economy continued to expand.

The goose was nice and plump when it was sold to
Babcock & Brown, an Australian investment group. The
Australians insisted theirs was not a private-equity firm. But it
certainly behaved like one. Babcock & Brown shovelled
another pile of debt on to the balance sheet of the phone
company. By 2009, Eircom had borrowings of €4 billion. At
this stage, the Irish economy had executed a volte-face and
Babcock & Brown admitted it had overpaid for Eircom.

But Mallabraca distanced itself from the private-equity
mishaps that had discredited such investors in Ireland. It
insisted it was not interested in investing in the Irish banks for

the short term only. It pointed out that it was willing to provide funds at a time when the banks had few friends and the economy urgently needed healthy financial institutions.

25 November 2008

The private-equity groups had barely unpacked their BlackBerrys before the union representing bank staff launched a broadside. The Irish Bank Officials Association (IBOA) called the private-equity potential investors 'the real sharks and predators' of the business world. IBOA general secretary Larry Broderick said he feared a merger of Bank of Ireland and Irish Life & Permanent, with finance from private-equity companies, could result in 3,500 job losses. In a clear indication the government was engaged with private-equity groups, Lenihan said that if there was private investment in the banks he would safeguard the public interest.

26 November 2008

Bank staff were not the only ones quaking at the prospect of private-equity piranhas swimming in their stream. So, too, were management and directors. With any private-equity deal, the first place where blood would spatter the walls would be the boardroom. In an attempt to block the investment, the financial houses scouted around for other sources of capital.

Irish banks run investment management operations that invest money on behalf of pensions, usually into the stock market. With the sharks circling, the Irish Association of Investment Managers said that a number of its members were interested in the banks. They included AIB Investment Managers, Bank of Ireland Asset Management and Irish Life Investment Managers. In other words, banks would advance money to banks to head off the private-equity boys at the pass.

In theory, it sounded terrific – particularly in the board-rooms of the banks, where their excessively well-paid jobs would be safe if the investment management companies poured in funds. But the cash would come from ordinary people, who were investing in pensions, and they would be plugging a hole in banks that were facing enormous bad debts.

As an investment strategy, this sucked.

It was no surprise when the idea was quietly buried. The private-equity candidates ordered up room service and settled down to wait.

28 November 2008

It was a clear, bitterly cold day. At 9 a.m., a solitary figure appeared. From the distance, he looked like a prosperous bookmaker staking his pitch at the Leopardstown Christmas Festival, in a black overcoat and black trilby. Michael Fingleton walked along Merrion Street towards the Department of Finance. The Irish Nationwide chief shied away from the television cameras outside the Edwardian stone building. 'No comment whatsoever,' was all that could be wheedled from him on his way in.

It was part two of the showdown: the Irish State versus the banks. This time, the Department of Finance had abandoned any idea of off-campus meetings, instead letting the bankers fend for themselves with the media outside.

Before 11 a.m., a chauffeur-driven silver Toyota Avensis pulled up outside the department. Irish Life & Permanent chairwoman Gillian Bowler emerged with chief executive Denis Casey. Unlike the other banks, they had brought one of Ireland's top corporate lawyers, Paul Carroll, managing partner of legal firm A&L Goodbody. Irish Life & Permanent was signalling it was not the marrying kind: try to force us into an arranged match with Bank of Ireland and we'll have the law on you.

To Lenihan's fury, Carroll proceeded to read a twenty-minute statement outlining the bank's legal objections to a merger with Bank of Ireland. One person at the meeting said they would 'never forget the faces on the government side for the rest of their career. That statement business really got the government's goat up.'

Unknown to the banking executives, it was not just the media watching them. Right across the street from the Department of Finance is the Merrion Hotel. The hotel is spread across four Georgian buildings. Built in the 1760s for the nobility and wealthy merchants, its suites overlook the Department of Finance and the meeting rooms used by officials and Lenihan – a convenient vantage point for guests if they happened to belong to a private-equity consortium with a keen interest in the negotiations.

At 3 p.m., a gleaming 2006-registered navy-blue Bentley Continental pulled up at the Merrion. With a price tag of a quarter of a million euro, the only thing understated about this vehicle was its colour. Nigel McDermott and Nick Corcoran of Mallabraca stepped out of the Bentley and went up to their suite. Their proximity to the nerve centre of decision-making, just the twitch of a curtain away, lent the day a surreal air.

The journalists were watching the bankers come and go as well as the consortium's movements.

The consortium was watching the bankers. And officials from the Department of Finance were watching the consortium.

The 1980s Rockwell song about paranoia, 'Somebody's Watching Me', sprang to mind.

There was plenty to see. Half an hour later, Bank of Ireland's chief executive Brian Goggin and chairman Richard Burrows walked across the street to their meeting. Perhaps in the knowledge that the cameras were rolling, they had been dropped off around the corner. Limousines disgorging banking executives tended to grate with shareholders feeling the pinch.

As Goggin and Burrows entered their meeting, McDermott and Corcoran received notification that their offer to invest €4 billion in Bank of Ireland had been rejected by the bank.

The pair were suspicious about the timing of their deal being shot down just as the bankers were meeting Lenihan. The consortium had also suggested an alternative, where existing shareholders would own just under half the bank. Under this arrangement, the consortium offered to invest €2 billion and current shareholders could invest a further €2 billion by buying new shares in a rights issue. If existing shareholders did not want to invest, Corcoran and McDermott's consortium would put up the rest of the money. Either way, Bank of Ireland would reap €4 billion. But Bank of Ireland had rejected the approach as 'outside our process'.

A Bank of Ireland source said, 'The real problem with the Mallabraca takeover was that they wanted a new board and a new management team for the bank. There was political support for Mallabraca, so we had to keep them onside to some extent. Lenihan was saying, "Why should the State put money into the banks when Mallabraca was prepared to do it?" Richard Burrows thought there could be something to the Mallabraca proposal but that came to a halt when it became clear they wanted to control the bank. Then there was a major bust up.'

Corcoran could see from his suite that Lenihan was now in his meeting with Burrows and Goggin. Corcoran rang Lenihan, who took his blue Nokia mobile phone out of his pocket, checked the caller ID, excused himself and left the room. Corcoran briefed Lenihan on the detail of what Bank of Ireland had rejected before the minister returned to the meeting.

The sharks were showing their teeth.

An hour later, AIB chief executive Eugene Sheehy and chairman Dermot Gleeson arrived in a chauffeur-driven black Mercedes. One of the officials in the Department of Finance rolled his eyes at the Mercedes idling outside. 'And they wonder why people call them fat cats,' he commented.

The banks were in a sticky situation. Legally, their shareholders were supposed to be their top priority. But with shares so low, whoever injected new cash could become the new owners of the banks, rendering worthless the stock owned by existing shareholders. The banks were discussing the possibility of selling assets to raise money – a Utopian plan in the face of the grimmest financial crisis since the 1929 Wall Street Crash. The other option they floated was going back to existing shareholders and trying to sell them more shares – again, a crackpot conceit in the middle of a stock-market wipeout.

After the round of meetings, Lenihan said he encouraged the banks to explore the possibility of 'private investment', but for the first time indicated that the State might put in money.

1 December 2008

Labour Party finance spokesperson Joan Burton criticised Lenihan's 'Farmleigh formula' of inviting private-equity funds, such as the Carlyle Group and JC Flowers, to rescue the Irish banks. 'This is like being rescued from a whale by a shark,' she observed.

14 December 2008

A fortnight of further falls in share prices underlined the stock market's confusion about the master plan for sorting out the banks. Where would the money come from: State or sharks? Would there be enough funding? Would the banks sell off subsidiaries abroad or try to issue new shares? On this Sunday night, before the markets opened for business, the government tried to clarify the situation. It explained it was willing to 'support' a recapitalisation programme of €10 billion. It said it would invest alongside existing shareholders and private investors. But this did nothing to settle the markets, because the government did not specify how much money it would invest.

21 December 2008

The dramatic departure of Anglo chairman Seán FitzPatrick on 18 December, followed by chief executive David Drumm the next day, intensified pressure on the government to straighten out this most troublesome of banks. Again on a Sunday, with the markets closed, the government set to work. It may have been the shortest day of the year, but it was long enough to send in the Seventh Cavalry. Taoiseach Brian Cowen, along with Brian Lenihan and Central Bank Governor John Hurley, lined up to announce that the State would inject €1.5 billion of public money into Anglo Irish Bank. More largesse was forthcoming, with €2 billion for AIB and the same amount again for Bank of Ireland.

AIB and Bank of Ireland would try to raise money by selling shares in a rights issues to bring in a further €1 billion each. If this did not work, the State would provide the deficit.

Commentators were sceptical about the banks' ability to raise money on the financial markets. Trinity College associate professor of finance Brian Lucey predicted that the State would end up supplying every last cent. If that happened, the government would invest a total of €7.5 billion in the three banks. He was broadly correct.

Arguments put forward by Sheehy and Goggin had worked. This was a shareholder-friendly package. For the bankers, it meant they did not have to set foot on the Via Dolorosa – either the sharks taking control or nationalisation – after all. Since the government's investment would be classed as preference shares, it worked like a loan. The State would be paid 8 per cent annually for lending the money over five years to the big two, AIB and Bank of Ireland. It would receive 10 per cent in the case of Anglo. Crucially, the existing shareholders' shares would not be diluted. This was of particular significance to pension funds, with a time frame that presumed an eventual recovery in bank shares.

For the financial institutions, there were strings attached. They had to sign up to a new code of conduct for people in arrears on mortgage repayments. They would be 'treated with respect', and the banks would work with them to ensure 'repossession is truly an option of last resort'. AIB and Bank of Ireland pledged to wait at least six months from the time arrears first arose before taking legal action on repossession of a customer's primary residence. The banks also had to guarantee lending to small businesses which would provide credit to keep the wheels of the economy turning.

12 February 2009

So a shotgun marriage took place after all. But it was between the State and Anglo rather than between Irish Life & Permanent and Bank of Ireland. The sudden nationalisation of Anglo on 9 January meant that life became tougher for AIB and Bank of Ireland, however. They were not able to sell assets, and the appetite among investors to buy shares was negligible. They could not raise that €1 billion each. Goggin and Sheehy had to return to the government, cap in hand.

At 8.30 p.m., Lenihan announced he would put €3.5 billion into AIB and the same amount into Bank of Ireland. He said, 'The big picture here is the survival of our financial system and, by extension, the future of our economy.'

The Minister for Finance had no choice: the banks needed liquidity. The only question was whether he may have been better off biting the bullet and nationalising all three banks. Many people still believed that could happen.

26 February 2009

The private team of Corcoran and McDermott knew they had been bested in the campaign for control of Bank of Ireland. With Bank of Ireland and AIB signed up to recapitalisation, the consortium turned its attention to Anglo.

RTÉ News reported that Mallabraca had been in talks with the government about taking a majority stake in the bank. Corcoran and McDermott contacted David Morgan, a former chief executive of Australia's largest bank Westpac, who had expressed an interest in running Anglo.

Morgan, who started his career as a child actor and featured in a movie called *Funny Things Happen Down Under* alongside Olivia Newton-John, had earned a reputation as a solid professional who could fix broken banks. Previously he worked with the IMF and served as senior deputy secretary in an administration run by Bob Hawke and Paul Keating.

Corcoran and McDermott said that their consortium would invest €5 billion in Anglo and absorb the first €750 million of losses. But with any deal of this nature, it would require a risk-sharing arrangement with government. One source said, 'The danger is this deal could be constructed so that these investors get all the upside, and the State gets all the downside. And with Anglo there could be a lot of downside.'

The National Treasury Management Agency (NTMA) was charged with negotiating about Anglo's future ownership. In a letter to the NTMA on 25 February 2009, Corcoran said that Mallabraca felt 'particularly uncomfortable' that the Anglo response to its proposal was being led by chairman

214

Donal O'Connor. He pointed out that O'Connor was a board member when the bank produced accounts now subject to serious investigations. Corcoran said that, 'while in no way questioning the integrity or bone fides' of O'Connor, he wanted him replaced as chairman.

The State had been forced to nationalise the black sheep of Irish banks: Anglo was the last institution it wanted to bring into public ownership. A mismanaged Anglo could gnaw an enormous hole in the taxpayer's wallet. Knowing this, Corcoran and McDermott bided their time.

11

Alpha Males in Denial

'It is well that the people of the nation do not understand our banking and monetary system, for if they did, I believe there would be a revolution before tomorrow morning.'

Henry Ford

While this juggernaut called the boom was careering along on bald tyres, banks delivered enormous profits to their shareholders. The two biggest planets orbiting the Irish financial sphere were Bank of Ireland and AIB. They were no fly-by-night operations, even if their behaviour left much to be desired. Twin pillars of the temple, they delivered handsome profits, paid generous dividends and employed tens of thousands.

But the lion's share of their profits stemmed from the credit boom. Intense pressure was applied by the banks' boards of governors and shareholders to deliver ever-escalating profits. Huge loans, which worried staff in the middle echelons of the banks, were approved at senior levels. Bank of Ireland, like AIB, kept lending long after it should have stopped from fear the business would go elsewhere. Elsewhere often meant Anglo.

The two heavyweight banks had a personality disorder. Externally, they projected a measured and trustworthy image, pinstriped to the core. Internally, executives were obsessed with growing profits, and this led them to approve lending for commercial and residential property which ignored stress test criteria.

The Irish stock market – of which 60 per cent was composed of the four quoted banks (AIB, Bank of Ireland, Anglo and Irish Life & Permanent) – went through the roof during the boom. In 1996, the ISEQ index of Irish shares was 2,725 points. It peaked in 2007 at just under 10,000 points. People with money to invest were steered towards the so-called blue-chip stocks, generally the banks. Pension funds were enamoured of those steady-as-she-goes banks which delivered, year after year.

But bankers became synonymous with capitalism unleashed. A gung-ho approach to profit growth was developed by all the Irish banks. They ran risks a professional card sharp would have hesitated to take and lent money faster than dealing out a hand of cards. This racked up bank profits, which, in turn, ballooned their bonuses. Stress-testing borrowers for ability to repay a loan ran a poor second to bankers shaking their money-makers.

At the end of September 2007, Bank of Ireland Private Banking was urging shares as an investment. It said bullishly, 'Recent turbulence in equity markets now presents a compelling buying opportunity for private investors.' It expressed itself 'confident that returns of between 15 and 20 per cent are achievable over the next 12 to 18 months from global equity markets'. But the downturn was already under way.

Listen to what director Kevin Quinn had to say: 'It is our strongly held belief that this recent volatility has led to an opportunity that private investors cannot ignore.' The stumble in share prices was only a hiccup in his interpretation

– an opportunity to make money by buying at somewhat lower than usual prices.

This was on a par with soliciting passengers to board the *Titanic* ten minutes before it struck the iceberg. Far from representing minor seepage, that dip in share values was the prelude to a full-scale tumble. Within eighteen months, the Irish stock market had retreated to its 1996 position, and stock markets around the world had experienced a 'once in a century recession', as Japanese Prime Minister Taro Aso described it. Bank of Ireland was virtually worthless.

Regarded as an august institution, Bank of Ireland was established in 1783, opening its doors to the public in Dublin's Mary Street. Twenty years later, it bought the magnificent College Green building which was first home to the Irish Parliament. Designed by architect James Gandon, this imposing colonnaded affair facing Trinity College was purchased for £40,000. Gandon also designed Abbeville, the stately home at Kinsealy in north County Dublin that became home to Charlie Haughey.

Bank of Ireland was known as the Protestant bank – the first Catholic chief executive was appointed only in 1991, when Patrick Molloy took over. It has a court rather than a board of directors, because the bank's charter was awarded by a British king, pre-Independence. Such anachronisms define Bank of Ireland.

By the time the Celtic Tiger was on the prowl, the bank was an impressive operation with subsidiaries in the North of Ireland and Britain, following the takeover of Bristol and West Building Society. It had even dipped its toe into US waters with the purchase of a commercial bank, First NH Banks of New Hampshire, although it later disposed of its interest.

While College Green is the flagship branch, Bank of Ireland has its headquarters on nearby Lower Baggot Street. From their eyrie on the top floor, the bank's executives needed no statistics to remind them of the building boom. The evidence was all around them, visible in the rapidly changing skyline.

From the outside, the building is a monolith of breathtaking brutality, with its copper and tinted glass facade. It interrupts a line of elegant Georgian buildings, some of which were controversially torn down to make way for Bank of Ireland's office block. But take the lift to the executive floor and a striking boardroom awaits, walled in glass from floor to ceiling on two sides. One side looks west towards the Dublin Mountains, where new housing estates cling to the foothills. The other side offers a panorama over the city centre, showing office blocks and apartment complexes springing up at jack-in-the-box intervals. For years, an army of cranes and building equipment peppered the horizon. This was not just a view: this was a ringside seat on the boom.

The economy was healthy, but the bank's financial results were positively bursting with vigour. Bank of Ireland recorded a 22 per cent jump in profits to €1.9 billion for the year ending March 2007. Its profits were growing five times faster than the economy. A decade earlier, the results for the year ending March 1997 showed a profit of €673 million.

No wonder every young graduate joining the bank wanted to work in the property and structured-finance teams. This was where the action was brewing. Property deals appeared to be infallibly productive.

The mentality hinged on being on the lookout for the next source of revenue at all times, which persuaded Bank of Ireland to take a step few of its customers matched. It decamped from property. In 2006, the bank sold its head office to developer Paddy Shovlin and Quinlan Private for more than €200 million and then leased it back. Sale and leasebacks of a number of branches followed. AIB did the same. The banks were raising capital to offer more loans, and offloading fixed assets was a way of expanding the loan book. After all, fixed assets made no return.

They were also calling the market, however, which they felt had peaked. This sale of their own assets was like an alarm bell, raised by themselves, which bankers chose not to heed. What chance had the rest of the country? But if the banks were selling their own properties, the big chill could not be far off.

At the height of the boom, Bank of Ireland was in Brian Goggin's stewardship. His ascent to the post of chief executive was as unexpected as it was abrupt. The serving chief executive, Michael Soden, quit unceremoniously in May 2004, in murky circumstances. Soden was caught viewing a website for escort agencies in Las Vegas before he was due to travel on a business trip to the US gambling resort. His defence – that he was looking at it for a friend but had no intention of using it himself – caused gales of laughter among bankers in the pub get-togethers in Larry Murphy's or Toner's at the end of the working week. Soden had contentiously outsourced his IT department, which resulted in Bank of Ireland staff joining an outside company. It was these workers who found him logged on to adult material – and blew the whistle without a shred of hesitation.

Soden, an Irishman who had worked in National Australia Bank, was a surprise appointment when he landed the job of chief executive in February 2002. Bank of Ireland traditionally appointed from within its ranks. Goggin was a strong contender but judged somewhat tame by comparison with Soden who arrived bursting with new ideas. When Soden clinched the post, Goggin's chances were dismissed as lost for ever. Colleagues said he seemed dispirited afterwards, a man with nothing to look forward to apart from his pension. 'He definitely had the air of somebody who had taken his foot off the pedal,' said one.

A former colleague of Goggin's said, 'The ultimate irony, in view of later developments, is that he was regarded as a very conservative banker. He did not get the job when it went to Soden because he was seen as too conventional, when someone more thrusting was needed. Brian Goggin did not like to take risks.'

At first, during Goggin's tenure, there was restraint – a consciousness of potential vulnerabilities. He tried to rein in operating costs, and in November 2004 the bank halted loans to first-time investors in the buy-to-let market. The managing director of its mortgage division, Joe Larkin, said at the time, 'A lot of people are trying to get into property knowing nothing about it and lacking the wherewithal to underpin the investment.'

Yet, in 2005, the year after Goggin landed his gold-nugget job, Bank of Ireland's thought processes underwent a shift. 'We weren't the ra-ra guys, we were a conservative bank. The culture was very sober, and Goggin embodied that. But that culture changed under Goggin. It lost its way,' said his colleague.

Bank of Ireland's customer loans stood at €68 billion in March 2004. By September 2008, they had more than doubled to €145 billion. Some €13 billion of this was in loans to developers of commercial and residential projects. In a number of cases, the money was advanced to buy land with nothing on it. This was all very well during a boom, but developers went bust in a crash – and the land would be worth a fraction of the price paid. Bubbling away inside Bank of Ireland, as in the other financial institutions, were loans to developers that left them exposed. Goggin, the arch-conservative, the Old Guard banker, got sucked into risk-taking. The safe pair of hands did not hold the tiller steady.

Goggin joined Bank of Ireland from school at the age of seventeen, in 1969. 'He quickly became a marked man for the future. He was the total banker,' said a Bank of Ireland source. Later he graduated from Trinity College with a Master's degree in management. He climbed quickly through the ranks to become chief executive of wholesale financial services in 1996 and to head up the asset management division in 2003.

He did not cover himself in glory in the asset management division. The unit suffered a major blow when four key staff members defected to Australian company Perpetual, as it set up a rival outfit in Dublin. When these trusted authorities walked away, investors withdrew large sums.

Some felt Goggin was fortunate to make chief executive considering the significant problems facing Bank of Ireland Asset Management. But he was regarded as rock solid, and the bank needed it after the Soden episode.

'He would often travel to international functions. He was one of the best CEOs for pressing the flesh,' recalled Adam McNulty. 'He was not a particularly egotistical person. He was very sociable. He would have a few beers with the staff, let his hair down.' Others recalled a man who had a tendency to order people about, and it rankled – his manner was sometimes regarded as brusque.

Together, he and the bank's chairman, Richard Burrows, made a credible pair. Burrows is a distinguished-looking patriarch, permanently tanned from sailing. He is a former chief executive of Irish Distillers, makers of Jameson whiskey, taken over by French drinks group Pernod Ricard in 1988. Rather than dispense with his services, the French company kept Burrows on the board. Burrows speaks with a suggestion of an Anglo-Irish accent and has very proper manners. Although a jolly man, he is no pushover. People who have worked in boardrooms say he can give executives a tough time when their performances are below par.

As chief executive, Goggin's image was pleasant, confident and articulate. He conveyed a hard-working impression by giving television interviews in his shirtsleeves – other captains of industry would fuss with buttoning up jackets and straightening ties for the cameras. The cameras never picked up his trademark highly polished shoes, however. He was scrupulous about them – they were his calling card.

Banking has given Goggin, who is married to Finula and has two daughters and a son, a prosperous lifestyle. He lives in the comfortable Dublin suburb of Foxrock, on the Avonmore estate, an enclave of large, modern detached houses. At the height of the boom, houses on his road easily fetched more than €3 million at auction. Coincidentally, a blogger called IrishHousePricesFalling used a property on Goggin's road as an example of diving property values. A neighbour's house went on the market at €3.3 million in May 2006 but was still on offer at €2.7 million that October. Perhaps the long-awaited reality check on property prices called early to his neighbourhood.

Goggin has a sense of humour. Following a controversy about the theft of Bank of Ireland laptops containing customer information, he was interviewed by RTÉ's business correspondent David Murphy. After leaving the chief executive's office, Murphy was called back by Goggin, whose grin matched the Cheshire Cat's. The journalist had forgotten his own laptop. Pointing gleefully, Goggin remarked, 'You wouldn't want to leave without that!'

When it came to championing the boom, Goggin led the field. Announcing his results in May 2007, he attacked those who called attention to the shaky state of the economy, and warned against the bogeyman of Ireland talking itself into a recession. Shades of Bertie Ahern here. Blindly convinced he was right, he insisted, 'There is no point in me telling a story which is inaccurate or false because it is only a matter of time before you get caught out.' Goggin did get caught out. Within three months, the credit crunch would squeeze the banking system, tighten it – and then twist the tourniquet again.

His remarks corresponded with a period when property

prices in some sectors of the market had been falling for six months. He must have known this. But he displayed the habitual arrogance of a senior banker. It was not a lack of information that killed the financial institutions: it was a mindset that left them prisoners of their own flawed decisions. Errors of judgement were not recognised and could not, therefore, be corrected. Top-tier bankers were united by a myopic – and dangerous – refusal to acknowledge their own mistakes.

Towards the end of his tenure, Goggin was a shadow of his former self. Colleagues spoke of him as a man in a daze – unable to absorb the scale of the disaster. 'He was shaken by what happened and seemed to have difficulty grasping the enormity of it,' said a source.

A senior Bank of Ireland executive observed, 'There were plenty of people saying the property market was overvalued – economists, the ESRI . . . I am just not sure Brian Goggin could have stood up and said "I am turning off the tap" and stopped lending. The bank would be in a better place if he had. But the share price would have been hammered, and he would have got the can.'

It happened anyway. Shortly before Christmas 2008, it was clear to people at a senior level in Bank of Ireland that boardroom support for Goggin was beginning to wane. One source said, 'He really could not cope with what was happening. His ability to deal with things was seeping away.'

On 19 January 2009, Goggin yielded his job, announcing he would stand down that summer. He put the best possible gloss on it, as other bankers have done. 'In June I will have completed five years as CEO, and I believe that the time is now right for a new chief executive to take the group forward through the next stage of its development,' he said. Mumbo-jumbo about taking a group forward is an indispensable part of every CEO's speech, at any stage in his or her career.

This meant that Goggin was leaving twelve months early.

Most chief executives at Bank of Ireland went at the age of sixty, and Goggin's contract had an option to leave in June 2010, at fifty-eight. Sources in the bank said that once recapitalisation was completed Goggin felt he should step aside. But at an extraordinary general meeting in March 2009 to approve recapitalisation, Bank of Ireland's chairman spelled out that Goggin did not have the board's support. 'It was clear that different times required different leadership, and, by mutual agreement, Brian Goggin stepped down,' said Burrows.

He did not stay until the summer, as intended. On 13 February 2009, the morning after the bank recapitalisation was announced by the Minister for Finance, Goggin made an unforgivable mistake. He agreed to an interview to welcome the deal. The briary question of money came up. Asked about his 2008 salary, Goggin told RTÉ business reporter Christopher McKevitt, 'I can tell you for a fact it will be substantially down on what I earned last year.'

'And how much did you earn last year?' inquired McKevitt.

'I think my total disclosed compensation in the report and accounts was €2.9 million,' said Goggin.

'For guidance, what would you expect to take home this year?' McKevitt persisted.

'It will be less than €2 million.'

(In fact, it later emerged that his package amounted to €1.1 million.)

Public anxiety about bank chiefs' salaries was at fever pitch, and that figure of almost €2 million was incendiary. Goggin had spent years in the cushioned upper echelons of management – he had not yet grasped the extent of taxpayers' outrage at being forced to bail out profligate banks. People were flabbergasted by the scale of this salary in view of the bank's abysmal performance and Goggin's admission that he had made mistakes. The sense was, as former US presidential candidate William Jennings Bryan put it, 'no one can earn a million dollars honestly'. Bankers were seen as reaping the rewards of failure.

A source at Bank of Ireland said Goggin felt he had been asked a factual question and gave a correspondingly factual answer. But its insensitivity enraged Brian Lenihan, under flak for his handling of the banking crisis. The source said, 'When Goggin did his interview with Christopher McKevitt, he was supposed to apologise. It did not come across with conviction and passion. He did not get it; he did not get why the general public was angry. Brian Lenihan was furious with Brian Goggin's interview and expressed that view by phone to the chairman, Richard Burrows.'

It was a PR disaster that sent out all the wrong signals, according to Minister for the Environment John Gormley. The timing was embarrassing for the government, just twenty-four hours after announcing it would funnel €7 billion of taxpayers' money into Bank of Ireland and AIB.

Goggin was finished.

Normally when a chief executive departs early, the move is announced by the company. But in a show of irritation with the banks, Lenihan did the job himself just four days after Goggin's tactless disclosure. He told the Dáil that Goggin would not be staying on after all but would be replaced within three weeks. And the salary of the new executive would be significantly reduced.

'Goggin signed his own death warrant with that interview,' said a former colleague. 'But he was a broken man already. You could tell it from the pre-scripted way he spoke, the amount of jargon he used, the total lack of conviction in his voice. Brian Goggin was someone who had been through the wringer.'

On 25 February 2009, Bank of Ireland announced an internal candidate would be the new chief executive – a move to facilitate Goggin's early departure. The following day, Goggin cleared his desk. At 11 a.m., he made an informal speech to staff. One person present said, 'His bottom line was, "I did nothing wrong and banks did nothing wrong."'

On 28 March 2009, a month after stepping down, Goggin went to his doctor complaining of feeling unwell. His GP sent him for tests, and he was whisked into the Beacon Clinic in Dublin's Sandyford in early April 2009. Following a successful triple heart bypass, he was discharged from hospital to recuperate at home.

The internal choice to replace Goggin was Richie Boucher, who had been chief executive of retail financial services, selected for his 'expertise, determination and pragmatism'. Stocky and greying, Boucher was no gentleman banker. He looked like a man who would flourish in the bear pit of a Wall Street bank trading floor.

A Bank of Ireland source said, 'It was basically Burrows who led the heave against Goggin. If there is one thing that boards of directors do well it is self-preservation.'

Boucher's unanimous appointment showed the bank's directors were out of touch with market perception and share-holders' views. Many doubted Boucher could restore Ireland's reputation in financial circles – as an internal appointment, he was part of the problem not part of the solution.

A former colleague said of him, 'He was one of the most aggressive guys and ruthless in the bank. He would be the epitome of the Anglo way of doing things, not Bank of Ireland. And he came from the corporate banking side, which was in an appalling state.'

Two days after Boucher was named chief executive, €7.6 million was stolen from the bank's College Green flagship following a tiger kidnapping, the largest robbery in the State's history. The bank was heavily criticised for failing to follow established protocols during the robbery – yet another example of its slack controls.

Richie Boucher grew up in Zambia, where his parents

emigrated in the 1950s, and went to boarding school in Southern Rhodesia, later transferring to the exclusive Clongowes Wood, the Jesuit boarding school in County Kildare. Developer Seán Dunne sent two sons there. Dunne built a €1 million floodlit all-weather rugby pitch as a donation, and a joke circulated that the school should be renamed Dunnegowes. Coincidentally, the school's huge working farm, if rezoned, would have represented a prime residential opportunity.

Boucher, who never lost his distinctive Southern African accent despite spending a relatively short time in Africa, is direct and feisty. He is generally regarded as having a ruthless streak. Long meetings are not to his taste, but he does prefer to deal with people face to face. Married to Sandra and living in Clontarf, he has a son and a daughter. A rugby fan, he trains a children's rugby team. He worked for Ulster Bank before being headhunted by Bank of Ireland in 2003. Three years later, he was made head of Bank of Ireland's retail financial services division, where he oversaw the company's land bank and development loans grow to €7.1 billion.

Agreeing to his appointment was a mistake on Lenihan's part. It signalled business as usual when a new broom was needed. More disturbing again, Boucher was indivisible from the hazardous relationship between builders and bankers. Boucher championed Dunne's pie-in-the-sky plan for a thirty-seven-storey 'Trump Tower' in Ballsbridge. In a radio interview with Marian Finucane on RTÉ in March 2008, Dunne described being advised by Boucher, his 'very good friend', on the purchase of the Jury's site, for which he paid €275 million in July 2005.

Dunne spoke to him by phone from Thailand, and Boucher recommended he return to Ireland to sort out the finance. But what was not generally known was that Boucher also told Dunne to get back because Bank of Ireland was not going to provide the finance. A Bank of Ireland source said that Boucher had decided 'he was not going to touch' a deal involving the purchase of the Jury's site. But Boucher was there for Dunne in October 2007 when he sent a letter on Bank of Ireland stationery to the planning department of Dublin City Council. 'I write to confirm my strong support for this landmark proposal which I believe will significantly benefit the city of Dublin and its citizens through helping enhance the concept of a living city and providing buildings of significant architectural merit befitting Ireland of the twenty-first century.'

Boucher would later be asked by shareholders why he used notepaper with the bank's letterhead. But he refused to answer questions about it at Bank of Ireland's extraordinary general meeting in March 2009, claiming it would breach client confidentiality. However, that argument was not watertight. Boucher's letter was kept on a planning file which could be accessed by members of the public. So, by sending the letter, he was breaking his own client confidentiality. A Bank of Ireland source said there was a 'business reason' for the letter, and it was not just about helping a friend. Boucher never gave an explanation.

At one stage, Carlow-born Dunne was reported to have loans accruing €11 million in annual interest payments on his Ulster Bank borrowings for sites in the area (although he told Finucane that his lending arrangements constituted 'good banking').

So it was a blow when, in March 2008, the council allowed part of the development but gave a thumbs-down to the diamond-shaped tower. The following January, after a week of public hearings and a record-breaking volume of submissions, planning authority An Bord Pleanála rejected all Dunne's proposals. Around €300 million was carved from the potential value of his development. If the Celtic Tigers had learned to swagger, Dunne was Swaggerer-in-Chief, with his partiality to Dom Pérignon and dropping in on business meetings by helicopter. But his gamble on a Hibernian Knightsbridge had detonated in his face.

No wonder Boucher's appointment was regarded with dismay as perpetuating the cartel. Labour's finance spokesperson Joan Burton said, 'This is a missed opportunity to signal a new beginning in Irish banking.' She noted Boucher was one of a number of senior bankers who had assured an Oireachtas committee that the fundamentals of the Irish banking system were sound – even as the meltdown thermostat was on red alert. Not exactly an encouraging sign.

Boucher's comments at the joint finance committee in July 2008 came less than three months before the banks were brought to their knees. The banker assured politicians in terms that cannot be misconstrued: 'If bad debts and the economy get worse, we believe we are sufficiently capitalised.' Boucher, number two to Goggin at the time, went on: 'We believe we have enough capital to meet bad debts of a significantly greater magnitude than we believe them to be. This issue has been examined. In life and business, one has expectations, and one has to ask what will happen if one is wrong. We are very often wrong but we have a strong belief that we have significant and sufficient capital to meet even worse scenarios than we envisage.' The stock market was shrieking the reverse: that Bank of Ireland and the other banks did not have enough capital to handle the bad debts they faced. It was why international investors had sold their shares in Irish banks. For good measure, Boucher also told the committee, 'Unequivocally we do not believe there is a Northern Rock lurking in Ireland.'

This was the man chosen to lead Ireland's largest retail bank.

Boucher was not the only member of his family to hit the headlines in the financial pages. His colourful brother Paul Boucher was a joint managing director of MMI money brokers, which arrange short-term inter-bank loans. In 1998, the Central Bank stepped in and halted trading in the company's stockbroking arm. It had been lending money to clients to buy shares in Irish exploration company Dana Petroleum. But a sudden collapse in Dana's share price left the division dangerously over-exposed.

Although Paul Boucher was not intimately involved in the stockbroking arm, he was a director of the overall MMI company. In court, Paul and other directors successfully defeated a fraud action taken by the liquidator. Paul always maintained he was in the clear. He has since left the world of financial services.

With Richie Boucher, Bank of Ireland continued its tradition of appointing from within. Mike Soden's tenure had caused shockwaves at the bank even before his fall from grace. Soden disapproved of the 'sense of entitlement' he identified at the bank. One of his opening moves had been to tackle the fleet of 2,300 company cars which he regarded as an extravagance. It took ten people just to manage the fleet. He argued he was running a bank and not a 'car rental business' and reduced vehicle numbers dramatically.

Soden also wanted to merge Bank of Ireland with AIB and to acquire British lender Abbey National, to create a super-institution so strong it could not be taken over. This was radical thinking. Shareholders were cool on the idea. Soden exacted his revenge after Boucher's appointment, insisting bank bosses associated with the crisis within Bank of Ireland and AIB should leave.

'Anybody who oversees the destruction of 99 per cent of the value of the two great banks in Ireland and says "We're not accountable, we're not responsible" – get off the bus right here and now,' he said.

Dermot Desmond took the initiative. He raised the sort of reservations Brian Lenihan should have expressed when

Boucher's name was first proposed. The businessman, a substantial shareholder, wrote to Bank of Ireland's court about Boucher's appointment. He said he was seeking clarification about the new chief executive's involvement in the bank's exposure to property lending. Boucher had been a member of the group risk policy and group investment committees, among other roles, so he 'must have been responsible for fatal errors of judgement, including advancing loans to developers on the strength of overstated land values and insufficient security'. Desmond saw 'a direct correlation' between Boucher's senior positions and the excess lending policies of the bank.

Desmond followed it up by sending John Bateson, finance director of his company IIU, to Bank of Ireland's extraordinary general meeting in March 2009. He read out a statement on Desmond's behalf, which said, 'It is difficult to understand the justification for allowing those who have caused the bank to be in this current mess to remain in situ and be trusted with getting it out of the mess.

'We appreciate the difficulty in recruiting a candidate of suitable calibre to become the next CEO, but we strongly believe that more time should have been spent to do so. We are not advocating a swift, blanket ousting of the current board and management but a changing of the guard over an acceptable time frame on the clear understanding that it will ultimately be a full, clean break with the past. There must be a new beginning.'

Restoring credibility and confidence would not be achieved by promoting existing management further up the chain.

Desmond was not the only angry Bank of Ireland shareholder. Pensioners who relied on their dividends for a substantial proportion of their incomes were affected. They turned up at the extraordinary general meeting in Dublin's Savoy cinema chanting 'go, go, go' at Richard Burrows and calling the board 'scumbag millionaires'.

Bank of Ireland's 16,000 employees were also disillusioned: many of them had shares and share options – and had watched them vanish in a puff of smoke. 'We used to get between 3 and 6 per cent of our pay in shares. A lot of people saved for fifteen years this way, in a nice upward trajectory. It seemed like a good deal. There was a decent yield,' said Adam McNulty. 'A middle manager would have had €100,000 to €150,000 in shares because we also had a save-as-you-earn scheme. I know one man who has lost €300,000. He says he resents every day he has to go in to work for them now. You used to have a lot of pride in working for Bank of Ireland – that has evaporated. Most of the staff were just working to the best of their ability. Now they have been left high and dry.'

McNulty said if anyone expressed doubts about how the bank would hold up in a downturn, they were fed reassurance: the loan book was in good shape, and the treasury had done sound work diversifying sources. Consequently, staff were as shocked as anyone by the level of the bank's exposure. 'The bank had been saying the loan book was high quality. They were saying they didn't have any Seán Dunne-style loans. Our funding sources would stand to us. But the house of cards collapsed so quickly that the bad-debts ratio ratcheted up more quickly. And then you have to go back and look at how prudent the lending policies really were,' he said.

At the March 2009 extraordinary general meeting to approve recapitalisation, a reference was made to Goggin standing down by the Bank of Ireland chairman. One shareholder shouted from the floor, 'And how many millions did he get?'

Goggin had always wanted to be chief executive. Be careful what you wish for. He achieved his heart's desire, only to be remembered as the man who broke Bank of Ireland – presiding over a 98 per cent wipeout in its share price. Suddenly Soden's transgressions seemed venial.

Goggin's sin was to avoid reality. But he could not avoid the consequences of avoiding reality. Still, he walked away with €1.1 million to keep him going for a year until his pension was activated. Not such a bad version of reality.

12

Champagne and Caviar Taken
off the Menu

*'Give me control of a nation's money and I care not who
makes its laws.'*
Mayer Amschel Bauer Rothschild, banking-dynasty founder

'Do you have an extravagant lifestyle?' That was the question
put to AIB chief executive Eugene Sheehy, at the bank's 2008
results meeting. He coloured but answered gamely. 'If people
think I do I would defy them to find it – because I don't. I am
here thirty-eight years. I would have hit the high numbers for
a couple of years. I expect to work here for another few years.
Working in the bank – it's a commitment to serve the organisation to the best of your ability.' Very red-faced by now, he
added, 'As you go up the ladder you are earning more money.
But it is not the reason you get out of bed and come to work
here – not for me. I see myself as an experienced banker who
wants to take the bank through this cycle.'

So, not a champagne-and-caviar lifestyle.

Although a uniformed waiter *was* putting the finishing
touches to a fine lunch Sheehy was hosting afterwards, in the

executive dining room.

There was no doubt he belonged to the aristocracy of money men, even if he was insisting he had seen the light – and the bankroll had never been his motivation. 'Of all the bankers, he was the one who would have been least worried about the cuts in salary for chief executives,' said a bank source.

Sheehy's talk of commitment and service suggested his line of business amounted to a calling. But should senior bankers be defrocked when their behaviour failed to meet appropriate standards of fiscal prudence? In a refrain echoed by other senior bankers, Sheehy insisted there was a world of difference between himself and financiers who had acted inappropriately. Mistakes were forgivable, he argued, awarding himself absolution.

This was his rationale for attempting to stay in tenure at a bank which had crumbled in value on his watch. Bank of Ireland's Brian Goggin, who could have applied the same argument, stood down fairly quickly. In March 2009, Sheehy said he had not offered his resignation to the board and had not considered it. 'I retire when I'm sixty,' he maintained. This would be in July 2014 – an optimistic time frame by anyone's standards.

AIB always had a whiff of being a risk-taker compared with Bank of Ireland. The culture was that bit more combative. It fought its corner just a little more tenaciously. Those factors might combine to explain why AIB managed to retain its chief executive when the guillotine was kept busy elsewhere.

'If Bank of Ireland is the David Niven of banking, AIB is the Gene Hackman and Anglo Irish is the Dell Boy.' That's how one senior banker remembers former AIB chairman Peter Sutherland's appraisal of the banking scene. A former roommate of Dustin Hoffman, Gene Hackman was a late starter and was told he would never make the grade as an actor. But he flourished long after others ran out of steam. There were parallels with Sheehy's late-developing career.

As Sheehy spoke about chaperoning his bank through 'this cycle' – better known as the recession – the 1980s were back with a vengeance in Ireland. Their return was signalled by a plague of 'to let' signs. The shutters began to be pulled down on shops across Ireland as the love affair with consumerism ended in tears. Customers who had cash were nervous to part with it. Fewer transactions meant lower profits – and traders could no longer afford their rents. Many of the leases in the capital were twenty-year agreements, with upward-only rent reviews every five years and no break clauses. This militated against breaking leases and moving to more cost-effective premises. It was cheaper to shut up shop.

Figures from the Central Statistics Office showed the sharpest decline in retail sales in more than twenty-five years during 2008. As clothing, furniture and lifestyle businesses quickly went to the wall, the amount of vacant space in the retail sector began climbing. In Dublin's Grafton Street, occupancy rates experienced a steep drop in 2008.

Retailer John O'Connor, of O'Connor's Jeans and Jack & Jones stores, said, 'There are a number of retailers who are simply unable to pay [rents]. It is reaching epidemic proportions. The rents were established in the middle of the Celtic Tiger era and are no longer realistic.'

Another problem for retailers was no longer being able to buy stock on two-month credit arrangements. Credit tightened, with suppliers unwilling to take a risk. They might only advance a retailer one month's credit – or even demand payment in advance. Credit served as the invisible oil that kept the cogs of commerce moving. Without it, they seized up.

Before the credit crunch, and long before Anglo became involved in Trotteresque enterprises, one bank was synonymous with financial scandals. That lender was AIB.

Perhaps it was the flipside of its comparatively robust culture. Or perhaps it was because a culture pervaded that refused to be embarrassed by shameful episodes which would have horrified Bank of Ireland had they happened on its terrain. AIB extricated itself from controversy as casually as a dog shaking off a paddle in a mud pool.

The bank was pilloried for its 53,000 bogus non-resident accounts, used by customers from the mid-1980s onwards to facilitate DIRT (Deposit Interest Retention Tax) evasion. It ended up making a €114 million settlement with the Revenue Commissioners. Separately, there was the revelation at the Moriarty Tribunal – investigating payments to politicians – of the bank's decision to write off about IR£400,000 (€508,000) owed by Charlie Haughey in 1980. The bank also wrote off IR£130,000 (€165,100) owed by another former Taoiseach, Garret FitzGerald. Benevolence? Hardly, when such goodwill only applied to political leaders.

Add to these events the fulminations over the 1985 rescue of the bank's Insurance Corporation of Ireland, with the government's assistance. And all this happened before the more recent flurry of scandals on foreign-exchange overcharging, the Rusnak fraud and the Faldor tax scam. It combined to paint a picture of a more aggressive culture at AIB than at Bank of Ireland, regarded as a gentleman's club. Both were heavy-hitters, but one found it trickier than the other to stay squeaky clean.

The culture of an organisation starts at the top and filters down. Hardly surprising, then, that problems were not confined to the boardroom but reared their head in the middle and lower ranks. When issues arose they were not escalated up the line to senior managers, so they were allowed to fester.

Despite their differences in ethos, like Bank of Ireland, AIB played catch-up to Anglo – both loath to be left behind during the lending bacchanalia.

The boom supplied days of wine and roses for AIB. Its headquarters, Bankcentre, are in Dublin 4. Banks always feel the need to have a landmark building to establish their credentials. Most of the buildings surrounding it are mature and venerable – it is directly opposite the stately Royal Dublin Society, for example – but Bankcentre is modern, sturdy and utilitarian.

The 1970s property is laid out over four blocks – named A, B, C and D – which vary in height from three to five storeys. It feels less like a bank headquarters and more like a university campus with its square, tinted glass buildings and sprawling site of almost four acres.

The interior is more eye-catching. Not for the profusion of cream orchids in pots on the executive floor (which could lead to its being mistaken for a smart showhouse) but for the art. This is the giveaway that heady quantities of money were made here. Art hangs everywhere on the walls of this floor, and so much of it is stacked in the vaults that paintings are rotated regularly. During 2009, a distinctive Jack Yeats racehorse scene in blues and greens, *A Race In Hy Brazil*, was a sprightly addition to the executive dining room. Even the foyer has designer egg chairs, while staff eat their lunch in a magnificent glass atrium – in-house catering provided because staff numbers, 4,500 of them in the HQ alone, were deemed excessive to unleash on Ballsbridge cafés.

One of Bankcentre's friskier features is a sculpture of a 17-foot hare called *Nijinsky*, inspired by the Russian ballet dancer. The work of Welsh figurative sculptor Barry Flanagan, it strikes a teasing note in solemn surroundings. The bronze hare has been described as 'playful, upbeat and accessible' by AIB's art adviser Frances Ruane, who said it was intended to create 'a welcoming bridge between the bank and the surrounding community'. A giant, bouncy hare to boost the spirits of the workforce was needed almost as soon as it was lifted into place.

Internationally, AIB operates mainly in the UK and Poland. It owns First Trust Bank in the North of Ireland and has a 22.5 per cent stake in M&T Bank in the US. At the beginning of 2008, it entered the Latvian, Estonian and Lithuanian markets by acquiring a mortgage finance business. Staff cuts seem inevitable, but in mid-2009 AIB had almost 24,000 employees: close on 9,000 in Ireland and almost 8,000 in Poland. It has a presence in thirteen countries although some operations are small – for example, in the Baltic states the only product it sells are mortgages.

AIB and Bank of Ireland regularly indulge in semantics about which is the largest bank in Ireland. AIB says it has 40 per cent of the business market and 35 per cent of the personal market, making it supreme. But Bank of Ireland is generally regarded as the biggest retail bank.

One of the most notable characteristics of AIB during the boom was the way it lurched from crisis to crisis yet managed to keep profits in the stratosphere. In February 2002, AIB's chief executive, the serene ex-seminarian Michael Buckley, was at home at 9 p.m. with his wife and three children when he received a long-distance phone call. It was the bombshell every banker dreads.

There was no shilly-shallying. Despite giving the impression of being a leisurely-moving countryman, Michael Buckley acted at warp speed. The next morning, he was on radio revealing the details of that call, in tandem with an announcement to the Irish Stock Exchange. The bank's US subsidiary, Allfirst, had been defrauded by a staggering amount – the final figure was $691 million. Within hours, Buckley's solemn face and measured tones were on news broadcasts across the world.

Allfirst employed a currency trader called John Rusnak, who boosted his bonuses to a total of $850,000 in a four-year period by gambling with the bank's money. Despite working in a complex area, his trades were simple. His strategy was that the yen would rise against the dollar. For five years, until 1997, he did well. Then Asia was hit by a market crisis and the yen fell dramatically. Rusnak lost $29 million. In the archetypal gambler's error, he threw good money after bad. Instead of owning up, he convinced himself he could recoup his losses and nobody would be any the wiser. And so began a spiral of enormous trades that bloated his losses. Many of his trades were vested with a patina of legitimacy because he forged documentation from Asian banks. These lent the appearance of authorisation for his transactions, implying that he was using the Asian banks' money. In fact, he was speculating with AIB funds. His laptop contained a folder called, pithily, 'Fake Docs'. In it, Rusnak kept letterheads from banks in Japan and Singapore, which he had copied from the Internet to falsify documents.

In order to check these transactions, Rusnak's bosses would have had to get up in the middle of the night and call the relevant bank in Asia. They never did. Larger banks, which ran complex treasury operations, had layers of compliance to deter fraud, but Allfirst was a small operation run on a shoestring. The trader lived a lie for five years.

Rusnak's home was a thirty five minute drive from the centre of Baltimore in Maryland. His commute took him through a rundown urban area, but his house was a large clapperboard property surrounded by houses of equally generous proportions. These homes were perched on a leafy hill overlooking Baltimore. It was a tranquil, prosperous setting – light years away from the frenetic environment he had constructed for himself in the workplace.

When the scandal broke, the bank presumed he had gone on the run, but he was actually coming clean to a lawyer and his family before cooperating with the FBI. His children's minder described him as a family man who attended church every Sunday with his wife Linda and children Katie and Alex. 'He was a nice, fairly busy man,' said babysitter Lea Schleimer. Neighbours were stunned to discover Rusnak's activities had drawn media from around the world to stand in February slush outside his home.

Luckily for AIB, it was in a rollicking financial position and could take the hit without going under, as had happened in the case of trader Nick Leeson and Barings Bank in 1995. Leeson, now commercial manager of Galway United football club, broke Britain's oldest merchant bank and spent four years in a Singapore prison for his fraudulent trades.

Chairman of AIB at the time, Lochlann Quinn – the no-nonsense businessman brother of former Minister for Finance Ruairi Quinn – was blunt in his appraisal of the bank's failures. 'We were asleep at the switch,' he said. The lack of adequate security measures to prevent Rusnak's fraud exposed glaring deficiencies within AIB. Jobs were lost at the bank's Dublin and US operations, but Buckley and Quinn remained in place. Rusnak pleaded guilty and received seven and a half years in jail. He was released early in 2009.

Buckley offered to resign, but the bank's directors convinced him to stay. 'The degree of shock that I was affected by was on the same scale as a family bereavement,' Buckley said later. Fortunately for him, he was shock-proofed from the subsequent banking collapse by having retired from AIB already – the Rusnak losses were only a taster of that down-ward pitch.

Buckley was no stranger to handling stress. He spent two years in the 1960s training to be a Roman Catholic priest, before realising that he did not have a vocation and transferring to a Master's degree in philosophy at the National University of Ireland. He always carried a smack of the seminary, and perhaps that helped restore confidence in the bank.

A major clean-up operation followed. The janitor chosen to protect AIB's interests was Eugene Sheehy – later to become chief executive. He learned one handy phrase Stateside, which he pulled out of the hat during the subsequent financial disaster. 'A lot has come out already about Irish banking,' he told a media briefing, 'and as the American saying goes: "Sunshine is the best disinfectant."'

While Sheehy was in the US sanitising Allfirst, AIB was confronted with another scandal, this one closer to home. Again, Michael Buckley found himself in crisis-management mode. The bank was found to have overcharged customers on one million foreign-exchange transactions. AIB had to refund €26 million and repay a further €8 million for overcharging on other products.

Trouble comes in threes. In May 2004, yet another AIB embarrassment occurred – and this one led straight to the boardroom. The bank's investment management division set up an offshore vehicle in the British Virgin Islands called Faldor, named after golfer Nick Faldo. Money was invested in it on behalf of four former bosses. These included former chief executive Gerry Scanlan and Roy Douglas, who had become chairman of Irish Life & Permanent after leaving AIB.

The investment management division of the bank topped up the Faldor fund with cash from other clients' investments. The scheme resulted in the four being targeted by the Revenue Commissioners. Scanlan made a settlement of €206,000, while Douglas paid €53,000. Diarmuid Moore, the bank's former director of corporate strategy, handed over €51,000, and AIB's late deputy chief executive Patrick Dowling paid €13,000.

The bankers were called into the Financial Regulator's office, floundering to explain away the Faldor scheme. After they left, Regulator Patrick Neary said to one of his officials, 'Don't feel sorry for them. Did you see the size of their cars in the underground car park?'

Eugene Sheehy was preoccupied with restructuring Allfirst in the US and had the Atlantic Ocean between him and these scandals. But he was in the hot seat when the crisis to dwarf all previous crises enveloped the bank.

In 2005, keen runner Sheehy breasted the finishing tape in the high-stakes race of his life when he was named chief executive designate of AIB. Sheehy, who has the spare build of a runner, enjoys competing in five-kilometre road races. He is a tall, elegant man with a gliding walk, perhaps honed by the walking holidays he enjoys. (In 2008, he did the famous Camino de Santiago de Compostela in northern Spain.) With his prematurely silver hair and gracious manner, a less suave version of Cary Grant springs to mind. Journalists had a field day using his hobby as a metaphor. It was pointed out that his distance of choice – neither a sprint nor a marathon – symbolised his rise to the top at the bank: at a steady jog rather than a meteoric sprint. Still, on the home strait he dazzled as he took the helm at Ireland's most valuable publicly quoted company, worth €13.5 billion at that time.

His career had been outside the norm. Able young bankers were generally star-spotted at an early age and moved up through the ranks. But Sheehy was a branch manager for years before finally being noticed. The decision to send him to the US showed he was viewed as an able operator.

His appointment as chief executive ended a period of uncertainty that had beset the bank. Many felt an outsider was needed to purge the organisation of its susceptibility to scandal. But with Buckley not due to retire until early 2006, the bank – led by chairman Dermot Gleeson – operated on default and appointed internally rather than bring in a new face. It cannot have escaped the board's attention that when Bank of Ireland introduced an outsider, in the form of Mike Soden, the relationship ended unhappily.

Sheehy's long career at AIB made him the archetypal insider. But propelling him into Buckley's shoes was doubly convenient because of his three years outside the country. This lent him newcomer status. His semi-detached role meant that the upheaval caused by the foreign-exchange and Faldor upsets cast no shadow on him. Working abroad was seen as a positive addition to a chief executive's CV – Buckley had run the Polish operation.

Born in Dublin in 1954, Eugene Joseph Sheehy inherited some of his business acumen and leadership skills from his late father Maurice, chief executive of Irish Sugar in the 1970s. After being schooled at Salesian College in Limerick, he joined AIB at the age of seventeen, in 1971. The next two decades were spent in the retail network, where he operated at manager level in various Dublin branches, including Dame Street, flagship of the old Munster and Leinster Bank. His people skills were among his defining traits in the branches and contributed to his popularity with staff. His CV included working for the Simon Community.

Sheehy was sent on a full-time M.Sc in organisation behaviour at Trinity College Dublin, where he won the Sir Charles Harvey Award. Senior management had finally spotted him and shunted him into the fast lane. Shortly afterwards, he was given overall responsibility for improving banking in the branches. He engaged with the trade unions after a strike at AIB in 1992 and helped to establish formal structures to deal with industrial relations. His approach was one of dialogue and consensus.

Having performed well, he was promoted to general manager of retail operations for AIB in 1999. Two years later, his rising-star status was confirmed when he became managing director of AIB. But the most obvious signal that Sheehy was a potential chief executive came in 2002, when he buckled on his six guns and hightailed it to the US after Rusnak's escapades.

Married and with a son and daughter, Sheehy lives in a townhouse in Dublin 4, in a relatively modest development – by senior banking standards – off Marlborough Road in leafy Donnybrook. 'He is a pragmatic man, he is not interested in a lavish lifestyle,' said an AIB source. 'He does not do fine dining. When you see a picture of his house in the newspaper alongside other chief executives' houses, his looks very ordinary. He is not interested in money.'

Sheehy's background was in branch banking. He spent years dealing with the public and their needs, unlike other bankers who came from the world of high finance where dealers did not bat an eyelid at trading in billions of euro. His appointment was a popular move among the rank and file, who regarded him as affable and also as one of themselves because he came up through the retail side. Reserved in temperament, he is seen as a low-key and unflappable person. 'He is not an individual who has huge emotional swings. Despite the collapse in the share price, I have never seen him angry or frustrated on the difficult days,' said a source at AIB.

Another said, 'He is a shy man. He is not interested in the cult of the chief executive. He does not particularly want to do television interviews. If he managed to get from appointment to retirement without anyone seeing him, he would be a happy man. If there is a positive article about him in a newspaper, it does not give him a thrill.'

Bringing down costs at the bank was one of his goals, and AIB had already signalled to the markets that it wanted to make the organisation more efficient. He cut costs in a passive way by leaving vacant posts unfilled.

But the momentum of cost reduction increased with the credit crunch. AIB's profits zoomed ahead during the boom – to the joy of its most important constituency, the shareholder. In 2003, its profit before tax was €1.01 billion. Compare this with 2006, when it reached €2.61 billion – an acceleration of 158 per cent in just three years.

In 2006, AIB showed the property market was peaking when it agreed a €378-million sale and leaseback of its Bankcentre headquarters with property developer Seán

Dunne and Hibernian Life and Pensions. Similar transactions involving a number of landmark branches followed. This coincided with Bank of Ireland's sale and leaseback of its headquarters. In 2007, AIB's profits dipped marginally to €2.5 billion, as the market showed signs of faltering.

The following year, the writing was on the wall. The figure underwent a dramatic revision with a 1,700 per cent increase in provision for bad debts relating to property. The bank had fallen back to 2003 levels, recording a profit of €1.02 billion.

The bad-debt provision was AIB's comeuppance for turning to the Anglo lending model. Credit officers in branches around the country lent out far too much on property, and the short-term business gains of this policy were not weighed against warnings of a downturn. The presumption was that a soft landing would take care of everything.

'The troops on the ground would have been under pressure, with clients going to Anglo,' said a senior AIB banker. 'They would have said Anglo is making decisions more quickly than us when people were applying for loans. They wanted devolution of decision-making. People felt Anglo was meeting the needs of professional customers. We felt we had to react to that, to match Anglo's responsiveness.

'So we set up business banking centres around the county with credit officers to offer loans to small and medium-sized businesses. But we would have been equally concerned with the competitive threat from Ulster Bank which had the support of Royal Bank of Scotland in the UK.'

Sources close to government said the devolution of decision-making on issuing loans was AIB's tender spot. Many loans did not go through head office, and AIB saw its loans to commercial and residential developers inflate to almost €22.6 billion by the end of 2008. The comparable figure at Bank of Ireland was €13 billion. Clearly, there was quicksand ahead.

By 2009, the Irish stock market had lost 80 per cent of its

value, largely due to the banks' performance, and Sheehy admitted, 'We are entering the phase of realism with admissions about bad loans.' It took long enough. The bank suffered a 62 per cent collapse in profits, down nearly €2 billion. It had set aside €1.8 billion to cover loans on property which seemed unlikely to be repaid. Although it registered a profit of €800 million, these looming debts meant the bank was on course to lose out dramatically. By how much was disputable. It could be €9 billion – or twice that, in a worst-case scenario.

'He is very bright, very able,' was the received wisdom on Sheehy. People continually said it about him, even after AIB's abysmal performance. 'He is meant to be very good,' they insisted. If he was so gifted, how come a litany of mistakes were made on his watch?

Sheehy presided over an apocalyptic share price. The number of customers falling behind with their mortgage repayments quadrupled between 2007 and 2008 – and that figure was likely to climb still further as unemployment bit in 2009 and 2010. Astonishingly, AIB decided to increase its dividend by 10 per cent in 2008 as a show of confidence to the markets – a step amounting to bravado. But Sheehy froze and then scrapped the dividend in 2009, admitting it had been an error.

Yet he was in no hurry to vacate his position: he clung on doggedly, even when his opposite number at Bank of Ireland had his departure date set for him and his replacement's new business cards were burning a hole in his pocket.

Sheehy's position was strengthened because he had the backing of the bank's chairman Dermot Gleeson, a former Attorney General whose words undoubtedly held sway with Brian Lenihan. AIB achieved what it wanted from negotiations with the government and retained its chief executive as others were losing theirs.

A banking source observed, 'Sheehy was considered the golden boy by government and particularly by the Department of Finance. But when you think about it, the guy had not done any better at his job than Brian Goggin. In fact, AIB's exposure to loans to developers for residential and commercial property was €23 billion, in Bank of Ireland it was €13 billion. The government was simply more impressed with Sheehy and the arguments put forward for keeping him by Gleeson.'

Gregarious Corkman Gleeson was a tough negotiator, with skills honed from arguing his case as a barrister. He was instrumental in helping Sheehy keep his job. 'You would want him batting on your side. He knew how government works. He knew the legal position – what the government could and could not do – and he would not be pushed around,' said a banking source. Another noted succinctly, 'He got what he wanted from the government: he got to keep Sheehy.' At least for a time – but he was not out of the woods yet.

Sheehy would have done well to learn from his predecessor's handling of the Allfirst crisis. Michael Buckley's fast reactions and efficiency stood out in stark contrast to Sheehy's fumbling and delaying tactics during 2008 as the scale of AIB's exposure to bad debts became apparent.

All the banks fudged the issue with the government. In the months following the original €440 billion guarantee, bankers remained economical with the truth. 'This is a whole new paradigm for the boardrooms of Irish banks,' Anglo's then chairman Seán FitzPatrick said in the wake of the State guarantee, noting they would have to pay attention to what politicians and the public wanted.

But bankers were slow learners. At AIB, senior executives were trying to pretend a drive-by shooting was an August Bank Holiday picnic. Sheehy and his senior executives maintained the fiction that all was well, even as their share price skidded downhill and international financial institutions worried about whether to lend them money. They had to be dragged by the scruff of those Thomas Pink and Henry Jermyn shirt collars to the recapitalisation table with the government. It only dawned on them that they were pariahs on the world markets – a status blindingly obvious to even casual observers – when they went to New York in December 2008. Here, they failed to raise the €1 billion target they had set themselves. Back to the government they trailed, to tap the public purse again.

Even after this lesson, Sheehy continued to trot out a devalued defence. 'The rate of change, the pace of change and what has happened here has been mirrored in other authorities. There are international comparisons,' he said, as late as March 2009. He was passing the buck.

The bank was sluggish to catch on to the notion of belt-tightening, even after the public funding lifeline it was thrown at the end of September 2008. Before Christmas that year, AIB brought a party of its corporate banking division to Carton House near Maynooth, a magnificent stately home, for dinner and an overnight stay – a jolly defended as an annual planning meeting. The corporates had gone there the previous year and had been impressed. But the previous year was another era.

The bank issued a statement insisting that this trip was being run on a 'reduced cost basis' compared with 2007, and there were no free beauty treatments or leisure activities lined up. Just that brainstorming session followed by dinner and bed, in a Palladian mansion where even the shepherd's pie was served with foie gras. Carton House had once been the home of Lord Edward FitzGerald, the 7th Duke of Leinster, but he ran up debts he could not pay and lost the house in the 1920s. A morality tale there, but it was wasted on AIB.

Commentators said that Sheehy was failing to make the tough decisions essential for survival. A senior banker said, 'Sheehy is not driven by money. But he is living in Cloud Cuckoo Land. He said "we'll pay a dividend." No, he didn't. He said, "we don't need to recapitalise." Actually, he did.'

As calls for his resignation circulated, Sheehy tried to

assert that he was going nowhere. For some months, he appeared to have won the battle to stay on, unlike his opposite number at Bank of Ireland. 'There is a big job to be done, and I think I can do it. I have the confidence of my board. I just want to get on with my job and do it,' he told the 2008 annual results press conference in March 2009. It was a smooth performance. But alpha-male bankers had enrolled in the School of Hard Knocks since the credit crunch, and the gloss had worn off their performances. Sheehy was as dashing as ever, but he had lost weight – his shirt was pristine, in true banker style, but the collar was loose on his neck. Determined though he was to lead the bank's fight back, he was not doing cartwheels. A rocky road stretched ahead.

Sheehy acknowledged that he had made mistakes and admitted to over-lending during the boom. The word 'regret' featured frequently in his vocabulary, but he insisted there was no wrongdoing.

The head of one of the bailed-out lenders said, 'It is not easy being a banker now. The managements are knackered. But they are hoping there will be some differentiation between the good banks and the bad ones.'

Sheehy certainly made a distinction between himself and Seán FitzPatrick. Choosing his words with care, he said some people had 'behaved inappropriately', and some have made mistakes.

Bankers may have complained privately about Anglo, but even when the bank's dirty linen was in full view they would not admit to their doubts. Sheehy adopted a 'see no evil, hear no evil, speak no evil' approach when asked if there were concerns in the industry about Anglo's lending practices. He ducked the question repeatedly at the March 2009 press conference. He said he did not know what went on in other organisations, nor was it his place to raise concerns with government about rival institutions.

251

But questions pursued him. Was he not perturbed about Ireland's reputation when scandal after scandal spewed from Anglo? 'It has been difficult and very troubling . . . it has been a very trying experience to explain to people,' he said. 'We immediately spoke to our own investors about how we were fixed and we reassured them that none of these things applied to us. When this happened, clearly it makes the slope steeper. But it doesn't stop us from saying the bank is clean . . . We may have credit quality issues but we are a resilient organisation.'

Resilient or not, the Fraud Squad raid at Anglo Irish Bank added to his woes when thirty media outlets abroad reported it as a swoop on AIB. The mix-up occurred because the two banks share a set of initials. It created headlines – and headaches. The bank had to spring into damage-limitation overdrive and hit the phones immediately, contacting investors and the media to correct the inaccuracy.

As bankers trailed behind serial killers in public approval ratings, Sheehy emerged as one with impressive evolutionary survival instincts. But he was hamstrung by his long association with the bank. Dermot Desmond's warning about Richie Boucher at Bank of Ireland was just as easily applied to Sheehy: 'A clean break is needed. The people who got the bank into the mess are not the people to get the bank out of the mess.'

A Department of Finance source said that Brian Lenihan had taken the stance that some of the bankers responsible for the deluge should stay behind and mop up. Sheehy was viewed as a useful cleaner-upper. But to others, this was a risible viewpoint.

Institutional shareholders began a heave against him, after the bank had to revise upwards three times how much it need-ed to survive – the figure climbing to €5 billion.

But he retained a surprising level of support within the board and the government, partly because of his people skills. An indicator of his talent peeked through when he acknowledged that staff morale was low – one of the few bankers to refer to the difficulties experienced by troops on the ground. Sheehy said, 'It is very important the staff know the bank has done nothing to be ashamed of, that it is going to support its customers through this downturn.' The mistake, he reflected in March 2009, was that the bank believed in a soft landing, 'The fact is there has not been a soft landing – and there is not going to be one.' The dogs in the street knew it by then, of course. Some might say that this pipe dream was the least of AIB's mistakes.

At the end of April 2009, Sheehy bowed to pressure and finally tendered his resignation, although he was to stay on until a replacement could be recruited. In the same shake-up, two other top guns announced they would step down: Sheehy's loyal supporter, the bank's chairman Dermot Gleeson, and AIB's finance director John O'Donnell. The AIB team was the last of the boom-time top guns to be cleared out. Just before they were due to put themselves up for re-election at the May 2009 annual general meeting, the patience of ministers and institutional shareholders finally snapped.

Both AIB and Bank of Ireland were left facing a public-confidence deficit when the banking crisis went nuclear. Financial systems had been operating on a basis of faith and trust, as opposed to regulation, but the trust model only worked if all the participants were honest.

Afterwards, customers lost faith in banks. Financial institutions had appeared to offer security; if that was called into doubt, what else did they have in their shop windows? Certainly not much in the way of returns, with deposit interest rates on the floor. Biscuit tins seemed safer for storing cash.

The dollar bill carries the legend 'In God we trust', but financial structures required trust to be placed in men, too. And not every banker was reliable.

13

Sticky Fingers

'Once you eliminate the impossible, whatever remains, no matter how improbable, must be the truth.'
Sherlock Holmes

In the command centre of the Department of Finance, officials were gathered for a hush-hush briefing in September 2008. 'Your mission, should you decide to accept it . . .'

They were charged with setting up a section described internally as 'the bad bank unit'. They never spoke about the division publicly. Its mission was, well, if not impossible then decidedly thankless: to monitor the banking tearaways. Two institutions were being watched closely: Anglo Irish Bank and Irish Nationwide Building Society. The operatives shadowing them had to battle not the Cold War but the Bank War. It was never to be talked about publicly.

As the first wave of casualties on the markets shunted the banks close to extinction in September 2008, the Minister for Finance decided to focus on the bigger banks in Accident and Emergency in urgent need of medical assistance. They were Anglo, AIB and Bank of Ireland. Irish Nationwide was left on a trolley.

Umpteen questions revolved around Irish Nationwide and its ruler, Michael Fingleton, a Napoleonic figure with the Corsican's breadth of ambitions – although, unlike him, he needed no generals because he ran a one-man empire. 'You may as well have called it the Michael Fingleton Building Society,' said a financial source.

Brian Lucey, associate professor of finance at Trinity College, had this to say about Fingleton's realm: 'When you think of Irish Nationwide, it reminds me of Churchill's famous quote about Russia, "a riddle wrapped in a mystery inside an enigma."'

Irish Nationwide was suspected to be a Pandora's Box. But while the building society had significant debts owed to other financial institutions, they did not require repayment until later in 2009. It made sense, during the first six months of the crisis, to leave Irish Nationwide to one side and to deal with it later. Brian Lenihan's attitude was 'sufficient unto the day is the evil thereof' – he had enough to contend with.

It was a source of black humour in political circles that Bank of Ireland, Anglo and Irish Life & Permanent all shed chief executives while Fingleton remained in position. If ever there was a banker who prompted speculation, gossip and innuendo, 'Fingers' Fingleton was the man.

The building society and its chief struck an unconventional note in the starchy financial community. Fingleton looked closer to a well-to-do turf accountant than a banker. With his goatee beard and penchant for raucous ties, he was never going to blend in with Brian Goggin or Eugene Sheehy.

He rarely held press conferences, and was a reluctant communicator. When asked questions by journalists, his face invariably settled into the pinched expression of somebody dosed with cod liver oil.

Away from formal settings, he relished the image of lovable rogue. He told one journalist, on first meeting him, 'The thing about me is that I know where the bodies are buried.' Usually bankers do their best to convey an air of prudence and respectability, but that was never Fingleton's style. The throwaway comment, made after a brief conversation as he entered Dublin's Shelbourne Hotel, spoke volumes. He wanted to convey two impressions: that he had power and that he was unlike other bankers. Both were true. In his own eyes, he was indestructible – and he liked people to know it.

'I found him friendly, but canny. I could never be sure if I trusted him, though,' said the chief executive of one of the bailed-out lenders. 'He is a grizzled old professional; a kind of a grand old man who wanted you to know where your place was. He always gave the impression he had been through it all before.'

Fingleton lives with his wife Eileen in Shankill, County Dublin – not far from his good friend Seán FitzPatrick, who was born in Shankill. A regular at race meetings – where that trilby he favours fits right in – he is also a keen sports fan and once said that, in another life, he would have liked to win 100 caps for Ireland in any sport.

He is well connected and an habitué on the social circuit – but then, business is conducted discreetly on these occasions. He was a regular at Michael Smurfit's annual dinner for the Smurfit Group. In 2006, Fingleton joined the paper and packaging tycoon on a four-day cruise to celebrate Smurfit's seventieth birthday. Smurfit hired the enormous motor boat *Sea Dream* because his own yacht was a tight squeeze for his 100-plus guests, who included Dermot Desmond and Bill Cullen, guru of *The Apprentice* television show. Coincidentally (except, is there such a thing in business?), Fingleton's deals include financing the purchase of the K Club by Smurfit and property developer Gerry Gannon.

He obviously has a weakness for cruising. Two years earlier, he joined developer Seán Dunne and his second wife

Gayle Killilea on their €1.5 million wedding cruise of the Mediterranean, aboard Aristotle Onassis's yacht *Christina O*. Two of the world's most famous wedding parties were held there: Onassis married Jackie Kennedy on the vessel while Grace Kelly and Prince Rainier of Monaco held their reception there. Dunne was another significant client of Irish Nationwide's – but then, business and pleasure mingle agreeably on the top deck.

In 2006, Fingleton attended a ball in St Petersburg to raise money for the charity Russia With Love. Also present were developers Bernard McNamara and Seán Mulryan. Fingleton has done business with Mulryan's building company Ballymore, amongst other developers.

The lender's personal branding has always outshone his building society's. Fingleton's influential connections were helped by his persona as a powerful individual who could direct Irish Nationwide's lending clout where he liked. Green Party Senator Dan Boyle, his party's financial spokesperson, described him as running the building society as 'his own personal fiefdom'.

Building societies are not bound by the same restrictions as banks. Fingleton flourished in an environment where regulation was lenient and nobody was peering over his shoulder. Irish Nationwide was not obliged to report its financial results as frequently as banks quoted on the stock market, such as AIB or Bank of Ireland. The only burden on it was to publish an annual report. If the situation deteriorated, there was no immediate necessity to inform members. This allowed him to operate an institution of national importance without either politicians or the public having much of a clue what went on behind closed doors.

Fingleton manned the controls at Irish Nationwide for thirty-seven years, during which time his career was written off countless times. But with a steely grip on the institution he revolutionised, he was the ultimate survivor – until the banking crisis, when even immortals lost their protective shields.

Running a building society that was largely his own creation, Fingleton took Irish Nationwide way, way beyond simply lending to property developers. He turned it into a property developer itself. Much of this property development was in Britain and Europe. But Irish Nationwide also developed a prime site in Booterstown, south Dublin. It bought the property more than twenty years ago when, for a time, it planned to relocate its headquarters there. Instead, Fingleton had sixty-two apartments built on more than an acre.

Fingleton did not follow a well-trodden route into banking. Born in 1938, the son of a garda, from Tubbercurry in County Sligo, he was an ambitious young man with an appetite for knowledge. Like many bright men of his generation, he furthered his education at a seminary but left before taking vows. While still in his twenties, he joined Allied Irish Finance, part of AIB. Hungry to get ahead, he took a degree in commerce and afterwards went off to work in the Dairy Disposal Agency, a State-owned organisation formed to sort out ailing creameries.

Self-improvement was still high up his agenda, and Fingleton attended night school, emerging as a chartered accountant. In 1969, his career veered off in a different direction, and he worked with the charity Concern in Nigeria, organising transport for food supplies. He returned to Dublin in 1972 to become company secretary to the Irish Independent Building Society, which later changed its name to Irish Nationwide. His thirst for knowledge continued, and he qualified as a barrister in 1973.

At the time there were many small building societies across Ireland. They had a profoundly different ethos to banks, existing for the benefit of their members. Finance for members to purchase homes was provided; when all the members had one, the society was dissolved. This model was replaced with a permanent building society where the organisation provided loans on a rolling basis.

It was in this mutually beneficial environment that Fingleton became managing director of the Irish Nationwide Building Society in the 1970s. Over three decades, he built it up from an operation with a staff of just five to a 400-strong workforce with branches in Britain, Ireland and the Isle of Man.

He pared costs to the bone and boasted about being obliged to wait three years for a company car. Despite the apparent culture of existing for the benefit of its members, Irish Nationwide took a tough stand against anyone falling into arrears. Under Fingleton, delinquent borrowers found themselves hit with penalty interest rates of up to 20 per cent. In a court action in 1998, Dr Emmanuel Buffet, a senior lecturer in mathematics at Dublin City University, described Irish Nationwide's system of fining arrears as 'pernicious'. He said someone who underpaid by €10 every month for twenty years would end up being billed €30,624, instead of €2,400. This was because Irish Nationwide charged a cumulative fine of 3 per cent per quarter. The society defended its policy as a deterrent against people using arrears for an overdraft facility.

For years he was known as the only banker willing to give mortgages to journalists who had been turned down elsewhere – any perceived risk from irregular earners was balanced by the boost in media relations. But the journalists who took out his loans frequently paid higher interest rates. In the long run, it meant he had more enemies than friends in the media.

Fingleton's lending practices did not only target journalists – they also facilitated politicians, with whom he made sure to stay chummy. In his early days he conducted some of his financial dealings with TDs on Wednesday nights in Leinster

House. There are those who suggest his longevity was due to well-placed contacts within political circles.

In 2008, he personally authorised a fast-tracked loan of €40,000 to Celia Larkin, former partner of Bertie Ahern. It was passed without the standard criteria being fulfilled, such as Larkin being asked to provide documentation including proof of income or other loans drawn down. Fingleton personally signed off on it.

But despite his connections, he blamed the Department of Finance for causing hitches that prevented his game plan from reaching fruition. Fingers had a grand scheme lined up for the building society – tactics that stretched far beyond transforming it from a home-loan lender to a developers' bank. He wanted to sell it for a €1-billion-plus price tag.

The society was owned by its members, so if it was taken over they would benefit from a once-off bounty. This happened in the cases of First Active and Irish Permanent. Under legislation, when a building society is converted into a company owned by shareholders, it cannot be bought by another company for five years.

Fingleton lobbied to have this restriction lifted so that if Irish Nationwide was acquired by a bigger player, members would land an immediate windfall. His political leverage stood to him and he was successful, but the process of having the legislation changed took longer than he anticipated. This delayed an Irish Nationwide sale.

Still, he expected it would be worth the wait. A takeover deal of this nature usually landed a golden goose in the laps of management coordinating it. At the peak of the boom, a variety of valuations were put on Irish Nationwide ranging from €1 billion to €1.5 billion. Either way, members could expect €10,000 or more if the company was sold.

Irish Nationwide hired investment bank Goldman Sachs to advise on a sale. Many members remained with the building society in the hope of a cheque in the post. Irish Nationwide took steps to deter carpetbaggers by setting a minimum stipulation of €20,000 on deposit to open a share account. Under building-society legislation, members were also required to have the account open for two years before the decision to demutualise.

The higher a building society's profits, the higher the price tag. It was no coincidence, then, that a jump in profits was registered as Fingleton plumped up Irish Nationwide for a sale. Pre-tax profits rose by 63 per cent to €391 million for the year ending 2007 compared with the previous year. Lending was ramped up.

The only prospective buyer was in Iceland, that 'reasonably large banking system with a small country attached' as the *Financial Times* labelled it. Would-be purchaser was Iceland's Landsbanki. But as the credit crunch snowballed, hopes of selling Irish Nationwide melted. The following year, the Icelandic bank had its assets in Britain frozen after Iceland's financial collapse, and Landsbanki was quickly nationalised in October 2008. Without a takeover deal, Fingleton's blueprint for a glorious exit strategy was back on the drawing board.

Irish Nationwide was beginning to look somewhat pointless. It could continue to operate as a building society, but its activities had given it a makeover as a finance house for property developers. In a crash, that left it facing substantial bad debts. New owners would be deterred from running it as a traditional building society because they would have to wrestle with this slew of bad debts.

Irish Nationwide, established in 1873, had taken an axe to its roots. Its 2007 annual report showed revenue from residential mortgages was €163 million, but the figure from commercial mortgages was a breathtaking €805 million. More than four-fifths of its activities were concentrated on financing developers, many of whom were close to Fingleton.

The Financial Regulator never intervened. Regulation was almost non-existent – yet bankers chafed at any. In an interview with RTÉ Radio in June 2007, Fingleton's good friend Seán FitzPatrick argued for 'appropriate regulation' – by which he meant none. Pushing for even lighter regulation, he claimed, 'If we try to shackle [entrepreneurs] instead of encouraging them, the country as a whole is going to suffer. Part of the shackling is with the huge emphasis on more and more regulation, and that can't be good for business. We haven't suffered the huge scandals that have occurred elsewhere. Of course there are always going to be some bad eggs in the basket but we have not got a history of abuse in the business world.' (At that time, Ireland was still in its prelapsarian phase in relation to banking shocks.)

There was precious little evidence of regulation at Irish Nationwide. And Fingleton was crafty in his dealings with the regulator. A source who used to work at the building society said he always arranged meetings with the Financial Regulator for late on a Friday afternoon. He knew the regulator's staff would not want the encounter to last for more than an hour because it would nibble into their weekend.

One senior banker said of Irish Nationwide, 'This was Fingers' own business, designed to deal with the needs of his pals. He made no secret of not running a building society. He was also sharing in the profits of the business – that was not the right thing to do. I could never understand how the regulator would allow it.'

Irish Nationwide financed property deals involving one of the country's most successful developers, Seán Mulryan and his Ballymore Homes group. Ballymore's chief operating officer David Brophy, is a director of Irish Nationwide. Wheels within wheels.

Irish Nationwide was also the majority shareholder in a

company owning a considerable amount of land in London's Docklands. It owned a stake in Clearstorm with Mulryan's Ballymore. They planned a series of towers up to 85 metres tall at Leamouth and Minoco Wharf, but Irish Nationwide sold the company, although the developments are proceeding. Developers Liam Carroll and solicitor-turned-property tycoon Noel Smyth were also backed by Irish Nationwide.

Unlike other lenders, Fingleton had no layer of middle management. This partly explained why Irish Nationwide's costs were so low. One Christmas during the 1980s he sent journalists a card portraying himself as Santa Claus. Even then he was viewed as closer to Scrooge than Santa – the building society was one of the most tightly managed operations in Irish banking.

His policy of running a lean organisation was not just a cost-cutting exercise; it also meant the normal checks and balances did not apply. He could lend to whomever he wanted, without restriction.

'It was scandalous at Nationwide. There was no management team. He ran the place with an iron fist,' complained the chief executive of one of the bailed-out lenders. 'It has no place in the new Ireland. I am surprised it was allowed to happen. I would criticise the Financial Regulator for not doing anything. The regulator could have insisted and been more aggressive. But the regulator's office was under-skilled in terms of staff.'

Not in terms of numbers, however.

In a court case in 2007, the building society's home-loans manager Brian Fitzgibbon made a number of allegations corroborating the view that Irish Nationwide was a one-man band. Fitzgibbon said, 'While protocols existed, they were never adhered to, and the entire ethos of the society when it came to lending was entirely informal and controlled by Michael Fingleton.

'I am also aware of a significant number of high-value loans which were personally approved by Mr Fingleton without any recourse to or compliance with the normal procedures.' He said the credit committee, in place within other lenders to put loans under the microscope, existed simply to satisfy the requirements of the regulator. Many loans were given the nod 'without any or limited compliance with procedures in place'. Celia Larkin's certainly ticked that box.

Fitzgibbon claimed he was dismissed because he was made a scapegoat for more than €20 million of loans given to corrupt solicitors Michael Lynn and Thomas Byrne. He claimed Fingleton directly approved a €4.1 million loan for Lynn's house in Howth, which was also mortgaged for a similar amount with at least two other financial institutions. He said he turned down a loan application from Byrne, which was subsequently approved by Fingleton after an appeal by a branch manager.

Mr Justice Frank Clarke ruled Fitzgibbon had established an arguable case that Fingleton had allowed 'deviations from the society's written lending policies'. Irish Nationwide reached a settlement with Fitzgibbon after the High Court said he should be reinstated.

The court case highlighted a culture where compliance with procedures was treated as window dressing and where a solo operator had absolute control. This should have set off warning bells in the Financial Regulator's office. Yet, Fingleton was allowed to remain in place. The following year, the regulator did instruct the society to strengthen its management team by hiring a chief operating officer, a chief financial officer and a chief risk officer. Their omission until then was an alarming blank.

Not only was the absence of middle management a problem. There were also issues at board level. In 2008, when Fingleton reached the age of seventy, he was no longer able to remain on Irish Nationwide's board under its own rules and had to step down. This did not happen. Instead, his title was changed from managing director to chief executive, and he stayed under a one-year contract that expired in January 2009. Yet still Fingers loitered, attending negotiations with the government about recapitalisation although no longer a member of the board.

Worries about Irish Nationwide were stoked in the wake of the State guarantee in September 2008. Fingleton's son, Michael Junior, who was working in an Irish Nationwide branch in London, circulated an unauthorised email soliciting deposits in the UK market. The email was despatched on 1 October, the day after Brian Lenihan tried to reassure his opposite number, Alistair Darling, that the guarantee would not send money flooding out of British banks. He did not allow for Michael Junior, whose email to an investment bank touted blatantly for business.

It crowed that the guarantee meant Irish Nationwide 'represented the safest place to deposit money in Europe'. It suggested that the building society's six-month and one-year fixed rates were now very attractive and added, 'Money in these accounts are guaranteed regardless of the size of deposit and represent the best value in the UK market.'

This enticement flew in the face of Lenihan's insistence that the scheme would not be exploited. The Minister for Finance was furious, and a spokesperson described it as 'predatory practice'. The Financial Regulator fined Irish Nationwide €50,000 for breaching its consumer code and 'failing to act professionally and with due regard to the integrity of the market'.

It was one of the rare times a bank had been fined by the Financial Regulator since the authority was established in 2003.

Despite the indignation of populace and politicians alike at this profiteering from the State guarantee, one person felt sorry for Michael Fingleton Junior. That man was Seán FitzPatrick, then chairman of Anglo Irish Bank and a long-time admirer of Fingleton. In a radio interview with Marian Finucane three days after the act of blatant opportunism, he spoke up for Michael Junior. 'I am sorry for the kid, the young son,' said FitzPatrick. 'He was a young man, he was motivated by the right ideas but obviously he wasn't directed.'

Finucane pushed him, saying people were cross about it. FitzPatrick replied limply, 'Of course it was wrong but I think it was misplaced.'

That show of support for the Fingleton family was telling. Two months later, FitzPatrick was forced to resign as chairman of Anglo. It transpired that his policy of corporate concealment of borrowings – totalling €122 million in 2007 – was facilitated by short-term borrowings from Irish Nationwide.

While FitzPatrick had to depart immediately, Fingleton clung on. Irish Nationwide's position was that it had not behaved inappropriately. But these borrowings, for which Irish Nationwide temporarily became responsible, were risky. Some of the money was lent to FitzPatrick to buy shares in Anglo, which ultimately collapsed in value. Other borrowings went on property investments.

Subsequently, the Financial Regulator sent a team of thirty to investigate Irish Nationwide's relationship with Anglo and the way it smoothed the progress of FitzPatrick's clandestine loans.

Those short-term loans to FitzPatrick from Irish Nationwide represented corporate cronyism in action. It was a classic case of bankers giving one another a dig-out.

The chairman of Irish Nationwide was Dr Michael Walsh, a former lecturer and an executive director of Dermot Desmond's investment vehicle IIU. Walsh was regarded by the Department of Finance as somebody the government could deal with during the crisis. In February 2009, an official from the department rang Walsh to set up a routine meeting with Irish Nationwide. Out of the blue, the chairman said he was resigning because of 'unfolding events' at the lender.

The government was being bounced into yet another crisis. One Department of Finance source said, 'We weren't happy at all about this. It's disgraceful that when the going gets tough some of these guys just leave.' Walsh wrote a letter to Irish Nationwide's company secretary saying it could not survive without significant government support and reorganisation. He said, 'I believe that the board and ultimately the minister should have an opportunity to provide new oversight and leadership.'

Irish Nationwide issued a statement indicating Walsh had not left because it was in financial trouble. It claimed that Walsh could no longer devote 'the increasing amount of time required' to the building society. A more credible explanation would be that there was a disagreement between Walsh and Fingleton about how the lender operated.

Irish Nationwide rapidly appointed vice-chairman Terence Cooney, an accountant, as chairman, a temporary measure to plug the gap. Cooney and Fingleton met Lenihan, who was worried that Walsh's statement may have fanned the flames by suggesting the building society needed further State aid. The reference to 'government support' in Walsh's statement was clarified as the guarantee. Panic over. For now.

By March 2009, the political pressure for Fingleton to stand down was mounting. At a time when all the top bankers were taking significant pay cuts – although still receiving huge sums considering their institutions faced enormous losses – Fingers was paid €2.3 million, including a €1 million bonus – this for running one small lender.

Nationwide had 400 staff compared with AIB's 23,000. But AIB's chief executive Eugene Sheehy was paid €1.1 million for 2008, less than half Fingleton's remuneration. Sheehy had taken a drop of 45 per cent on the previous year. But the five years to the end of 2007 had netted Fingleton a total of €7.2 million. What an exceptional reward for running a building society of just fifty branches, whose credit rating was recently downgraded by two leading international rating agencies.

More salt was rubbed in the public's wounds when it was revealed that €27.6 million had been paid into Fingleton's pension. This information came from the building society's 2007 annual report in which it said a group pension scheme was transferred to a retirement benefit scheme outside the group. What it did not specify was that Fingers was the only beneficiary.

The occupants of Leinster House frothed but conceded they did not have the power to reverse a pension deal. However, Fingleton was also under fire over a contentious €1 million bonus paid in November 2008. This only became public in March 2009, around the same time as his pension payment, during inquiries by a government committee on pay.

He was not about to get away scot-free twice. The government asked the Attorney General to investigate whether this was in breach of its bank guarantee scheme, which accorded it powers to clamp down on bonuses. There were calls for a 'super tax' on the bonus if Fingleton did not give it back, citing the US Congress vote to impose a 90 per cent tax on bonuses paid to companies helped by taxpayers.

Irish Nationwide took legal advice and argued it was contractually obliged to pay the bonus. Fingleton resisted for two weeks before bowing to mounting pressure and agreeing to surrender his million.

In a bluster of self-justification he said that the bonus was a contractually binding agreement which he was legally entitled to receive and had been agreed long before the guarantee scheme. He had 'no obligation to be beholden to any other third parties in this regard' but wished to repay the money to conclude the matter once he had established his right to it.

He said that he had decided to voluntarily return the bonus because of the effect on his family 'with a continuing twenty-four-hour media siege on his home' and also because of his concern 'for the effect it may have on the society' which he had served for almost forty years.

Senator Dan Boyle said that Fingleton personified all that was wrong with Irish banking. 'That he has remained so long in position while others have fallen on their swords is a complete mystery. He should not continue in that position of trust in what is, after all, supposed to be a mutual society,' said Boyle.

In an attempt to show change was on the way, Irish Nationwide briefed journalists that it had identified a replacement for Fingleton. But it said this individual had turned down the position because of the cap on executive salaries which would limit his pay to €360,000. This conveniently made Fingers' overdue departure appear to be the government's fault. The reluctant alternative turned out to be former Green Property finance director and IBI Corporate Finance executive Daniel Kitchen, who joined the building society as a non-executive director in late 2008. He was also the Irish Stock Exchange's nominated director on the Irish Takeover Panel.

The building society said that it had homed in on Kitchen as a potential chief executive after a selection process involving a company of headhunters. But the search did not exactly trawl far and wide if the candidate pinpointed was already on its own board.

On 24 March, Brian Lenihan met the two government-appointed directors to Irish Nationwide, Aidan Kearns and Rory O'Farrell. In a statement afterwards, the minister said that the management team 'must be reviewed' and that disclosures about Fingleton's remuneration 'require investigation'.

He held a further meeting six days later, after which the Department of Finance let it be known there would be a change of chief executive. On 2 April, Irish Nationwide announced that Fingleton would retire at the end of the month while Kitchen would become non-executive chairman and temporarily assume the role of chief executive until someone else could be found.

Fingleton clung to a fig leaf, maintaining he had only stayed on at the board's request and that he had intended to step down voluntarily at the end of April 2009. But multiple meetings between Lenihan and the building-society board suggest that the government wanted Fingleton gone before announcing further measures to support the financial institutions.

Regardless of who runs the building society in future, the taxpayer will have to finance the clean-up of an almighty mess left by Fingleton. The group experienced a dramatic reversal of fortunes in 2008, with 80 per cent of its loan book devoted to property developers. More than €8 billion had been advanced to borrowers in the highly vulnerable commercial property sphere.

Losses to property developers represent a slow-spreading cancer in the banking system, their potential yet to be fully realised. Not only that, but in a note to bondholders in 2008, the building society said it was owed €320 million by a single customer. Any lender concentrating large quantities of loan funding on a few big customers was acting in a dangerous manner. If those clients failed, the impact was relatively greater, especially in the case of a small lender such as Irish Nationwide.

On 17 April 2009, Irish Nationwide revealed it owed far more to other financial institutions than was previously suspected. The building society published results for 2008 revealing it had bonds of €2.23 billion which had to be repaid

270

in 2009 – it had been borrowing from other banks and lending to property developers. It said its ability to raise money depended on an extension of the State guarantee.

2008 was not a vintage year for Irish Nationwide. It lost €243 million, compared with turning a profit of €309 million in 2007. Its results showed it had escalating bad loans, which meant €464 million had to be written off in 2008. The results contained no explanation as to why, despite such atrocious figures, Fingleton was deemed to deserve a €1 million bonus for that year.

Irish Nationwide had tried to reduce its lending in 2008 – functioning like a zombie bank. In other words, instead of lending out incoming money it diverted the funds into reducing its loan book. But it was still owed €8.1 billion by commercial property developers, and a further €2.2 billion by residential mortgage-holders. The moral from its results was clear: the building society's foray into financing speculative developments had left the taxpayer highly exposed.

But its losses did not stop Irish Nationwide from engaging in wishful thinking. It said: 'When the financial environment improves the society intends to reinstate the sale process to release maximum value for members.'

Fingleton was given free rein to run a building society that financed property developers, and the authorities permitted such an unhealthy situation to continue unchecked.

Who gained? Fingleton, who became a very wealthy man, and the developers, who secured finance for their projects. Who lost? The taxpayer, summoned to cork up the black hole in Irish Nationwide's books. Who was held to account? Nobody. Fingers retreated into twenty-four carat gold retirement. He was far from being the only banker treated so tolerantly.

A senior banker remarked, 'Fingleton revelled in the role of swashbuckler. But you always came away from an encounter with him feeling that you were a bit of an idiot, for some reason you could not quite fathom.'

Citizens of Ireland shared those sentiments.

Irish Nationwide was not the only building society to stage a breakout during the boom. Despite its upright image, EBS also went AWOL – with spectacular consequences.

The institution was set up in 1935 to cater for the teachers who wanted to buy a home. For decades, the Educational Building Society, as it was then known, was a genuine mutual which adhered to the precept of looking after the needs of members. But in the immortal words of former Taoiseach Bertie Ahern, as the 'boom was getting boomier', the EBS, led by its chief executive Ted McGovern, had a rush of blood to the head and began to finance developers building homes and commercial buildings.

'When they went in, oh boy, did they go in big – and at exactly the wrong time into exactly the wrong kind of stuff,' said one banking source. Another former banker observed, 'The EBS really had a case of late-onset madness.' Each proposal to lend to a property developer had to be approved by the EBS board. In total, 62 proposals came before it. Not one was turned down by the directors.

Scottish-born McGovern, dark-haired and sporting a moustache, was a fanatical Glasgow Celtic supporter. The chartered accountant worked with First National Bank of Chicago, then joined Bank of Ireland in 1985. That year, the bank bought the ICS building society. McGovern worked at ICS and was appointed chief executive in 1995. Six years later, he landed the number-one job with EBS.

For most of his term, McGovern was uncontroversial – until 2005 and 2006, when this late-onset madness flowered, just as the first cracks spidered through the property market. At that point, he latched on to lending to developers. An EBS source said, 'In 2005 we were being crucified for not being Irish Nationwide. There is great profit margin and up-front fees in lending to developers. We were being hammered in the media for not having profits like Nationwide.'

At the same time, McGovern was also feeling competitive pressure from Bank of Scotland's Halifax, which was gobbling up customers in the mortgage market. 'Our idea was to use the money from lending to developers to cross-subsidise our traditional business,' said the EBS source.

As McGovern led his forces straight towards enemy lines, a non-executive director of the building society launched a series of attacks on him and the board. Ethna Tinney, a radio producer with Lyric FM, was scathing about a €5 million pension top-up for senior management and about McGovern's pay of €760,000. She was selected to join the board as part of a process of reaching out to members of the public, to give them a voice in the building society. Ironically, the idea of bringing the people into the boardroom was conceived by McGovern, a decision he must have regretted as Tinney clashed with him.

At a stormy annual general meeting in April 2007, Tinney put herself up for election knowing she did not have the support of the board. Chairman Mark Moran, a former chief executive of the Mater Private Hospital, said the board was 'not satisfied with her performance', and Tinney was ousted by a narrow margin. She said her purpose in standing 'was to raise issues and get them out in the public arena'.

Her case damaged the credibility of the board, sharply criticised for blocking her reappointment by many members in attendance. The ruckus highlighted boardroom divisions. Two months later, McGovern resigned at the age of fifty-three with a handsome €1.86 million pay-off.

In January 2008, Fergus Murphy took over as chief

executive and cast a cold eye over the building society's adventures with developers.

Murphy was born in 1964 and lives in Enniskerry, County Wicklow. He began his banking career in 1986 as a dealer with Irish Intercontinental Bank, now KBC, before heading to France where he spent five years working with BNP Paribas. In 1994, he joined Dutch banking giant Rabobank, staying for thirteen years. Initially he worked as the group's Irish treasurer before managing its investment book. In 2000, he became managing director of Rabobank Ireland and engineered its takeover of ACCBank for €165 million. Next stop was Singapore, where he ran Asian operations covering ten countries and led a series of takeovers. He returned to Dublin to lead ACC but left six months later, joining Shelbourne Developments – the fast-moving property company headed by the over-ambitious developer Garrett Kelleher.

Shelbourne's most conspicuous project was the Chicago Spire on Lake Michigan, expected to be the world's tallest building when completed. But the credit crunch was causing funding complications for the project, which meant that Murphy would have to spend more time in the US than he had bargained for.

One of Murphy's reasons for returning home from Singapore was to be close to his mother after his father's death. His wife Catherine and their three children – a son and two daughters – had also relocated recently from Asia. It was not practical to uproot them again. He quit his post as president international with Shelbourne after only a month.

Speculation has whirred about the Chicago Spire and whether Kelleher may have overreached on the scheme. One veteran property developer commented, 'It is always unwise to build a monument to yourself.' Kelleher organised a star-studded launch with film star Liam Neeson to promote the project. Apartments started at $750,000 and penthouses cost up to $40 million. But the financial collapse led to the Spire being postponed in 2008, pending a recovery in the markets, although its underground section was complete.

Murphy found a home at EBS, running the rule over its €500-million worth of loans to property developers. A number of the projects looked decidedly dodgy, particularly with the property market in a downward trajectory. Instead of lending for prime sites in cities, which might bounce in a recovery, some of its lending was to projects on the outskirts of regional towns. They were a riskier prospect.

Three months into the job, Murphy stopped loans to developers. But the stable was empty, the horse already across the field. The EBS had been lending to projects at the top of the market, and in a full-bodied way for a slight institution. It tried on the halo of having acted in the interests of members, but this was soon cracked. In common with the other banks, EBS needed taxpayers' money.

In April 2008, Ethna Tinney was voted back on to the board after yet another turbulent annual general meeting, with the newspapers dubbing her the 'Comeback Queen'. She launched an assault on the beefy pay-off awarded to McGovern. Chairman Mark Moran said the building society had taken independent advice and had benchmarked it against other similar situations. The building society also had to admit lending €15 million to rogue solicitor Thomas Byrne, which finance director Alan Merriman conceded had been an 'embarrassment and a concern'.

But bigger problems were brewing. The following March, EBS announced its results for 2008 and said it had to set aside €110 million to pay for bad debts because of lending to developers. It lost €38 million from dealings with builders.

Then something remarkable happened. Moran and Merriman revealed they were resigning.

They were right to do so. The chairman and the finance

director had supervised a regime that resulted in a small, well-run institution trying to imitate Irish Nationwide's questionable practices, and found itself in a nettle-bed instead of in clover.

The unusual element here, however, was that it was the first time any of Ireland's bankers – let alone two at once – had recognised the error of their ways and had left of their own volition, as soon as bad debts were announced. Chief executive Fergus Murphy was not required to join their strategic withdrawal because the policy of lending to developers predated his arrival.

As he left, Moran said, 'When I became chairman I set out my stall that EBS would be a very transparent organisation and we would adopt the highest standards of corporate governance. Our total motivation is to do the right thing for our members and, by taking these decisions, where the chairman of the board and the finance director are stepping down, I think we are demonstrating to our members the accountability they expect.'

But the bad debts meant that EBS would need €300 million from the government. It was disappointed that a building society with a previously spotless reputation should have developed herd instincts – although to a lesser extent than others. However, the brisk departures of Moran and Merriman helped restore confidence in EBS's ability to ride out the financial storm.

With the worldwide banking system in fragments, and not everyone in favour of gluing it back together, Murphy proposed an alternative strategy. Following reform in Ireland, he believes there could be a role for a solid mutual building society. 'A core part of the solution should be a government-sponsored mutual like the fifty-five buildings societies in the UK,' he said. 'The stock-market-quoted banking model is broken. The man in the street is crying out for a community model.'

PART IV

The Fallout

14

Who's Sorry Now?

'Banks are wonderful things, when they work. And they usually do. But when they don't, all hell can break loose.'
Nobel Prize-winning economist, Paul Krugman

Everybody regrets the trouble they find themselves in, but nobody is sorry for what they did – because nobody admits to any misdeeds. Post mortem justifications from the culprits all echo the mindset that led to the crisis in the first place: arrogance and wilful blindness emerge in their rationalisations for what went wrong. The universal position has been to point the finger elsewhere, in an endless chain of blame shifting: politicians at bankers, bankers at regulators, regulators at politicians, politicians at regulators. Nobody is prepared to accept responsibility for the state of affairs in Ireland, in which a synchronised worldwide recession degenerated into a wholesale disaster.

However, legal innocence is not interchangeable with ethical innocence. A hallmark of the crisis has been a disconnect between the banking elite and the rest of the country. The top tier has no sense of responsibility for its behaviour. Greed, it seems, does not do repentance.

279

The bonfire of the vanities that defines the banking crisis has been the most intensely dissected scandal in Irish society in living memory. The circumstances are compelling because they impact directly on everyone's lives. Few can fail to relate to an upheaval that has precipitated job losses, pay cuts and higher taxes; an upheaval that has truncated public services, corroded pensions and eroded living standards; an upheaval that has contributed to a sense of the social fabric unravelling – a suspicion that civilisation itself has been compromised.

The very institutions that were once viewed as citadels of decorum have destabilised the Irish State. Banks were large employers. They were patrons of the Arts. They sponsored community, sporting and charitable events at not just national but also local level. Banks were the warp threads in the tapestry of society.

Anglo Irish Bank sponsored, among other things, the RTÉ National Symphony Orchestra, a writer-in-association bursary at the Abbey Theatre and a mentoring programme with the Warrenmount Community School in Dublin's Liberties. Over ten years, Bank of Ireland donated €12.5 million to fund sixty scholarships at the National College of Ireland in the IFSC. AIB has run the Better Ireland Programme, which addresses social exclusion for children – €2 million was donated to that cause in 2008. Irish Life & Permanent contributed €250,000 to a service that carries out handyman's jobs for the elderly. EBS has worked with the Simon Community to tackle homelessness. Irish Nationwide says it has been involved in a range of community and charitable ventures.

In many cases, the financial institutions have been able to write off their largesse against tax. Still, their intervention enhanced people's lives. With banks now facing heavy losses, sponsorship will be curtailed. This is inevitable, but the repercussions will cause hardship for charities and communities.

The banks invested heavily in their reputations – that

status has had a stick of dynamite tied beneath it. They have mutated from a cohesive force to a divisive one, with widespread resentment at their bailout – not just because they were prodigal, although they were; not just because they were greedy, although they were; but because people feel looted by them.

Somewhere along the line, the idea of what constituted a banker became muddied, and sensible behaviour was no longer desirable. Senior bankers, once upstanding citizens, came to represent a spoke in the wheel of crony capitalism.

The banking collapse was more than simply a business scandal. The concept of Ireland as a meritocracy was debunked. The country was revealed as operating on an incestuous basis of networking, with the 'invisible government of monetary power' exposed as the real head of state. It italicised the government's incestuous relationship with developers, but it also accented bankers' complicity in bloating the property bubble.

In Seán Quinn's case, the idea has taken root of a moneybags' elite playing their financial games behind closed doors. In Anglo Irish Bank's case, the transparency of public companies has been compromised. Thousands of small investors, as well as pension funds representing larger groupings, believed they had placed their money in an open, accountable, listed company – instead, it was Seán FitzPatrick's private source of finance, and David Drumm and Willie McAteer's optical illusion.

In the aftermath, the world is a different place. Less secure, certainly, but perhaps less Darwinian as well: there is a realisation that the law of the jungle cannot be the only code. People understand the need to work together to rebuild what has been destroyed – refining the model in the process. President Mary McAleese urged people to unite and fight to restore Ireland's damaged reputation in a March 2009 speech to the Independent Broadcasters of Ireland's annual conference in Dublin. A willingness to do this exists within the business and political spheres. Yet, public misgivings also surface that those who share the blame for the financial maelstrom may never be held accountable for their actions.

One upshot of the new reality is an acceptance that banking is too important to be left to bankers. People have lost faith in institutions that continued to reward senior executives, even as small shareholders were disinherited. There was too much greed and not enough fear in the financial sector, as former US Treasury Secretary Lawrence Summers put it. Banks were shameless, even when caught red-handed.

A curious philosophy took root in the Department of Finance – a conviction that the vibrant property sector was a side effect of Ireland's remarkable economic growth. When commentators repeatedly quibbled that the sums flowing into the tax coffers from property deals were unsustainable and could not fund the country's operating costs, they were scolded, ridiculed . . . ignored. This happened right up to and including Brian Cowen's tenure as Minister for Finance.

The Department of Finance argued that a sizeable proportion of stamp duty came from stock-market transactions and that not all the booty was generated by house and apartment sales. When the property market froze, tax revenues fell to earth faster than a plane with empty fuel tanks. So much for the theory about stock-market activity.

Who is responsible? Since 1997, Fianna Fáil has been the largest party in government and has held the Ministry of Finance without interruption. Under this political party, the boom went unchecked – stockpiling problems for the downturn. Its leading figures courted the legions of property developers, who evolved from small-time builders to real-estate moguls during the highpoint. Government policy was actively to promote property development, not to deter it.

There was no political will to introduce measures that would slacken the whirlwind of lending to developers; any impediment to their relentless expansion was discouraged.

Bertie Ahern is presented by his apologists as a crypto-socialist spreading the wealth during his eleven years as Taoiseach between 1997 and 2008. In fact, he was a pawn of the property developers, ranting against anyone who questioned their expansionism, consistently clearing obstacles from their path. His regime dilated the bubble with an extensive variety tax incentives to invest in property − even as growth in the construction sector reached patently unsustainable heights.

Ahern used the boom − created under a false premise − to court popularity with voters, as jobs and money flooded through the economy. His philosophy was, 'When we have it we spend it − when we don't have it we'll deal with it.' But dealing with it was far from the walkover his breezy analysis implied. There was no future-proofing against economic shock and an unemployment explosion, as he consistently chose populist policies above fiscal caution. Ahern turned the ship of state into a wreck. Had the boom been less inflated, the bust would have been more manageable.

Brian Cowen was Minister for Finance (like Ahern) before becoming Taoiseach. No effort was made to contain the property market during his tenure in the Department of Finance, although the writing was already on the wall. His time there was distinguished by inaction rather than action. Public spending continued to roar at full throttle, oiled by property taxes. (He even owned at least three investment properties himself, two in Dublin and one in Leeds.) But he allowed spending on wages in the public sector to rise by 14 per cent annually, with inflation at less than one-third of that figure. This was storing up trouble. As Taoiseach, he dithered and allowed the crisis to become further enflamed. Since the country plummeted into recession in late 2008, Cowen's leadership has been considered passive. While imaginative solutions have been devised by world leaders including Barack Obama and Gordon Brown, Cowen has appeared to flounder. He has failed to instil public confidence in his management of the crisis.

Charlie McCreevy was Minister for Finance during the critical period of the property bubble, between 1997 and 2004. He gave away hundreds of millions of euro in subsidies or tax incentives to builders, speculators and investors. The runaway train of the property market had its brake cables cut by him. Instead of approaching his role with discipline and judgement, he behaved as though he was Willy Wonka with a conveyor belt of goodies to distribute.

Financial regulators were effete, bureaucratic and failed to do their jobs as watchdogs, yielding to lobbying by bankers opposed to any restriction on lending. They should have intervened in the free market so beloved of McCreevy and acted as a restraint on the banks. But regulators did not challenge bankers, nor did they restrict lending to developers. They second-guessed what would best please their political masters rather than take unpopular – but crucial – steps to prevent a banking crash. They became enablers, not guardians. The Central Bank and the Financial Regulator failed the people they were charged with serving.

Property developers were avaricious and had bulletproof self-belief – imagining themselves as Donald Trump figures. They borrowed madcap sums for projects that crashed about their ears when property prices began to slide – and they took down the entire banking system, which had foolishly backed them.

Non-executive bank directors failed to rein in their chief executives. They anticipated no risks attached to increased lending. But they had a responsibility for the overall direction of the bank and to protect the interests of shareholders. Their function extended beyond simply listening to information supplied to them.

And then, of course, there are the bankers. Their lending was excessively ambitious and their analysis was deeply flawed – they foresaw no danger in the small, relatively unimportant city of Dublin achieving property prices on a par with New York or London. The greed that fuelled the now discredited bonus system encouraged recklessness the likes of which has never been seen before – and should never be allowed to unfold again. Bankers were dishonest in confessing to the extent of their bad debts. And they prevaricated about shutting down property developers as a way of cutting their losses.

As with the property boom they helped to broker, bankers lived in an unsustainable bubble. But the more it earned them, the less they questioned its viability.

Bankers continued to defend their princely salaries, even after the banking system crashed. The chief executive of one of the bailed-out lenders said, 'People running banks are only getting half of what the chief executive of Paddy Power is getting, and in that case you have some guys who are spending social welfare on gambling. Running a bank is technical, and it's tough.'

Any analysis of their behaviour at the crescendo of the boom, and in their denial phase afterwards, shows they lost all common sense. Then again, greed will do that. They steered their countries' economies over a cliff. Yet amid the wreckage, their mantra was to bleat about being victims of unprecedented market forces. Dick Fuld, Lehman Brothers' chief executive, told a congressional panel that his bankrupt investment bank was prey to a 'crisis of confidence'. Not grasping executives? Not alpha males on the ultimate binge?

While the entire banking industry has been damaged by scandal, it is worth remembering that two classes of bankers operated in Ireland:

(1) those who made mistakes by lending too much money during the boom – hugely imprudent although not corrupt;

(2) those who bludgeoned such regulations as did exist and demeaned Ireland's banking system in the eyes of the world – these bankers behaved inappropraitely.

AIB, Bank of Ireland and EBS fit category number one. They abided by the rules – but the rules were the problem. The regulations were both woefully inadequate and improperly implemented by the regulators. This is why they faced going bust without taxpayer support.

Anglo Irish Bank, Irish Life & Permanent and Irish Nationwide fall into classification number two. They transformed a banking collapse into a labyrinth of scandals that blotted Ireland's reputation and reduced the country's appeal as a location for foreign investors to set up new businesses. Light-touch regulation was the great ally of these banks.

One former banker said, 'Try applying light-touch regulation in criminal law and see what you're left with. Light-touch regulation is no regulation.'

In any review of the growth in bank lending, the speed with which bankers scooped up money and lent it on was dizzying. From 2004 to 2008, lending to customers at Anglo almost tripled from €24 billion to €72 billion. Over the same period, lending at AIB nearly doubled from €67 billion to €129 billion. The scale of this expansion was unnerving – particularly as it coincided with the final years of a boom.

In disclaiming any liability for the crash, bankers, politicians and regulators insist that their woes were caused by the international crisis. Other countries were tussling with similar quandaries, they point out. However, this does not withstand closer inspection. It is abundantly clear that the recession did not impact identically everywhere. Spain, like Ireland, had a property boom and bust – without a concurrent banking collapse. During the glory days, a stern set of regulators at the Bank of Spain kept lenders virtuous by demanding they set aside provisions for bad loans, even though customers could repay borrowings. The strategy worked. Spain's unemployment crisis and property collapse created difficulties for its banks. But they were largely able to cope without State support because the regulators had been unflinching.

Ireland may have been caught in a global bush fire, but its own financial institutions kindled the situation with lending policies that caused a gold rush.

The headline names departing the banking industry in a trail of anything but glory will not be forced to practise petty economies if they manage to keep their behemoth pension entitlements. These are all payable on retirement, generally at sixty-five, and are adjusted for inflation.

Seán FitzPatrick's arrangements are fascinating, in light of the extraordinary events at Anglo Irish Bank. An estimated pension of €13.5 million was transferred from the bank into a separate scheme before he stood down as chief executive in January 2005. If the government wanted to claw back some of the pension in view of his behaviour, it could not do so because the fund is now outside the bank's control and cannot be altered.

FitzPatrick was a member of Anglo's defined-benefit pension scheme. His pension entitlement at the 2004 financial year-end was €533,000 a year. Before January 2005, the trustees of the Anglo scheme paid a transfer value to his 'personal pension fund' in lieu of giving him a €533,000 pension on retirement. The figure was not disclosed but amounted to approximately €13.5 million based on information in the 2004 and 2005 annual reports.

This payment was concluded before the introduction of legislation in December 2005, which imposed a surcharge on blockbuster executive pension funds. If FitzPatrick drew on his personal pension fund before 7 December 2005, he would have been able to take 25 per cent of it tax-free. He could have transferred the balance to an Approved Retirement Fund

(ARF), which grows tax-free in retirement, subject to taking out at least 3 per cent a year as taxable income.

If anyone ever doubted Michael Fingleton's entrepreneurial talents, they need look no further than his handsome pension arrangements. Fingers, like FitzPatrick, benefited from a transfer by Irish Nationwide to his personal pension. The 2007 annual report shows a transfer of €27.6 million. To put the scale of this retirement package in context, it dwarfs the controversial £16 million pension paid to Fred 'the Shred' Goodwin, former chief executive of Royal Bank of Scotland – a fund the British government unsuccessfully demanded he repay.

One of Irish Nationwide's defined-benefit pension schemes was ended in January 2007, and a transfer value of €27.6 million was paid out to another pension scheme 'outside the control of the group', according to the annual report. It does not name the members of this terminated scheme. However, from the size of the transfer value paid, and Fingleton's disclosed 2007 package of €2.3 million, he was clearly the beneficiary of the €27.6 million.

As with FitzPatrick, Fingers is unlikely to be hit by the government's surcharge on executive pensions in excess of €5 million. In theory, Fingleton should be liable for the surcharge and income tax. However, that legislation was not retrospective. So, if he held €25 million in the fund in 2005, for example, only the excess would be liable for the surcharge. Since the stock-market collapse, his €27.6 million has probably fallen below 2005 levels – meaning he would not be liable for any surcharge.

Fingleton may have transferred the pension to an ARF. The fund can grow tax-free, and he can take the first €1.3 million without paying tax on it. But he is required to withdraw a minimum 3 per cent of the fund every year, which is liable to income tax. One possible reason why both FitzPatrick and Fingleton may have moved their pensions would be to benefit from the ARF option so that, on death, the money can be left to their children at a favourable tax rate (just 20 per cent).

When David Drumm reaches retirement age in 2031, his annual pension will be worth €271,000 in today's terms. Unless his name is cleared, he is unemployable in the front line of any Irish financial institution. But he has a young family to raise and is now spending considerable time in the US in an attempt to revive his career.

Despite his misconduct, Drumm may be entitled to compensation for losing his job. In a statement in January 2009, Brian Lenihan acknowledged that Anglo directors who lost their positions would 'retain their right to pursue compensation for loss of office'. He added that while it would be wrong to prevent such claims, they 'will be defended as appropriate'.

Drumm and Anglo's former finance director Willie McAteer have outstanding deferred bonus payments awarded in 2006, which were due for repayment in December 2008. Anglo's new board has been taking legal advice about whether the money should be paid.

Brian Goggin can access his retirement package from the age of fifty-eight in 2010. When he stepped down, he was on a salary of €1.1 million. He retains this level of remuneration until his pension is activated, in lieu of the final year of the contract he expected to fulfil. When his pension becomes operational, he will be paid €733,000 annually from the Bank of Ireland defined-benefit pension scheme. Unlike some other former bankers in this checklist, Goggin is not under investigation for any misconduct and keeps all his pay and pension.

Eugene Sheehy and AIB's finance director John O'Donnell, both born in 1954, receive pensions upon leaving AIB. Sheehy was entitled to an annual pension of €526,000 and O'Donnell to €261,000. But these figures will be slightly reduced because they are departing before their normal retirement age of 60.

Denis Casey received one year's pay of €890,000 in return

for standing down from his position early. His pension will be worth an annual €430,000 in today's terms when he retires.

Irish Life & Permanent's head of treasury David Gantly and finance director Peter Fitzpatrick were also paid a year's salary when they stood down and are entitled to substantial pensions at sixty-five. Peter Fitzpatrick's is €284,000 a year in today's terms.

The banking clean-up operation will be not just lengthy but tortuous. Straightening out the banks demands huge expenditure – a necessary evil. The final bill is an unknown factor, although it is an issue of significant national importance which will impact on the country's economic welfare. In the case of financial institutions such as Anglo, their readiness to lie about some of their activities casts lingering doubt on the true extent of their lending.

AIB has loans to developers of €23 billion; Bank of Ireland, €13 billion; Irish Nationwide, €8 billion; Anglo Irish Bank, €17 billion; and EBS, €500 million. (Irish Life & Permanent did not fund developers – a small mercy in the overall scheme, but a mercy nonetheless.) These figures add up to €61.5 billion. How much will be recouped? Here are two sketches that illustrate the dilemma.

First: a bank lent €10 million to a developer building fifty apartments which he hoped to sell for an average price of €300,000, netting him €15 million. The developer is going bust, and the bank faces the prospect of being handed the keys to a site with a half-built shell. Nobody will pay €300,000 for one of these apartments, and it will cost money to finish the development. How much of the €10 million will the bank retrieve if it sells off an incomplete development, in a falling market where demand is low, to another developer? Is it worth extending more finance to the first developer so the job is finished?

Second: a developer has borrowed €10 million for a greenfield site on the edge of a regional town to build homes and offices. The developer paid €15 million for the site and made up the difference from his own funds. After the property crash, the value of the land has fallen by 70 per cent. The developer is not paying interest to the bank on the €10 million and has nothing to sell to repay the loan. Should the bank wait until the property market rebounds and let the interest accumulate? Or should it sell the site now and lose €7 million?

These common scenarios are minnows compared with other deals, such as the €412 million purchase of the Irish Glass Bottle Company site in Dublin's Ringsend in 2006, which has nothing built on it. Davy stockbrokers told its private clients, who invested money in the deal, to write off 60 per cent. Finance was provided by Anglo and AIB.

Each sorry tale of a developer in over their head will have to be unpicked with care. Some money can be recovered. In April 2008, three of Ireland's leading stockbrokers – Davy, NCB and Goodbody – estimated the banks faced bad debts of €25 billion between 2008 and 2010. The banks all have a certain amount of capital to absorb some of the bad debts. But not enough. This is why the State is injecting cash.

UCD professor of finance Morgan Kelly wrote in the *Irish Times* in February 2009, 'The ability of the State to continue funding itself ultimately depends on the size of these bad debts. If they are of the order of €10 to €20 billion, we will survive. If they are of the order of €50 to €60 billion, we are sunk.'

Ireland has no clear idea of the potential scale of the abyss in its public finances. Since the introduction of the banking guarantee, the taxpayer is committed to meeting this bill – however humongous it should prove to be. The State does not have the resources to pay these debts and must borrow the money – at a time when more creditworthy countries are also rushing into the debt markets to raise finance.

Even if the banks are now being honest about their situations, they are hazy about the final cost. Kelly's doomsday synopsis includes mortgage lending to homeowners as well as loans to developers. Loans to developers are the Achilles heel – they amount to some €61.5 billion. Not all of that will go up in a puff of smoke. But a lot of it is beyond recovery.

To plug the gap, the government has infused a total of €7 billion into AIB and Bank of Ireland by way of preference shares. These shares are different to ordinary shares and act as a loan. The State is paid 8 per cent interest. But the fear is that those shares may have to be converted into ordinary shares as property losses accelerate and banks gobble up their capital reserves. Converting the shares will dilute existing shareholders' shares, rendering their investment virtually worthless.

Stockbrokers estimated the entire Irish banking system required an additional €3 billion. But they had a worst-case scenario, predicting that if 10 per cent of the bank lending went unpaid, the amount of additional capital needed would rise to €13 billion. This is on top of the €7 billion already allocated to the two big banks. However, the International Monetary Fund estimated the total cost at €24 billion. The truth is that nobody is sure.

Apart from the crisis of over-lending to developers, the banks face mortgages in arrears, businesses collapsing with debts and car loans going unpaid. These tribulations coincide with a period when Ireland's public finances are in unprecedented turmoil and will take years to repair.

Bank staff are as winded by the fallout as members of the public. 'The atmosphere is terrible in banking now,' said the chief executive of one of the bailed-out lenders. 'When I get dropped off at the office by taxi, I get them to leave me around the corner because I don't want them to see I work for the bank. We are all being tarred with the same brush. We are all rapists and murderers now; we are like the priests and sexual abuse – everyone regarded as guilty. There are decent people in banking too, and they are worried about job security.'

They are also worried about being a target for public anger. Shay Brennan, son of deceased minister Séamus Brennan, hesitated before running in his father's vacant Dáil seat in a summer 2009 by-election because, it was said, he felt his job at Anglo Irish Bank would tell against him with voters. Pubs, shops and buses have reported an unusual quantity of umbrellas with the Anglo logo left behind – abandoned by customers unwilling to be seen carrying them.

The chief executive of the bailed-out lender said, 'People think Ireland is the only place with some nasties in the banking system. We aren't.'

All the same, certain senior bankers pumped the Celtic tiger full of steroids and a rampage ensued. What they did will never wash off.

15

Culprits, Clean-up and Closure

'I never wonder to see men wicked, but I often wonder to
see them not ashamed.'
Jonathan Swift

As the government grappled with what to do about banks'
over-lending, it became clear the State would have to deal with
the bad loans that were suffocating the banking system. The
normal mechanism of banks lending to customers and being
repaid had ground to a halt. Billions lent to developers would
never be recouped. Many developers were not even paying interest on their loans and had been allowed to leave the amount
owed to accumulate, like a ticking time bomb. This 'rolling up'
of interest, as it was known, allowed developers to buy a site,
to build on it and to sell property before they had to pay back
the banks. It was a special arrangement between banker and
developer and – while invidious – it worked in a boom. But
when the market went into arrest, developers could not build
on sites they had bought, and the banks did not get paid.

Banks might have been expected to start seizing developers'
assets and selling them. They were reluctant to do this for two
reasons: they had an overly chummy relationship, and it would

put the developer out of business. Bankers hoped if they kept the developer afloat the market would recover and their debts would eventually be met. Furthermore, shutting down a big developer would mean a black hole in the bank's accounts.

Land bought at the peak of the boom for swollen price tags was left untouched as prices tumbled. Projects stalled, workers were laid off, and sites closed. Meanwhile, developers' debts continued to increase. This paralysed the entire banking network and required government action. But after the diplomatic spat following the introduction of the State guarantee, Brian Lenihan and his officials were cautious about going out on a limb again. For weeks, he kept in close contact with Joaquín Almunia, the EU Commissioner for Economic and Monetary Affairs (from Spain), while John Hurley, Governor of the Central Bank, held discussions with Jean-Claude Trichet, President of the European Central Bank.

Ireland was about to become a guinea pig. Together, Europe and the Irish government concocted a plan which could be replicated in other jurisdictions. Ireland was the first country using the euro to be pummelled by the banking crisis, now it would be first to establish an innovative but risky new entity to buy bank loans with State money. Trichet and Almunia knew Ireland's problems would be experienced by other countries. If a formula was agreed it could be reproduced elsewhere – particularly in Central and Eastern Europe, where similar banking dramas were materialising.

On 6 April 2009, on the eve of an emergency budget, Lenihan said he would take steps to deal with 'foolish' lending by the banks. In the following day's budget, he announced a new vehicle called the National Asset Management Agency (NAMA). It would buy back the loans by banks to developers at a knockdown price. If a bank had lent €100 million to a developer, the agency could purchase that debt for an agreed figure – €30 million, for example, with the bank taking a €70 million loss. The new agency, rather than the banks, would now deal with the developers. Over a period of years, it could try to manage the loan as the property market recovered. But this would be a long-haul prospect, possibly ten to fifteen years. And the taxpayer would be carrying the load all the way. No matter how you look at it, this could be an expensive solution. But inaction was not an option.

Conscious of this, the Minister for Finance was vehement. He said, 'All borrowers will be required to meet their full legal obligations for repayment. There will be a hardening of the approach to these borrowers – taxpayers' money is at stake.' If a developer goes bust, the agency seizes the assets on which the loans are secured.

There was considerable surprise at Lenihan's assertion, in the budget, that the potential maximum book value of the loans transferred to the new agency would be between €80 billion and €90 billion. The figure was expected to be lower.

But the government was embarking on a blockbuster solution – one with Europe's fingerprints all over it. Instead of buying back just the bad loans, it was buying the healthy ones as well. The scope of the scheme was more radical than anyone had anticipated.

While the six financial institutions had loans to developers of €61.5 billion, some of these developers had completed schemes, such as shopping centres and hotels, which were open for business. These were not development loans but investment borrowings. The government realised the banks, in many cases, were over-exposed to individual developers and feared that if they went bust it could cripple that bank. So, instead of taking on only the bad loans to developers, the State acquired a swathe of the Irish banking system instead.

Loans which were delivering a revenue stream for the banks would also be taken over by the new agency. More than half of the loans to be bought back belonged to AIB and Bank of Ireland.

Effectively, the government changed legislation to ladle up almost a quarter of bank lending, put it into State control and pay as little as possible to the banks. The ramifications were enormous. When it was put to one Department of Finance official that the banks may not like the proposal, he responded, 'Well, that's kind of the idea, isn't it?' The softly-softly approach was over.

The plan was described as 'a step in the right direction' by UCD Smurfit Business School lecturer Elaine Hutson, because it contained potential benefits for the taxpayer. If the banks required more capital, the State would provide that by way of ordinary shares. If the banks recovered, the taxpayer could own valuable shareholdings. But it also brought the banks one step closer to nationalisation. And the Irish people did not yet know the extent of the stake they were holding in the banks – it may be 2010 before that figure emerges.

However, there were disadvantages to the plan. The State would have to borrow billions to buy the developers' loans. That meant a significant increase in Ireland's national debt – and at a time when the public was experiencing steep tax rises, including an income levy being doubled as the government scrabbled for cash to run the country.

The State was buying the banks' loans with government bonds. The banks were then in a position to take these bonds and place them on deposit with the European Central Bank in exchange for cash. This would allow the banks to access cash to start lending again.

The key issue was the price at which the property loans would be purchased from the banks. The new agency would want to pay the minimum, while the banks would be keen to recover the maximum. Many academics argued that the State could get best value for taxpayers by nationalising the banks.

This would allow the government complete control over how much the banks were paid for their assets. Either way, the State seems likely to end up with majority shareholdings in AIB and Bank of Ireland, because both will require so much fresh capital to plug the gaps in their balance sheets. Barely two weeks after NAMA was unveiled, AIB admitted it would need to raise a further €1.5 billion in addition to the €3.5 billion already provided by the government. This shortfall could entail shedding overseas operations. The agency would have to be staffed by professionals from the property and investment communities. But stockbrokers pointed out it might be difficult to shield the agency from political inter-ference. The agency could put developers out of business who were in the process of construction – leading to hundreds of job losses. Politicians might be tempted to intervene, particularly at a time of high unemployment.

The day after the budget, Lenihan's second inside six months – a reflection on the state of the Exchequer – he held a press conference to outline how the plan would work. The venue was the Dublin office of the National Treasury Management Agency (NTMA), a State body that manages Ireland's debt and has been credited with sound policy since its inception in 1990. The location was chosen because Lenihan had decided the NTMA would set up and run the new troubleshooter NAMA.

One of the first phone calls NTMA chief executive Dr Michael Somers received after the announcement was from property developer Johnny Ronan. Ronan's company, Treasury Holdings, owns the building that houses the NTMA. Never slow to spot a business opportunity, Ronan wondered if Somers needed more office space for the new agency. The NAMA was being set up to straighten out developers – and already one of Ireland's leading property entrepreneurs saw where money could be made from it.

At the press conference, Lenihan was flanked by Somers and economic consultant Peter Bacon, hired to advise on the scheme. Bacon, an urbane man with slicked-back hair, well-tailored suits and a smooth way with words, was known for his previous reports on calming the housing market. Bacon is a director of one of property group Ballymore's subsidiaries – Ballymore's chief operations officer is on the board of Irish Nationwide. It serves as yet another example of the close connections between Irish boardrooms.

During the press conference, copies of Bacon's proposal for the new framework were circulated. The document referred to the relationship between developers and bankers, spelling out what everyone suspected: their relationship was too cosy. It said a new agency to buy the property debts might break the 'crony capitalist connections' between banks and developers which had deterred financiers from seizing the property of customers who were not paying up. This would be useful in cases where one developer owed a huge proportion of a bank's debt and had a superglue relationship with that institution.

It was clear from Lenihan's remarks that his patience had snapped. Many wondered what had taken him so long. As soon as the State guarantee was introduced in September 2008, he could have demanded sweeping changes in the banks. But he seems to have wanted them to undertake reorganisation of their own volition, rather than have the government force reform on them – and possibly end up in the courts. Lenihan's leniency was finally at an end. He said that any postponement of liabilities 'carried a cost'. Immediate reaction from the markets welcomed the fact that the government was eventually doing something about the over-lending crisis. Policy-makers had prevaricated because, quite simply, they did not want to do it. Many believed, as Lenihan admitted, that it felt as if they might be 'giving bankers a free lunch'.

Regulation was also being dealt with, at last. Ireland was to have a revised system which would follow the Canadian banking regulatory blueprint. This is a conservative model, and the embodiment of rude good health in an era of ailing banks. Canadian banks are only allowed to lend out twenty times their capital base, compared with thirty times for EU banks. 'The world needs more of this "boring" banking,' Canada's finance minister Jim Flaherty said in Rome in February 2009. Few would disagree.

Lenihan was advised on regulation by Sir Andrew Large, a former deputy governor of the Bank of England, who recommended a new structure. The role of the Central Bank would be reformed, placing it at the epicentre of banking supervision. A new commission would be set up under the governor of the Central Bank.

Large was also to help with appointing a new chief of financial regulation. Lenihan said that this individual would be a 'person of calibre, reputation, experience and expertise to lead reforms of financial regulation'. But assertive, proactive regulation was never hardwired into the Central Bank's DNA. The regulators rarely worked in the commercial sphere and appeared unaware of pressures to meet targets and generate profits. They also seemed ignorant of the tricks of the trade that allowed bankers to circumvent the rules. Simply establishing a new head of financial regulation was not enough. And, by allowing the Central Bank to stay at the heart of the new structure, the government showed its approach to regulation was little more than a cosmetic change. The new regime looked suspiciously like a re-jig of the old.

While the solution to address bad loans held by banks was new, the structure of the banks remained intact. There were still six Irish-owned financial institutions. But, in the new order, there may not be enough customers for all to survive. Many argue that bank restructuring needed to be more extreme. One former executive director of a bank is convinced that merging existing banks is the only viable long-term solution.

'We need to look beyond what is happening now to create something robust and profitable,' he said. 'We need to take Irish Life & Permanent, EBS, AIB, Bank of Ireland and Irish Nationwide, merge them and create two high-street banks which could make profits of €750 million each in total. That would have market capitalisation of €3 billion to €4 billion. Then you would create one corporate bank encompassing treasury and capital markets. Separately, you would have a good life-assurance business with Irish Life.'

However, such an uncompromising solution would result in as many as 10,000 job losses. At a time of rising unemployment, this would have political reverberations. 'It would be unpalatable because of the job implications. But we need a robust banking system, not a bunch of weakened deer depending on support from the State,' insisted the banker.

Compressing five high-street institutions into just two would impact on competition. But some level of competition in the Irish market would be provided by the foreign-owned players, such as Ulster Bank, National Irish Bank, and companies that offer services over the Internet, such as Rabobank and Northern Rock.

The damage wreaked on Ireland as a brand is almost impossible to calculate. The international community needs reassurance that the myriad scandals are being dealt with quickly and efficiently and that they will not be repeated. One way to broadcast the message that the State is equal to dealing with its errant bankers is by establishing well-resourced investigations. Ireland has an obligation to do this – not for reasons of vengeance but for the State's viability. It would be a mistake to hold no one accountable.

Public anger is mounting at the government's dawdling

DAVID MURPHY & MARTINA DEVLIN

pace. The pinched taxpayer wants to see corrupt bankers brought before the courts and justice served. Indeed, if judges rule that prison sentences are warranted, it may prove effective as a vote of confidence in the Irish banking system. And there is no doubt that an enduring legacy of the crisis is a lack of public trust in the banks.

With the exception of EBS, all the financial institutions use the words 'Ireland' or 'Irish' in their title. These are now debased words in banking terms, and rebranding would be constructive.

A phased clear-out of all the bank directors and senior executives responsible for unsustainable lending needs to take place. Simply replacing chief executives is inadequate – the slate must be wiped clean.

For a variety of reasons, chief executives from five of the six financial institutions have had to step down. Fergus Murphy of EBS is the only survivor, spared because he was appointed in 2008 as the banks were already in trouble.

While a distinction should be drawn between corrupt bankers and those who made costly mistakes, Ireland is too small a country to allow the architects of the frenzy to remain on the scene. This applies equally to politicians. The government has squandered its mandate. Many believe that Brian Lenihan's grip on the banks needed to be firmer, with more decisive measures implemented earlier in the crisis. Britain was prompt in recapitalising its banks during the early stages of the crisis in September 2008, but Ireland did not take that step until spring 2009.

Lenihan failed to clean out the bank chiefs quickly. In the cases of Michael Fingleton and Denis Casey, a charade ensued before they stood down. In other jurisdictions, go means go. In Ireland, it means prevarication – and unjustifiable pay-offs. The minister was also weak in allowing Bank of Ireland to replace Brian Goggin with an internal candidate, which did

302

little to restore investor confidence that Ireland was making a fresh start. So, while Lenihan always tried to do the right thing, his epitaph may well read 'too little too late'.

The fault lies in the political system. Ireland could learn from the US presidential model, where expertise is imported into government after a leader is elected. A finance minister is his or her country's chief financial officer. Why shoehorn a lawyer, or a teacher or an architect for that matter, into a pivotal position for which they have no training? Surely it makes sense for a leader to seek out the most able people in the country and appoint them to key posts. The expertise is supposed to be available to politicians via government departments – but that prowess has been lacking in the Department of Finance.

An alternative solution could be to draft in experts to share their skills and help Ireland through its 'economic Pearl Harbor', as billionaire Warren Buffett described the international crisis on US television. These authorities, from entrepreneurs to captains of industry to academics, could be appointed to the Senate and then brought into government.

Ireland also needs to take corporate governance seriously and immediately to implement rules about who is allowed to sit on boards. Guidelines which companies can choose to ignore are worthless. Business leaders were regarded as demigods and were rarely challenged by either their boards or the authorities. Such a supine attitude has to be dropped.

The bulwark against companies taking a wrong turn is a strong board with independent non-executive directors. According to the combined code on corporate governance, directors cannot be considered independent if they hold 'cross-directorships' or have significant links with other directors. The current system operates like an old boys' club.

Before Seán FitzPatrick's secret loans became public, the cross-directorships on the Anglo board were a classic example of this network in action. FitzPatrick, Lar Bradshaw and Donal O'Connor sat on the boards of Anglo and the DDDA where O'Connor was chairman. FitzPatrick was chairman of print and packaging giant Smurfit Kappa, where Gary McGann was chief executive, while McGann also sat on the board of Anglo. Ned Sullivan was chairman of food group Greencore and a non-executive director of Anglo, while FitzPatrick was also on the Greencore board. This system of interbreeding must be dismantled.

The media was complicit in the myth of Ireland's economic hegemony. It accepted the banks' assurances at face value for too long and believed their self-aggrandising and unfounded piffle. Bankers were operating on the basis of nothing more substantial than boundless optimism, and a discerning media could have questioned the banks' lending more vigorously. Newspapers revelled in stories of houses achieving record prices and peddled property porn.

The Irish people must also accept some culpability. The boom gave us our first real taste of material wealth: we licked our lips and liked it. But it seems we lacked the maturity to handle the avalanche of easy credit. A wise man has money in his head but not in his heart – for many, the reverse became the case in Ireland. The general population hurried to claim victim status as the recriminations mounted, but people had dived into the greed. In the process, we disregarded the corruption, the corporate cronyism, the stickiness of that interface between politics and business. So long as the jobs market was buoyant, credit was cheap and everyone could buy treats, a blind eye was turned.

Attaching blame to politicians, bankers, property developers and regulators does not give Irish people immunity. Bankers did not force anyone to live beyond their means. Who needed a recession to understand that weekend shopping trips to New York on the never-never were profligate? That driving ostentatious motors on borrowed money was foolhardy? That taking out a 100 per cent mortgage on top of crushing personal debt was wanton? Nobody was under an obligation to embrace the gimme-gimme values that evolved. Yet many tolerated a political and cultural ethos which they knew in their hearts was wrong.

Householders released equity – sometimes only notional equity – from their homes to purchase investment properties, holiday homes and apartments off the plans. Were they sufficiently warned of the risks? Unlikely. But anyone borrowing from a bank makes a choice: signing on the bottom line means accepting responsibility. Those who took stupid decisions cannot denounce bankers without also looking to themselves.

Irish people condoned too much that stank to the heavens, in part because we were sharing in the good times and it was a heady experience. Nobody needed a banking collapse to understand that the way land was rezoned for housing was questionable, or that the intimate relationship between property developers and politicians was a recipe for profiteering. Anyone who ever bought an item from a shop with dual sterling/euro price tags could see at a glance they were being ripped off. But the murmurs only reached a crescendo when recession hit. Until then, there was public collusion in the fallacy that Ireland had powered to the front ranks of the world's go-getting nations.

People cannot conveniently blank out how much they enjoyed the bling. The handbags and the Manolos, the power showers and the plasma screen television sets. But the money was borrowed, and fun came at a price: the economy was trashed. Nor did bling deliver contentment. And while being poor did not lead to happiness, neither did prosperity – the foundations were too rickety.

During the tiger years, a disproportionate value was

DAVID MURPHY & MARTINA DEVLIN

loaded on possessions and appearances. The heedless pursuit of more, and yet more again, delivered stress and overwork; we binged on consumer goods to compensate. Debt became the swipe card used to access treats, but it was a wolf in sheep's clothing. Many people benefited financially, at least temporarily, but lost in other ways. The pace of life reached helter-skelter levels, while time was in short supply. Time to spend with family and friends, to appreciate our environment, to dawdle and reflect. Prosperity was no recompense for a frenetic and self-absorbed tempo, when perceived wants were pursued at the expense of genuine needs. Even before the banking catastrophe, it was becoming clear that the boom-time attack of 'affluenza' was ultimately unfulfilling.

Is there any prospect of deliverance from the grimmest economic shockwaves in the State's history? Yes: salvation is possible if we can recreate a time when people are allowed to have a value independent of their possessions, or lack of them. If we can acknowledge that we are a society and not an economy. If we can accept that we are more than the sum of our plummeting house prices, our profligate bankers, our shrinking employment levels, our thwarted wealth aspirations. If we can recognise that such components do not comprise the parameters to our world – and that Ireland cannot be defined as an economic machine which has crashed. Redemption lies in amending those misshapen realities.

Revisionism was quick to rear its head in the aftermath, noted the chief executive of one of the bailed-out lenders. 'Lots of people are saying they were forced to take out mortgages. But that's not true,' he said. 'People were clamouring to buy their fourth investment property in Turkey.'

Little wonder ordinary people became smothered with debt. It has led to a new occurrence in Irish life – jingle mail, in which keys to a property are returned to a mortgage lender by borrowers who cannot maintain their repayment schedule.

A new expression is also being heard in banks: '
forgiveness'. This conveys recognition that lenders will hav
write off considerable sums on mortgages because nor
sanctions cannot be applied against defaulters. Not every
chanced their luck with investment properties. In a number
cases, homeowners risk losing the roof over their hea
because both income-earners in a relationship find themselve
out of work due to the downturn, financial problems pushe
to tipping point by the slide of their house or apartment int
negative equity.

Were the Irish lied to? Of course – by bankers and by
politicians, among others. But a banker's job is to boost
profits for the bank, a politician's is to serve the electorate.
Fianna Fáil could undoubtedly have taken a firmer stance in
guiding the country towards a soft landing. But the electorate
allowed Fianna Fáil to stay in government. Responsibility, it is
clear, falls across the board.

Change is inevitable – some of it painful – but there may
be benefits if a sounder and more trustworthy financial
system emerges. However, the problems facing Irish banks are
far from new. 'Owners of capital will stimulate [the] working
class to buy more and more of expensive goods, houses and
technology, pushing them to take more and more expensive
credits, until their debt becomes unbearable. The unpaid debt
will lead to bankruptcy of banks, which will have to be
nationalised, and the State will have to take the road which
will eventually lead to communism.' As a prediction of the
factors that precipitated the recession, this analysis is spot-on.

The source? It comes from Karl Marx's *Das Kapital*,
written in 1867, which makes him uncannily prescient. But the
only people listening were Marxists – who never did make it
into bank boardrooms.

Acknowledgements

Many people helped in the writing of this book, including colleagues of David Murphy's on RTÉ's business desk, and northern editor Tommie Gorman in Belfast. Thank you one and all.

We would also like to thank the *Irish Independent* for kindly allowing us to reproduce a number of photographs. Gratitude is particularly due to the newspaper's assistant editor (news) Cormac Bourke for trawling through files to locate them, and to the photographers who took them. They are: Tom Burke, Damien Eagers, Steve Humphreys, Frank McGrath and Martin Nolan.

Many who assisted us cannot be named, but among those who can are Tony Gilhawley and Adam McNulty. Thanks also go to our editor Ciara Considine and publisher Breda Purdue of Hachette Books Ireland.

Finally, a sincere thank you from Martina Devlin to the Ireland Fund of Monaco for the pitch-perfect timing of its 2009 writer-in-residence bursary at the Princess Grace Irish Library in Monaco – it delivered space and time to work on the book.